# CREATING HEALTHY ORGANIZATIONS

GRAHAM LOWE

# Creating Healthy Organizations

## Taking Action to Improve Employee Well-Being

Revised and Expanded Edition

UNIVERSITY OF TORONTO PRESS
Toronto Buffalo London

© Graham Lowe 2020
Rotman-UTP Publishing
University of Toronto Press
Toronto Buffalo London
utorontopress.com
Printed in Canada

ISBN 978-1-4875-0515-8 (cloth)
ISBN 978-1-4875-3165-2 (EPUB)
ISBN 978-1-4875-3164-5 (PDF)

---

**Library and Archives Canada Cataloguing in Publication**

Title: Creating healthy organizations : taking action to improve employee
    well-being / Graham Lowe.
Names: Lowe, Graham S., author.
Description: Revised and expanded edition. | Includes bibliographical
    references and index.
Identifiers: Canadiana (print) 20200152378 | Canadiana (ebook) 20200152408
    | ISBN 9781487505158 (cloth) | ISBN 9781487531645 (PDF) | ISBN
    9781487531652 (EPUB)
Subjects: LCSH: Employee motivation. | LCSH: Job satisfaction. | LCSH:
    Employee health promotion. | LCSH: Quality of work life. | LCSH:
    Leadership. | LCSH: Corporate culture. | LCSH: Organizational change.
Classification: LCC HF5549.5.M63 L68 2020 | DDC 658.3/14 – dc23

---

University of Toronto Press acknowledges the financial assistance to its
publishing program of the Canada Council for the Arts and the Ontario Arts
Council, an agency of the Government of Ontario.

 **Canada Council** **Conseil des Arts**
**for the Arts** **du Canada**

 ONTARIO ARTS COUNCIL
CONSEIL DES ARTS DE L'ONTARIO
an Ontario government agency
un organisme du gouvernement de l'Ontario

Funded by the   Financé par le
Government   gouvernement
of Canada    du Canada  | **Canadä**

 MIX
Paper from
responsible sources
FSC   FSC® C016245

*To Ella, Keith, and Penny*

# Contents

# Figures, Tables, and Boxes

**Figures**

## Tables

## Boxes

# Preface

How can you future-proof your organization by making it humanly sustainable? *Creating Healthy Organizations* answers this question, showing how to forge stronger links between employee well-being and the future success of any organization. In the chapters that follow, I make the case for resilient and humanly sustainable businesses, focusing on the importance of improving employees' well-being as the starting point.

In *Creating Healthy Organizations*, I describe how to strengthen the links between people and performance in any organization. The book provides an insightful new perspective on the drivers of organizational performance by integrating leading practices and research from workplace health promotion, human resources, organizational change and leadership, employee engagement, and corporate sustainability. *Creating Healthy Organizations* makes an evidence-based case for building resilient and sustainable businesses.

In the book, I argue that the cornerstone of a healthy organization is a vibrant work environment that supports all employees to achieve their personal health and wellness goals and, at the same time, feel inspired to contribute, learn, and collaborate. In a healthy organization, employees experience well-being because they are able to develop their capabilities and derive a sense of purpose from helping to achieve company goals, all within a psychologically and physically safe work environment. I encourage readers to view improved business performance and a better quality of work-life as complementary goals. This synergy is supported by an organization's culture, business strategy, approach to leadership, and day-to-day working relationships. As a result, healthy organizations provide measurable benefits to all stakeholders: employees, managers, customers, owners or shareholders, and society.

Organizations in all industries now operate in an environment rife with ever-greater risks and uncertainties, and sweeping transformations. Whether grappling with climate change, trying to recruit in a highly competitive labor market, or assessing the implications of the latest digital technologies for their business, employers increasingly recognize that survival depends on getting the fullest commitment and energy from each and every employee. Yet at the same time, employee stress, burnout, work–life conflict, and disengagement have become significant problems, threatening future organizational performance.

Observing these broad trends, I can see promising signs of progress. The goal of making entire organizations healthier has moved into the mainstream of corporate wellness. Scholarly research has advanced beyond making a business case for workplace health promotion to now emphasizing how successful interventions are based on a culture of health, integration with occupational health and safety systems, and closer ties with communities. More companies are addressing mental health issues, striving to make workplaces psychologically healthy and safe. As well, extensive resources are now publicly available in many countries to guide actions aimed at developing healthy, safe, and thriving workplaces. Expanded corporate sustainability frameworks – the evolution of what was called corporate social responsibility ten years ago – have opened the door to discussions about the sustainability of a company's human resource practices. And there are new possibilities for strengthening corporate cultures, as environmental and human rights goals align with what employees also value.

As I reflected on these trends, I saw a pressing need for an updated, practical guide that would help "change agents" – basically anyone committed to finding ways to make their workplace better – at all levels and positions take advantage of opportunities for creating healthier organizations. To be successful, those seeking to make workplace improvements also need to know how to overcome the challenges likely to be encountered, and the key success factors that can guide them and their coworkers in the workplace change process. This thoroughly revised and updated edition of *Creating Healthy Organizations* fills this gap in knowledge and practice. The book's new subtitle – *Taking Action to Improve Employee Well-Being* – underscores my emphasis on the "how" of change.

I offer readers an evidence-based, practical guide to how they can strengthen the links between employee well-being and performance in their organization, regardless of size or sector. You do not have to face an "either/or" choice of which goal to pursue. As I show, any successful actions designed to improve the well-being of employees will have positive ripple effects on many aspects of an organization's performance, ranging from reduced individual absenteeism and presenteeism to supportive and collaborative working relationships, the generation of new business ideas, more effective work processes, and more positive customer or client experiences.

Here are three clear indications that the 2020 edition of *Creating Healthy Organizations* is essentially a new book. First, I estimate that at least 80 percent of the content is new. That's because I draw on a greatly expanded evidence base and a wider range of consulting, workshop, and conference experiences over the past decade. Second, the 2010 edition of the book had 177 endnotes; this new edition has 456 endnotes, with only a small percent of these kept from the earlier edition. And third, of the ten figures, six tables, and nine boxes in this 2020 edition, all but four present new evidence or resources.

Even with this updated and expanded base of research and evidence, *Creating Healthy Organizations* is first and foremost a book for practitioners, written in an accessible style and conveying actionable insights. It is aimed at a diverse audience of managers, employees, and professionals. The book's "how-to" focus on improving employee well-being as a route to improved organizational performance will appeal to managers and executives. The emphasis on integrating mental, physical, and social well-being within a culture of health and safety will be of interest to professionals in human resources, occupational health and safety, and workplace wellness. These points also speak directly to the members of workplace health and safety and wellness committees, helping to strengthen their role in positive workplace change. The book's focus on the working conditions that inspire employees to thrive in their jobs will resonate for human resource professionals, given their continued pursuit of higher levels of employee engagement. Sustainability practices, reporting, and strategies are prominent themes. This makes the book relevant for anyone responsible for developing and implementing a corporate sustainability strategy, especially if they are looking for ways to incorporate internal people practices into that strategy. Consultants and non-government organizations in the areas of workplace wellness and workplace mental health will find the book's broad, integrative perspective useful. So too will policy-makers in the areas of workplace health promotion and occupational health and safety. And above all, a large and diverse audience for this book is the many change agents who can be positioned anywhere in an organization and are motivated by a vision of a better workplace with more fulfilling jobs.

That said, I also know that the 2010 book has been used in a variety of university and college courses, and by researchers in a range of disciplines that include human resources, organizational behaviour, change management, health and safety, health promotion, workplace wellness, sociology of work, and corporate sustainability. My hope is that the 2020 edition will be even more useful for teaching and research.

Researching and writing this book was a collaborative enterprise. As a consultant, workshop leader, and conference speaker, I have had the privilege of hearing and seeing hundreds of examples of individuals and organizations moving in their own way down a healthy trajectory. Many individuals generously shared with me their stories and practical advice. Others provided me with opportunities to observe firsthand how they went about translating their vision of a healthier organization into tangible change. I also have continued to learn more about the challenges faced by those individuals and teams actively committed to making their workplaces better. These numerous change agents have provided practical insights about how to seize opportunities to move down a healthy organization pathway.

Some of the new evidence I feature in the book comes from recent employee surveys conducted by Great Place to Work Canada for its annual lists of Best Workplaces in Canada. I am indebted to Priscila Porto and Alison Grenier at Great Place to Work Canada for generously sharing these data with me. I also make extensive use of recent surveys of Canada's workforce conducted by EKOS Research Associates. My thanks to Frank Graves, president of EKOS, for making these survey data available and for his continued collaboration with me on Rethinking Work surveys to document Canadians' work experiences.

An enormous volume of new academic research relevant for this book has been published in the past decade. Similarly, the "grey" literature – such as government, NGO, and think-tank reports – and media coverage of healthy workplace issues have continued to grow. To keep up with all this, I have benefited greatly from research resources provided by the Institute for Work and Health (IWH), the Centre for Industrial Relations and Human Resources (CIRHR) at the University of Toronto, and the University of Alberta. The IWH's weekly *Research Alerts* summarizes the latest scholarly journal articles on a wide range of topics relevant to occupational health and safety. The CIRHR's library's weekly e-publication, *PWR: work&labour news&research*, pulls together academic, government,

NGO, and media reports on workplace issues. And as a professor emeritus at the University of Alberta, I had full access to the university library's extensive online databases of academic journals, which were essential for tracking down relevant articles.

Many colleagues and clients have contributed stories, insights, and information that I have used throughout the book. I am very grateful to all of these people. In particular, I would like to acknowledge the various contributions of the following people: Mark Attridge, president of Attridge Consulting; Martin Bell, CEO of Urban Systems; Charles Boyer and members of the Council on Workplace Health and Wellness at the Conference Board of Canada; the late Ronald Burke, professor emeritus at York University's Schulich School of Business; Brian Davey, director of the Health Services Department at World Bank Group; Hardy Wentzel, CEO of Structurlam; Merv Gilbert and Dan Bilsker, who are experts on psychologically healthy and safe workplaces; Sonia Jacobs, formerly vice president, Canadian Partnerships, at NRC Health; Fatima Jorge, workplace integration lead, Alberta Health Services–Alberta Cancer Prevention Legacy Fund; Jonathan Lai at the University of Alberta; Barry Litun, executive director of the College of Alberta School Superintendents; Tracy MacDonald, executive director of Facility Engagement at the Kelowna General Hospital Physicians Society; Sharon McFarlane, health and safety advisor at Christchurch City Council in New Zealand; Lisa McGuire, CEO at the Manufacturing Safety Alliance of British Columbia; Shandy McLean, formerly the director of Health Strategies and Stakeholder Engagement at the Alberta School Employee Benefit Plan; Cam Mustard, president and senior scientist at the Institute for Work and Health; various colleagues at the Ontario Hospital Association and Accreditation Canada; Robert L. Quigley, senior vice president and regional medical director, Americas Region, International SOS Assistance; Janice Riegen, clinical nurse specialist, Healthy Workplaces at the Wiatemata District Health Board in New Zealand; Lisa Allen Scott, senior scientist, Alberta Health Services–Alberta Cancer Prevention Legacy Fund; and Valerie Smith, chief transformation officer at the Royal Victoria Regional Health Centre.

Jennifer DiDomenico at the University of Toronto Press (UTP) offered the encouragement and constructive feedback I needed to complete this book. Also at UTP, Breanna Muir in marketing and Leah Connor in production contributed to the successful launch of this new book. And Rebecca Russell's detailed copy editing made the text more readable.

I also owe a big thanks to numerous participants at my workshops and conference presentations. More than anything, my conversations with these individuals confirmed to me the need for a thoroughly updated practical guide to creating healthier organizations.

Graham Lowe
Kelowna, British Columbia
November 2019

# CREATING HEALTHY ORGANIZATIONS

# Introduction

You're about to enter into the world of competitive video gaming, known as e-sports, which has taken off in the last decade. Rogers Arena in Vancouver, home of the Vancouver Canucks hockey team, hosted in August 2018 what was touted as the e-sports Super Bowl. In the darkened arena, 15,000 fans cheered on professional teams of e-gamers as they battled it out on screen for the international *Dota 2* championship and over $25 million US in prizes. The gaming industry is propelled by a seemingly insatiable interest among young people in video games, especially mobile applications and virtual reality headsets. So it is not surprising that e-sports have become big business. The National Football League and ESPN, a TV sports network, have joined up with video game maker Electronic Arts to launch the *Madden NFL 19* Championship Series (MCS). The hugely popular *Madden NFL 19* tournament will be internationally broadcast on ESPN – just like NFL football, on which the video game is based. With numerous tournaments planned, one industry expert claimed that the Madden global ecosystem "allows anyone to go from couch to champion ensuring MCS competition is accessible to the masses."[1]

And that's setting off alerts about the health consequences for e-gamers in this booming twenty-first-century industry. To have a reasonable chance of entering high-level e-gaming competitions, young men and women, often in their teens, are expected to spend fourteen to sixteen hours a day practicing in dark rooms resembling factories, cut off from contact with the outside world to eliminate distractions and subsisting on Ramen noodles. The e-sports professional gaming market is estimated to be worth $1.5 billion US by 2020 with a fan base of 600 million.[2] It is an offshoot of the global gaming industry, which is estimated to be worth around $140 billion annually – about the same as the entire film industry.[3] Players don't receive salaries, just prize money. The expectation of winning motivates many thousands of aspirants to put in long hours of unpaid work and fund their own travel costs. That's why *League of Legends* teams in North America and Europe have called for better treatment of players, including job security, fair pay, and other career supports.

Taking better care of e-gamers' health has become an industry priority.[4] The repetitive hand, wrist, and arm motions required can lead to career-ending injuries. Several high-profile e-sports "athletes" have suffered from pneumothorax, or collapsed lung, due largely to their hunched-over posture and lack of exercise. E-sports teams are known to rely on performance-enhancing drugs to improve concentration during games. Gamers can crash and burn mentally under the strain of long hours, isolation, and competitive pressures. And obviously the brutal schedules gamers face training and competing leave little time for proper nutrition, exercise, or sunlight. Responding to this rapidly growing occupation, the World Health Organization in 2018 recognized "gaming disorder" in its international classification of diseases.[5] Gaming disorder results when playing video or digital games basically takes over a person's life to the exclusion of other daily activities and the impairment of their physical and mental health.

## Work Transformed

This vignette about e-gamers highlights the relentless pace of change in the world of work, which raises the fundamental question I take up in this book: How can you future-proof your organization by making it humanly sustainable? Doing so requires stronger links between employee well-being, as a worthy goal in itself, and the future success of the business. In the past decade, there has been a steady stream of scholarly research and proven workplace practices that look beyond the health behaviors and attitudes of individuals to get at the underlying organizational factors that contribute to workers' well-being. My goal is to synthesize and integrate leading practices and research from workplace health promotion, human resources, organizational change and leadership, employee engagement, and corporate social responsibility (CSR, also called "sustainability"). The result, I believe, is a compelling case for building resilient and sustainable businesses by focusing first and foremost on improving employees' well-being.

Digital health technologies are advancing by leaps and bounds. Worksite health programs delivered on websites can improve a range of health outcomes for participants.[6] An emerging trend in workplace wellness is the growing use of employer-subsidized wearable activity tracking devices ("wearables"). There is growing interest among employers and employees in using wearables, such as Fitbits, to promote health and wellness, including making them available to spouses and partners.[7] Setting aside for the moment growing concerns about the privacy of personal data, artificial intelligence (AI) has even greater potential to transform workplaces, for better or worse. AI applications already are enabling real-time tracking of health status, sleep, stress, happiness, and potential health and safety risks and hazards. AI also will be used to monitor the effects of healthy workplace changes.[8] Or in a far darker scenario, AI could lead us into a Brave New World where workers' thoughts and actions are monitored and regulated. These are the stark choices now confronting organizational decision-makers.

The global financial crisis was tightening its grip on the economy as I wrote the first edition of *Creating Healthy Organizations*. A big part of the solution to the economic malaise, I argued, was to foster a healthy, resilient, and productive workforce. For employers, this still remains a pressing people challenge, but for different reasons. The financial crisis is ten years behind us now. In many countries, the job market is booming, unemployment is at a record low, and an aging workforce is leading to worker shortages in many occupations and industries. Yet with inequality rising and incomes flatlining for all but the top tier of professionals, managers, and business owners, financial stress has become yet another sign of low job quality.[9] More than ever, the yawning gap between the haves and have-nots in the labor market now extends beyond the economic to the quality of work-life. Experiencing well-being through work should be a defining feature of a sustainable twenty-first-century society.

Finding effective ways to make organizations healthier is more important than ever. Yet fewer people are working in what early twentieth-century German sociologist Max Weber famously labeled a bureaucracy, with its rigid hierarchy of authority, narrowly precise job descriptions, and lifelong careers. Work structures have become more dispersed, decentralized, and fluid. Digital technologies can give workers greater freedom and flexibility in how, where, and when they work. But the very same technologies can also impose virtual prisons that monitor, control, and regulate every detail of a worker's behavior. And they are spawning a new cadre of freelancers who use digital platforms to do short-term "gigs," with no secure attachment to a traditional employer – and therefore no access to corporate health, safety, and wellness programs.

My profile of e-gamers highlights the future challenges of protecting and promoting workers' health and safety in a digital economy with a destructured workforce where fewer people have a continuous employment relationship with a single organization. Most e-gamers are freelancers who are not tied to an organization the way a continuing employee would be. Yet some belong to teams, which can advocate collectively for better working conditions within the e-gaming ecosystem. So e-gamers are part of a swelling pool of precarious workers. The latest research tells us that poor health, anxiety, and financial insecurity are associated with the uncertainty surrounding any work that does not conform to the twentieth-century ideal of a steady full-time job with one employer.[10]

Gig economy workers and other freelancers or contract workers are self-employed. As such, they fall outside of the organizations that employ the majority of workers, even though they may be part of the extended networks of such organizations – just as some e-gamers are linked to the NFL. As we'll see, there is good potential for companies who are committed to CSR or sustainability goals to positively influence the working lives of individuals in their supply chains and business networks. This is how to expand the concept of a healthy organization to include those who are not "employees." With the spread of corporate sustainability practices and reporting, we can expect to see more and more companies addressing the health, safety, and overall well-being of workers in their business networks.

Yet for now, healthy-organization resources will be less helpful for those who are self-employed. So who are we talking about? In Canada, about one in seven workers were self-employed in 2018, accounting for about 15 percent of all employment, which is a small increase from 12 percent in 1976.[11] The largest group of self-employed consists of knowledge workers in professional, scientific, and technical services. In 2018 one-third (33.5 percent) of the self-employed gave independence and freedom as their main reason for choosing this form of employment – two widely sought-after features that have the potential to contribute to a worker's health. There are some signs of progress within this corner of the labor market. For example, agriculture has the highest proportion of self-employed (57 percent in 2018) of any industry. Farmers face climate change, volatile global markets, and chronic financial pressures, all of which contribute to high levels of stress, anxiety, and depression.[12] In response, farmers are developing their own mental health support resources, such as the Do More Agriculture Foundation.

This is a positive example of how workers who are outside typical work organizations are coming together to advocate for their own well-being. The widespread use of social media makes this sort of mutual support and joint action much easier than it was ten or fifteen years ago. Another example is the pathbreaking legislation passed in California, expected to take effect in 2020, requiring app-based companies such as Uber and Lyft to treat contract workers as employees, with all the legal protections and security that brings.[13]

## Progress at the Front Lines of Change

Since I wrote the first edition of this book, the concept of a healthy organization has moved into the mainstream of corporate health and wellness. The healthy organization is becoming a focal point in the fields of human resources, workplace health promotion, leadership, organizational performance, employee well-being, and CSR. Scholarly research has advanced beyond making a business case for workplace health promotion to report on the prerequisites for successful workplace health promotion interventions and explore the links between employee well-being and organizational performance.

A simple principle I learned from researchers at the Institute for Work and Health (I served on its Scientific Advisory Committee) is that work is a determinant of health and health is a determinant of work. Compared with the state of knowledge a decade ago, we now know much more about the dynamics of this complex relationship. We now have a solid foundation of evidence on which to design strategies for maximizing positive influences in both directions. In a nutshell, if people's jobs, work environments, and organizational supports and resources can be designed to contribute to their overall well-being, then their positive physical, mental, and emotional experiences of work will enable them to work "smarter." They win, the employer (and shareholders or owners) wins, customers or clients win. And as we'll see, benefits also flow to society. This is the basic formula for a humanly sustainable organization.

Many individuals have been diligently pushing the leading edge of these changes. The publication of the book's first edition brought me invitations for about 100 conference talks, webinars, and workshops. These events provided me with a front-row seat from which to listen to and learn from numerous "change agents," which included front-line employees, managers, and professionals in human resources (HR), occupational health and safety (OHS), workplace wellness, organizational development (OD), training, and other positions. I've picked up clear indications from diverse audiences that more focus is needed on the "how" of healthy workplaces. For example:

- A talk in Toronto for a human resource leaders' network brought out many HR consultants. They understood the rationale for better aligning HR programs and wellness. What they now wanted was a "deeper dive" into what changes could forge closer HR–CSR links, improve employee and customer experiences, and promote the sustainability of organizations.
- The chair of the board of trade in another large city also chaired the community's Healthy Living Alliance. Her key message at a conference: we have lots of activity in this area and don't need more resources, so please help us locate and figure out how to use what's available inside workplaces.
- At national OHS conferences in several countries, it was evident from my discussions with participants and from listening to other presentations that mental health had moved up the OHS agenda. The practical question that kept coming up: How can we expand traditional OHS to incorporate psychological dimensions of health promotion and illness prevention?
- At a healthy workplace conference, an insurance company executive stated that long-term disability often is caused by stress resulting from interpersonal conflict with a boss or an

overwhelming dissatisfaction with one's job. In other words, what looks like a personal health issue is symptomatic of how people are being managed and the quality of relationships between employees and their supervisors.

- At a healthy organization workshop in New Zealand, participants (mostly managers and business owners) understood the need to support resilience in their workforces. In that country, setbacks such as a devastating earthquake did not detract from a strong sense of momentum on workplace health and safety. The discussion centered on actions that promoted both well-being and performance.

## Expanding Wellness Initiatives

More companies are expanding their wellness focus to address workplace mental health issues. For example, CGI Inc., a Montreal-based information technology company, designated May as Mental Health Month, with a focus on the support employees can receive from the company, colleagues, and their personal network.[14] As Marie-Soleil Ferland, the company's health and wellness lead for Canada, explains: "At the beginning we were talking about mental health on the soft side, with yoga and massage days, and then we realized that we needed to have a stronger strategy if we wanted to really help members go through their journey."

Other employers are adopting new approaches to health promotion. Take Winnipeg-based Canada Drugs, which set up an on-site garden for its 200 employees as the centerpiece of its wellness program.[15] The garden gets employees outdoors, and on every payday they can enjoy the garden's products at a company-sponsored barbecue. In addition to the garden, the company's wellness strategy includes monthly employee educational sessions on wellness-related topics, a health risk assessment app, healthy vending machine options, digital health coaching, and various employee-led fitness events.

A leading Canadian provider of health benefits and disability insurance acquired a smaller company that specialized in workplace health promotion. The goal was to move into the organizational health space, supporting clients (mostly large employers) to do the same. So it set about developing self-assessment tools that clients could use to answer the questions "Where do we start and how do we pull it off?" For this company, it made sense to offer clients new heath, wellness, and prevention resources as an "add-on" to their disability insurance and drug benefits businesses. This approach was based on the realization that 40 percent of drug claims were for mental health issues. So the company saw a big opportunity for "bringing it all together," as the lead managers told me.

The CEO of a pharmaceutical company was less interested in the potential return on investment from workplace wellness initiatives than in knowing how actions in this area would improve employee engagement and morale. The CEO realized that thinking among healthy workplace advocates – especially in his own company – needed to expand in order to bridge this gap. This CEO articulated the growing recognition among corporate leaders that the healthy workplace conversation had to shift away from costs, which are lagging indicators, to emphasize promotion and prevention.

When Toronto-based FreshBooks, a small business accounting software firm, moved into its first office in 2007, the big workplace perks for employees – many of whom were in their early twenties – included a ping-pong table and video games.[16] But employees' needs evolved, and a decade later many of them were parents with young children who needed family-friendly benefits. As Levi Cooperman, a company cofounder and vice president, states: "A lot of the folks we hired in their early 20s are now aging into their 30s and we have about 35 to 40 people with young children on an employee base of 260, so a pretty good chunk of our folks have children." Recognizing the difficulty of obtaining childcare in Toronto, the company partnered with childcare provider Kids &

Co. to offer all employees with preschool-aged children guaranteed access to spaces.

These five examples highlight the big question a growing number of organizations must answer as they plan the future of their workplace health and wellness programs: How can we design and implement changes that will get at the root causes of employee well-being? Answers to this question, the details of which will vary for each organization, must target the organization's culture, systems, and structures. This includes how work is organized, how people are managed, workplace relationships, and the company's values that define what really matters for its success.

## Making Tangible Progress

I have contributed a number of presentations and workshops to the Conference Board of Canada, whose members include many of the largest private and public sector employers in Canada. These organizations exemplify leading workplace wellness practices. As part of my research for this new edition, I asked members of the conference board's Council on Workplace Health and Wellness to share their experiences over the past five years.

When asked to describe their most important success in making their workplace healthier, they indicated that there clearly is momentum in the area of workplace mental health, with more initiatives being launched, more leadership support, and more encouragement for employees to speak up about mental health issues in the workplace. As one council member put it: "We are moving to a focus on psychologically healthy workplaces." Other organizations strengthened their existing wellness programs by improving return-to-work outcomes, collaborating with HR and other organizational units to achieve healthy workplace goals, and broadening the definition of occupational health and safety to be more holistic and inclusive.

I also asked council members what they saw as the best opportunity for future progress in this regard over the next three to five
years. Here's what stood out: being able to dedicate more resources
to workplace wellness; having more employees champion wellness;
fostering shared accountability for workplace health; and measuring and communicating successes. There's general agreement that
Canadian employers – at least many large ones – have made good
progress in recent years and just need to continue building on these
successes. As one of the council members advised: "Stop focusing
on calculating ROI [return on investment] and instead focus on how
employees value your program."

Finally, council members identified the greatest barrier they
would need to overcome as they moved forward. The barriers mentioned are the common ones faced in many organizations: leadership changes; market changes that impact the company's revenues;
maintaining employees' interest and increasing their participation
in existing programs; reaching out to those employees who are not
yet engaged; competing corporate priorities; a perceived lack of urgency regarding workplace health issues; and a corporate emphasis on operational success rather than people. So despite making
progress, employee well-being has not yet become enshrined as a
top priority for some leaders. One council member described this
barrier as "a lack of urgency to include wellness as part of a healthy
work environment ... it continues to be a 'nice-to-have' rather than a
necessity for healthy and resilient employees."

## Momentum for Change

Extensive resources are now available in many countries to help
with the *process* – or the "how" – of making workplaces healthier.
Above all, these resources and activities highlight the need for a con-
cise, practical analysis of the challenges one can face trying to create

a healthier organization, the hurdles that must be overcome along the way, and the success factors that can energize the process. So far, there is no comprehensive synthesis of what we know about these issues that can help practitioners and other change agents to take an evidence-based approach to improving their workplace. That's the knowledge gap I intend to fill with this thoroughly revised and updated edition of *Creating Healthy Organizations*. By "practitioners," I am referring to those individuals occupying positions with formal responsibility and authority for their organization's health, safety, wellness, and HR programs and goals. However, some of these individuals may be perfectly content with the status quo. That's why I also use the term "change agent" to speak directly to individuals who have a personal commitment to creating a better workplace. Based on my observations, change agents are motivated to champion healthy change, and they find a way to do so regardless of their formal position in an organization.

More researchers, policy-makers, and practitioners are recognizing the need to take a more holistic approach to improving well-being, combining a focus on individual and organizational factors. There have been some pathbreaking efforts in this direction over the past decade, which I summarize throughout the book. These initiatives are a big step beyond wellness programs. Corporate wellness programs have done much to encourage and support employees and their families to adopt and maintain healthy attitudes and behaviors. However, while these programs cover a wide range of targets and goals, their main thrust has been to get more employees to quit smoking, eat nutritiously, and exercise more.[17] Reflecting on this limitation, more researchers are calling for an expanded focus on all aspects of an organization that influence health and performance. As Dee Edington and Jennifer Pitts propose, a "win-win philosophy" for achieving organizational health "is designed to create workforces and workplaces where excellent health, meaningful work, high performance, loyalty, happiness, and quality of life are the norm."[18]

The push for an integrated approach to worker well-being has advanced the furthest in the United States. The US National Institute for Occupational Safety and Health (NIOSH) advocates for an integrated and comprehensive approach to workplace health and safety called "Total Worker Health" (TWH). NIOSH provides on its website a compendium of resources for planning, assessing, and evaluating TWH programs, policies, and practices.[19] The TWH framework for improving worker well-being is based on multidisciplinary research and on input from an expert panel. The TWH framework comes out of the occupational health and safety area, where NIOSH sits. For well over a decade, workplace health promotion experts have recommended an integrated and comprehensive approach to workplace health, safety, and human resources.[20] Reflecting the growing interest in the TWH approach, NIOSH sponsored the second International Symposium to Advance Total Worker Health in 2018, focusing on the following theme: "Work & Well-Being: How Safer, Healthier Work Can Enhance Well-Being."[21]

In a complementary initiative, the American College of Occupational and Environmental Medicine and Underwriters Laboratories hosted the Summit on Integration of Health and Safety in the Workplace in 2014.[22] Experts attending the summit recommended a framework for integrating workplace health and safety strategies and relevant metrics modeled after the Dow Jones Sustainability Indices, which were the first global sustainability benchmarks measuring a corporation's economic, environmental, and social impact. The goal is OHS, wellness, and CSR integration: "Participants at the ACOEM/UL summit identified nonintegrated institutional silos as one of the greatest obstacles to achieving a true culture of health in the workplace."[23] So far, few employers have adopted a truly integrated approach, despite the potential synergies to be gained. Required is a strategic and systematic integration of policies, programs, personnel, and strategies to enhance the well-being of workers and their families. The key message for all stakeholders coming out of the summit: "Safe and healthy employees are less likely to be injured while on the job, they are more likely to be vibrant, engaged, and high performing ... all of these things are good for the bottom line."[24]

Elsewhere, the government of the United Kingdom commissioned an independent review of modern working practices by Matthew Taylor, chief executive of the Royal Society of Arts.[25] It sets an ambitious but necessary goal: "All work in the UK economy should be fair and decent with realistic scope of development and fulfilment." The UK government agreed that this commitment required measures against which the quality of work could be evaluated. The five principles defining the quality of work articulate the underpinnings of a truly healthy organization: worker satisfaction; good pay; participation and progression; well-being, safety, and security; and voice and autonomy. Moving in the same direction, the Australasian Consensus statement on the health benefits of work makes recommendations for governments, insurers, businesses and worker advocates to enhance health and productivity in Australia's and New Zealand's workplaces.[26] The statement advocates improvements in workplace culture and the creation of 'good work' from which individuals, employers and the community can benefit. The statement also aims to avoid no work or bad work, because both can make people sick.

Canadians have made substantial progress in the past decade promoting workplace mental health.[27] The Mental Health Commission of Canada (MHCC) has provided influential research, resources, and advocacy for a greater focus on mental health issues, particularly in workplaces.[28] The National Standard of Canada for Psychological Health and Safety in the Workplace was launched in 2013, a joint initiative of the MHCC, the Canadian Standards Association, and the Bureau de normalisation du Québec.[29] This consensus-based voluntary standard for psychological health and safety is widely recognized as a breakthrough in mental health promotion, enabling the integration of psychological health and safety within existing occupational health and safety systems, human rights policies, and HR practices.

## Connecting Well-Being and Sustainability

Sustainability is another accelerating trend, helped by the fact that the concept has found its way into the business mainstream. Deloitte's *2019 Global Human Capital Trends* report highlights the pressures on organizations to become more human-focused by giving higher priority to their impact on society, income inequality, diversity, and the environment.[30] Deloitte calls this newly emerging organization a "social enterprise" because it balances the goals of revenue growth and profits with respecting and supporting its stakeholders and the environment. This describes a sustainable company, which behaves as a "good citizen" internally and externally. The Deloitte report advocates for the large-scale reinvention of enterprises so they are better able to address societal issues (such as diversity, inequality, and the environment), customer and employee satisfaction, and employee engagement and retention. Deloitte's ten human capital trends do not specifically include employee health, safety, or well-being. However, one trend is improving the employee experience, which emphasizes putting more meaning back into work. This includes providing workers with opportunities to have a positive impact on their organization and on society – two features of a healthy workplace.

As more businesses around the world take environmental sustainability actions, HR has a vital role to play. Indeed, "green human resource management" is a growing trend, helping companies and their employees make more sustainable use of resources internally and externally.[31] Green HR practices help employees acquire the awareness, knowledge, and behaviors they require to achieve their company's sustainability goals. And the company's commitment to

these goals is infused in all aspects of employee recruitment, retention, development, and engagement.

Green offices are another sustainability trend that signals the closer
integration of environmental and employee goals. Features of the
physical work environment – such as workspace design, temperature,
air quality, color, light, noise, and plants – can influence employees'
well-being, work concentration, and job performance.[32] Green office
buildings have positive effects on workers' physical and psychological health and productivity.[33] For example, Microsoft's "sustainable"
Silicon Valley campus, opened in late 2019, is home to more than
2,000 employees. It is designed to provide "the best employee experience" in the industry.[34] It will achieve net zero non-potable water
consumption, the buildings meet LEED (Leadership in Energy and
Environmental Design) Platinum certification, there's a four-acre living roof, and construction utilizes sustainably sourced mass timber
in place of concrete and steel. The design is intended to promote
employee collaboration and productivity. And it surely will reinforce for Microsoft's employees that their personal environmental
values are reflected in the company's actions.

## Mixed Signals

What I've described so far amounts to a groundswell of positive
change. However, many workers have had their job demands, time
pressure, and performance expectations steadily ratcheted up in the
twenty-first century. The widespread use of information technology
is a contributing factor.[35] Thus, not all relevant trends are headed in
the same positive direction. On one hand, we know far more now
than a decade ago about the dynamics of work and health. There
are also more practical resources available that can be used to make
workplaces healthier and safer, and a growing emphasis on the
importance of addressing the underlying organizational drivers of

workers' mental and physical health, safety, and well-being. Yet on the other hand, studies in various countries show increasing levels of stress, work–life imbalance, disengagement, and job dissatisfaction across large swaths of the workforce.

Here's a sampling of these negative work trends:

Jonathan Karmel, in his book *Dying to Work*, documents that the workplace fatality rate in the US has increased since the 2008 recession. In 2015, thirteen workers were killed on the job each day in the US and another 50,000 deaths could be attributed to work-related illnesses. As Karmel writes, "for most workers in the United States the right to a safe and healthy workplace has been made difficult to achieve over our country's history and remains so today in the twenty-first century."[36] Furthermore, Stanford University professor Jeffrey Pfeffer reaches a stark conclusion from his extensive analysis of how work environments affect workers' health: "The workplace profoundly affects human health and mortality, and too many workplaces are harmful to people's health – people literally are dying for a pay check."[37] As Pfeffer documents, much of work's harmful health effects arise from job stress. A significant barrier to progress on workplace safety and health in the US is the relentless pressure from business lobbies and right-wing think tanks to deregulate worker health and safety – pressure that has intensified since the 2016 election of Donald Trump as president.

We now have a more complete picture of the costs of job stress. Australian researchers estimate that depression resulting from job-induced stress costs Australia $890 million annually, mostly in terms of lost work time and job turnover.[38] A survey of over 16,000 US workers confirms that stressful working conditions (resulting from job insecurity, work–family imbalance, and hostile work environments) can contribute to physical injuries. In other words, psychological risks are also risks to physical health.[39] Turning to Canada, in our book *Redesigning Work*, Frank Graves and I document rising levels of work stress, work–life imbalance, and job dissatisfaction using Rethinking Work national workforce surveys going back to the early 2000s.[40] These surveys also reveal the benefits of healthy psychosocial job conditions: lower absenteeism; greater job satisfaction; stronger commitment; lower turnover; and greater use of one's knowledge and skills. Stress and work–life imbalance are organizational problems that require organizational, not individual, solutions. When the Rethinking Work survey asked employees who experienced stress to suggest solutions, a reduced workload and better people management practices were at the top of the list.

Employers are responding to these workplace deficiencies, but too slowly and often using the wrong tools. The Conference Board of Canada surveyed 205 Canadian employers in 2016 and found that while workplace wellness programs have become more prevalent since 2009, only one-third of employers surveyed had a formal wellness strategy, while about half took an informal approach to wellness.[41] According to Conference Board research, lost productivity due to depression and anxiety alone are costing the Canadian economy billions of dollars annually. However, the 2017 Sanofi Canada survey of health benefits plans found that employers were becoming more cautious about investing in wellness, despite a positive assessment of the contributions of these programs.[42] The Sanofi Canada survey also found that according to employees, their organization's corporate culture was less supportive of health and wellness in 2017 than five years earlier. It is too early to say if these findings indicate longer-term trends. Regardless, they should encourage those employers who care at all about their employees' well-being to redouble their efforts.

## Chapter Outline

On the bright side, there are sure signs of progress when it comes to understanding and improving worker well-being. And there certainly are far more useful resources available than there were a decade ago. While we know that some leading organizations are having success tackling the organizational causes of job stress, work–life imbalance, and disengagement, many more employers must be convinced to also move in this direction. While not all major trends are moving in a positive direction, the potential is there for this to happen. As I document in this book, we know what will work. To help readers figure out how best to move their organization toward well-being and sustainable performance goals, I have organized my discussion as follows:

- Chapter 1: The Healthy Organization. This opening chapter updates my healthy organization framework, providing an even stronger case for building a healthy organization that is grounded in a positive culture, a vibrant work environment that truly inspires employees in their work, and an inclusive approach to leadership. With these foundation pieces in place, any organization will be much better able to achieve humanly sustainable success.
- Chapter 2: Beyond Workplace Health Promotion. Here I examine how existing wellness and workplace health promotion programs can provide a springboard for a more holistic, comprehensive, and integrated approach that will enable employees to thrive. Especially important in this regard is expanding the focus of wellness beyond physical health to encompass psychological well-being, and also to integrate wellness into a unified strategy that finds synergies with occupational health and safety, human resources, and corporate social responsibility.
- Chapter 3: How Vibrant Workplaces Inspire Employees. This chapter delves into what a healthy organization feels like through the daily experiences of employees. The chapter connects the "big dots" of employees' capabilities, resilience, well-being, and engagement. A healthy and safe work environment not only supports employees to be well; it also enables

them to develop and apply their capabilities, bringing creative energy to their work. This is the key connection between
well-being and sustainable business performance.

- Chapter 4: Positive Cultures. This chapter explains how a positive culture based on strong, widely shared people values is
what links together employee well-being goals with achieving
the organization's mission. Above all, a positive culture fosters
a sense of community in the workplace. People trust each other
and treat one another – as well customers and other external
stakeholders – with respect and fairness. Everyone in the organization understands that this is the ethical way to behave.

- Chapter 5: Inclusive Leadership. This chapter shows how defining and achieving healthy organization goals must be a shared
responsibility. While demonstrated support from senior leaders
is a key enabling condition for change, equally important is the
active participation of all the organization's members, right down
to the front lines. Ideally, all employees should feel motivated and
encouraged to make their work environment healthier and safer
as part of a shared commitment to continuous improvement.

- Chapter 6: Healthy Change. Drawing on my experience as an
organizational consultant, I offer insights, backed up by solid
research evidence, that are intended to help you design a change
process that fits the context and needs of your organization,
leading to sustainable improvements. There is no standard recipe for doing this, so I challenge each reader to adapt ideas and
actions that make the most sense for where their organization is
today and where it wants to go.

- Chapter 7: Sustainable Success. This chapter expands on significant developments in the past decade in the area of corporate social responsibility, or what is now more often called sustainability.
The next big step is firmly positioning worker well-being goals
into corporate sustainability strategies. The pursuit of sustainable
business practices dovetails with healthy organization ideals. This

is an encouraging development, one that I use to illustrate what it means for an organization to become humanly sustainable.

- Chapter 8: Measuring Progress. Here I review expert, evidence-based advice for how you can measure your organization's progress along its path to becoming healthier, safer, and more humanly sustainable. I highlight the measurement implications of taking a more holistic and integrated approach to promoting employee health, safety, resilience, well-being, and performance. Emphasis is given to the effective use of your existing measurement tools and data, particularly surveys and corporate human resource and health benefits data.

- Chapter 9: A Practical Guide to Creating a Healthier Organization. This chapter is an action-oriented summary of the insights, resources, and evidence provided throughout the book. I provide a tool called the Healthy Organization Assessment, which can help you to determine how far your organization has come and what the best next steps should be. I also provide a detailed action checklist that can guide whatever healthy workplace improvements you and your coworkers consider necessary. Readers are encouraged to use these and other tools presented throughout the book to design, implement, and evaluate their own strategy. Your focus can be a team, work unit, department, or your entire organization. Whether you sit at the executive table or are a frontline worker, you can be a change agent who helps your organization achieve humanly sustainable future success.

# CHAPTER 1

# The Healthy Organization

A potentially seismic shift is underway in workplaces. Human resources, workplace wellness, and occupational health and safety experts are focusing increasingly on how employees' work environment influences their well-being and job performance. Managers are searching for ways to fully engage employees and unleash hidden talents. More companies are making and delivering on sustainability commitments, or what's also called corporate social responsibility (CSR). These converging trends are opening up new opportunities to improve the quality of work-life, organizational performance, and communities – all at the same time. Imagine a future in which boundaries have dissolved between employee health and safety, performance, and CSR, and where these goals are central to every manager's job. We still have some distance to go before these silos break down. Progress requires an overarching well-being strategy that tightly integrates occupational health and safety (OHS), wellness, employee engagement, and CSR actions and goals.

These are the tailwinds of change pushing organizations toward a healthier future. The purpose of this chapter is to provide the basic ideas you will need on that journey, starting with my model of a healthy organization. This model rests on a simple premise: healthy organizations thrive because they are humanly sustainable, cultivating a mentally and physically healthy and safe workforce as a means to higher performance levels and a better world. The model promotes holistic, long-term thinking, showing how OHS, wellness, human resource management (HR), and CSR can have a more positive impact on employee well-being and organizational performance when combined than they currently do as separate areas. Tacking into the tailwinds of these changes requires executives and boards to build employee well-being goals into their corporate strategy, giving high priority to coordinated actions in the work plans for all areas of the business.

This chapter makes five main points:

1 Employee well-being is an organizational performance and sustainability issue, not simply a matter of personal health.
2 A healthy organization rests on these pillars: a positive culture, an inclusive approach to leadership, and a vibrant workplace that inspires employees.
3 This model of a healthy organization illustrates how the underlying drivers of well-being and performance are closely connected and systemic.
4 All internal and external stakeholders will benefit from employers taking an integrated approach to engagement, occupational healthy and safety, wellness, and CSR.
5 Healthy organizations put in place conditions for humanly sustainable success, renewing their workforce capabilities and relationships with customers and communities.

## Integrating Well-Being and Performance

I am challenging you to take a big step beyond what you now think of as a "healthy workplace." My concept of a healthy organization combines ideas about what contributes to employee well-being and organizational performance from different areas of expertise. Economists want to know how firms can achieve more output for the same units of input, ideally by working smarter. Managers and organizational experts are concerned about how businesses achieve better performance. Health promotion professionals want to know how to involve managers and employees in creating health-promoting work environments. Occupational health and safety professionals strive to foster a safety culture as a shared responsibility of everyone in the workplace. And the growing field of CSR emphasizes that social responsibility applies to everything a company does, especially how it treats its employees.

For too long, these have been separate agendas pursued in organizational silos. The healthy organization model unifies them into a powerful change tool. Over the past decade, there have been increased calls for a systemic view of the determinants of employee health, safety, and well-being. From this broad perspective, health becomes a defining feature of the entire organization. A holistic approach also emphasizes the importance of a healthy change process. Encouraging employees and managers at all levels to co-create healthy and productive work environments builds on the World Health Organization (WHO) definition of health promotion as "the process of enabling individuals and communities to increase control over the determinants of health and thereby improve their health."[1]

Improving the well-being of workers and communities is a fundamental goal of a healthy organization. We'll see in chapter 2 that workplace wellness strategies have broadened and deepened to address organizational factors, with the goal of improving employee well-being. This evolution of workplace health promotion is reflected in the WHO's definition of health as "a state of complete physical, mental and social well-being and not merely the absence of disease or infirmity."[2] As such, well-being is a de-medicalized term for a person's overall health. However, some experts point out that "complete" well-being is not a realistic goal in the context of twenty-first-century chronic disease trends and an aging population, replacing "complete" with "optimal."[3] Viewed through the lens of a healthy organization, well-being is a dynamic and ongoing process whereby individuals and groups develop the capacity to learn and adapt to new circumstances and cope in the face of social, physical, and emotional challenges. Thus, what's "optimal" is continuously evolving. As we'll see in chapter 3, this perspective on well-being intersects with the psychological concept of resilience.

Here's an example of healthy change that tied together all these pieces. A Toronto-area hospital was planning a move to a new facility. How it planned the move illustrates the internal workings of a healthy organization. Senior leaders and unit managers focused on maintaining staff well-being during the move. Numerous opportunities were created to directly involve staff in the changes associated with the move and to provide them with supporting resources. Using pod prototypes for medical-surgical wards, teams used Lean methods to improve the ward design. Lean healthcare applies the quality improvement principles from Lean manufacturing, pioneered by Toyota, to maximize patient care or service quality while minimizing waste in every process, procedure, and task. Lean methodology was used to actively involve clinical staff in shaping their new work environment, using staff expertise to benefit patients and themselves in the new facility.

While Lean methodology has been widely applied in healthcare, particularly in the US, Britain, and Canada, its success is contingent on many factors, and in some cases it may not benefit hospital workers.[4] However, what this and other Lean healthcare examples I describe in this book clearly show is the Lean approach to quality improvement can enhance employees' quality of working life, as well as benefit patients, as long as the staff play a meaningful role in designing and implementing the improvements. To provide additional context, in this particular hospital senior leaders supported staff well-being during the redevelopment process by revising the hospital's wellness program to promote staff resilience, an important individual and collective skill during the inevitable disruptions caused by the move. To address move-related stress, leaders ensured there were no vacation blackouts leading up to the move. A successful move ensured that high-quality patient care could be maintained. Staff felt they were the ones driving toward this goal, which contributed to high levels of job satisfaction and work engagement.

The growing consensus among practitioners and researchers is for a more integrated, comprehensive, and strategically aligned approach to well-being. This is reflected in the increasing use of the term "organizational health." Moving down this path requires actions that address the systemic (i.e., organizationally embedded) drivers of well-being and performance rooted in job design, work environments, culture, and organizational supports. Wellness consultant Laura Putnam's review of successful wellness programs concludes that actions at the organizational level are what determine a wellness initiative's positive impact. She explains: "The key is infusion, or a full integration of well-being and vitality, into daily conversations, daily work rituals, and core business objectives so that wellness is woven into every aspect of business as usual within the organization."[5] OHS experts also are calling for close links with wellness. Researchers at the Institute for Work and Health, a global leader in occupational health and safety research, recommend that "wellness and OHS programs share the goal of protecting and improving worker health and given these overlaps it makes sense to integrate both."[6] And an integrated and coordinated approach to health, safety, well-being, and performance is now widely endorsed by the influential International Labour Organization, the World

Health Organization, and the US National Institute for Occupational Safety and Health.

## Building Momentum for Change

Let's now widen our discussion to look at other signs of momentum – the tailwinds I referred to earlier. For one thing, corporate wellness programs are becoming more common. About 71 percent of large global employers had a defined wellness program for their employees in 2017, according to a survey by the Top Employers Institute.[7] The survey queried 1,300 employers who were audited and certified by the institute, confirming that North America is leading the way in wellness programs, with 80 percent of employers offering them. This compares with around 60 percent of employers in Asia. Employee assistance programs (EAPs) have grown the most in the last four years. However, while EAPs can provide useful wellness resources for individual employees, especially regarding mental health, they are not set up to target organizational influences on health. Furthermore, it's notable that wellness programs are most prevalent in the US, where there is a growing benefit gap between low- and high-income workers. Few low-wage workers in the US receive health insurance from their employers, which means they lack the most basic requirement for achieving good health.[8]

Some governments are playing a constructive role by introducing policies and legislation intended to make workplaces healthier and safer. For example, Canada and other countries are considering legislating employees' "right to disconnect" on the basis of a 2016 French law giving workers the right to turn off their electronic work devices outside of business hours in order to reduce unpaid overtime, stress, and burnout.[9] More jurisdictions in Canada and elsewhere are introducing "presumptive legislation," whereby workers' compensation systems accept psychological injury claims by first responders (e.g., firefighters, police, and paramedics) as work related. Also encouraging is that governments and their health promotion partners are sponsoring healthy workplace resources and programs, adding to momentum for change. Employers now have at the click of a mouse a much wider range of free tools for making their workplaces healthier.

I've already mentioned the launch of the National Standard of Canada for Psychological Health and Safety, which has provided public resources that are widely used by employers, employees, professional associations and unions, workplace health advocates, and occupational health, safety, and wellness professionals.[10] Canadian and American employers also have shown interest in the American Psychological Association's awards program for achieving psychologically healthy workplaces.[11] Reaching a much wider audience, the International Organization for Standardization (ISO) has added guidelines for promoting and protecting psychological health and safety in the workplace for its widely used OHS management system (ISO 45001-2018). The broader scope of this new standard "enables an organization, through its OH&S management system, to integrate other aspects of health and safety, such as worker wellness/wellbeing."[12] The ISO is also adapting Canada's Standard for wider use, with its forthcoming ISO 45003 guidelines for psychological health and safety in the workplace.[13]

Australia has launched a national strategy to create mentally healthy workplaces. The government-funded "Heads Up" initiative provides employers, employees, and health promotion organizations and professionals across the country with free tools and resources.[14] A pathbreaking national survey on workplace psychological safety was conducted in 2017, a partnership between R U OK, an Australian mental health promotion NGO, and Harvard Business School professor Amy Edmondson. In announcing survey results, R U OK pointed out that untreated mental illness costs Australian business $11 billion every year due to absenteeism, lost productivity, reduced business growth, and compensation claims. The study defined a psychologically safe workplace as having "a climate of interpersonal trust and mutual respect in which people feel comfortable being themselves to make mistakes or take risks in their work."[15] This definition underscores the importance of an organization's culture, as I outline in chapter 4.

Also in Australia, the state of Victoria's Achievement Program aims to improve health and well-being in the workplace.[16] The program is guided by a healthy workplaces framework based on the WHO's healthy workplaces model, providing employers with an easy-to-follow framework to guide their actions. Employers are encouraged to build on their existing healthy workplace initiatives, making continuous improvement to embedding health and well-being into the organization's culture in ways that also improve morale, safety, and productivity. The state government recognizes health-promoting workplaces, linking health promotion to the much sought-after goal of being "an employer of choice."

Along the same lines, the Canadian province of Alberta's Healthier Together Workplaces online program provides employers in the province with interactive promotion and prevention resources to help create healthier workplaces with healthier employees and a strong culture of health.[17] The program guides employees through the steps necessary to gain leadership support for workplace health, assess workplace health needs, and then plan, implement, and evaluate a comprehensive workplace health program. Employers whose workplaces meet established criteria can receive public recognition from Alberta Health Services (AHS, a provincial government department responsible for healthcare), helping to position them as an employer of choice. To create the program, the Alberta Cancer Prevention Legacy Fund partnered with AHS, clinical networks, workplace health and safety organizations in the community, and employers.

In England, the City of London's Healthy Workplace Charter provides tools, an accreditation process, and awards based on an organization's level of support for employee well-being, health and safety, and healthy behaviors.[18] In the US, the HERO Health and Well-Being Best Practices Scorecard (HERO Scorecard) benchmarks workplace health management practices. The scorecard is a collaborative effort between the nonprofit Health Enhancement Research Organization (HERO) and global consulting firm Mercer. The Wellness Council of America (WELCOA) provides a variety of resources for building healthy workplaces that are widely used in corporate America.[19] WELCOA members can make use of benchmarks, checklists, and training and also participate in Well Workplace Awards, all with the goal of promoting employee wellness.

Community partners also are promoting a convergence between OHS and wellness. Canada's Safest Employers awards, presented by *Canadian Occupational Safety* magazine, recognize companies from across Canada who have achieved outstanding results promoting the health and safety of their workers.[20] It recently added two special awards, one for wellness and the other for psychological safety. And in California, the state's Commission on Health and Safety and Workers' Compensation provides guidelines for employers, including clearly defined principles of wellness–OHS program integration.[21] California also links employers' legal responsibilities for providing a safe and healthy workplace with the voluntary provision of wellness or health promotion initiatives.

This last point about employers' legal responsibilities is a crucial one, reflecting how the legal duty of care has expanded in many jurisdictions to include psychological injuries. The basic legal expectation is that employers will exercise due diligence to prevent injury or illness caused by a person's job or work environment. For physical injuries, due diligence has meant implementing and enforcing a robust OHS management system. Now, due diligence has expanded to include the prevention of psychological injury. Furthermore, the duty of care also includes the protection and promotion of the health and safety of employees who travel or spend time working off-site. In Canada, courts and tribunals have recognized post-traumatic stress disorder, acute stress, anxiety, phobias, panic disorder, depression, and other mental health disorders as work related. An employer's duty is to minimize or eliminate risks that can cause these problems and promote a psychologically healthy work environment free from harassment, bullying, violence, and undue stress. Employers are also obligated in Canada to accommodate a worker who has suffered a psychological injury, just as they would one with a physical injury. Despite differences in legislation and workers' compensation systems, broadly similar trends are evident in other advanced industrial nations.

## Healthy Organizations in Action

Before talking about the healthy organization model, I'd like to describe three organizations that in their own distinct ways exemplify the model: the World Bank, SAS Institute, and Urban Systems. These examples show how healthy organizations operate in ways that assure a promising future for their customers and clients, their employees and society.

The World Bank Group (WBG) showcases how multinational organizations can take care of a large, diverse, and global workforce. Headquartered in Washington and with offices in more than 130 locations around the world and staff from 170 countries, the WBG provides financial and technical assistance to developing countries, with the twin goals of eliminating extreme poverty by 2030 and creating shared prosperity through inclusive, sustainable economic growth and development. The World Bank's CSR commitment rests on the belief that it must safeguard the well-being of its employees and the ecosystems, communities, and economies in which it works.[22] To do so, it applies the same sustainability principles to its internal operations as it does externally, publicly reporting its progress.[23] The bank continually strengthens its human capital by fostering staff health, safety, and well-being. Because some employees work in areas of high conflict and violence, it is especially committed to reducing the impact of stressful work. Employees have a voice, with 80 percent participating in a recent engagement survey. Results showed high levels of engagement, with 92 percent of respondents being proud to work for the bank, and three-quarters saying they would recommend it to friends as a great place to work and agreeing that the bank is the best place to work in development.

The WBG takes an evidence-based approach to workplace health and safety. As Dr. Brian Davey, director of Health Services at WBG, explained at the 2018 Duty of Care Summit in Chicago, employee healthcare costs are driven by risks that can be managed through well-designed programs informed by a careful analysis of employee healthcare data. A survey of its staff revealed that 33 percent did not have a primary healthcare provider; furthermore, 60 percent said they would participate in health promotion programs if they were available.

Health risk assessments and biometric screening completed at the head office and international offices helped to pinpoint health risks among staff and their dependents. These risks ranged from back pain, high cholesterol, and high blood pressure to stress, anxiety, and depression. In response, the bank's revised Health and Global Wellness program took a preventative approach, making it easier for staff to access health resources through on-site healthcare services, disease management programs, telemedicine, and wellness resources. Through an evidence-based redesign of its health services portfolio, service offerings at the WBG headquarters were expanded to include full primary care for staff, dependents, and retirees on an outsourced service model, bringing much-needed care close to where employees work and live. Even with this service expansion, the WBG Health and Safety Directorate is reporting annual savings of approximately $2.76 million through increased utilization of contracted in-network services, reduced internal staffing costs, and significant staff time savings from on-site health service availability.

An outstanding example of a healthy private sector organization is SAS Institute, a leader in analytics software that unleashes the power of clients' data to improve decision-making. Based in Cary, North Carolina, and with over 14,000 employees around the world, SAS is widely recognized for its successful HR practices and caring culture. At SAS, innovation and business growth are built on long-term relationships with employees and customers. It has very low staff turnover. As SAS president and CEO Jim Goodnight explains: "We've worked hard to create a corporate culture that is based on trust between our employees and the company, a culture that rewards innovation, encourages employees to try new things and yet doesn't penalize them for taking chances, and a culture that cares about employees' personal and professional growth." SAS employees understand that their work matters and is valued by senior management. All employees are treated with dignity, so part-timers receive paid sick days and health insurance. SAS also has created a robust accountability framework using metrics and ongoing employee feedback. SAS's caring culture places importance on work–life balance, so the company provides on-site childcare and flexible work options such as telecommuting and compressed workweeks.

SAS has been on *Fortune* magazine's 100 Best Companies to Work for in America list for twenty-two years. Nine out of ten (89 percent) of SAS employees surveyed in the US for the 2019 *Fortune* list said it is a great place to work. Between 93 percent and 96 percent reported that the company's facilities contribute to a good working environment and that they are able to take time off from work when necessary; feel that new employees are made to feel welcome; are proud to tell others they work for SAS; and feel good about the ways SAS contributes to the community.[24] SAS also has been named by Great Place to Work (who compile the *Fortune* list and similar national and global lists) as one of the world's best multinational employers, one of the top ten

Best Workplaces in Canada in 2019, one of the Best Workplaces for Women, and one of the Best Workplaces for Giving Back.[25]

Caring for its people extends to caring for its communities and the planet. Some of SAS's products battle cybercrime, improve customer experiences, protect endangered species, and improve education, child welfare, and public safety. The company actively engages in public policy discussions, particularly regarding how technologies can address challenges in these areas. For example, it hosts public safety summits in the US, which bring together community members and law enforcement officials. In 2019, SAS Canada was recognized as a Best Workplace for Women.[26] In 2018, SAS Canada launched the Women in Analytics Network to strengthen diversity in the data analytics field. Guided by the SAS values of authenticity, work–life balance, and passion, the network's goal is to build a community of women, inside and outside of SAS, who will advocate for women in the field of data analytics. The SAS Women in Analytics Network was featured as a best practice in research reported by Great Place to Work and the We Empower program of UN Women, the European Union, and the International Labour Organization.[27]

Urban Systems is a Canadian example of a medium-sized company that has put in place all the building blocks of a healthy organization. Urban Systems is an interdisciplinary professional services firm providing planning, engineering, environmental science, communications, and urban design services to governments, Indigenous communities, land developers, and private industry. The company's 550 employees work at fifteen offices in Canada's four Western provinces. In 2019, Urban Systems was recognized for the fourteenth consecutive year by Great Place to Work Canada as one of the country's best workplaces on its annual list published in the *Globe and Mail*, a national newspaper.[28]

Like SAS, Urban Systems has a deep understanding of how culture matters for a successful and sustainable business. The company's website provides a clear description of its "spirited culture," emphasizing how the company encourages collaboration, innovation, and a true spirit of service to its clients and communities.[29] The word "vibrant" is used to describe how Urban Systems' employees are committed to enabling communities to be prosperous, sustainable, resilient, and healthy. The company takes care of its employees and they take care of each other. Each office has a social committee that organizes fun events, such as summer BBQs, lunch and learns, and mixers with clients and community members. And there's an annual year-end event where the team's work is appreciated and celebrated. Urban Systems' leaders walk the talk when it comes to fostering a culture of collaboration, innovation, and a spirit of service. Martin Bell, the company's CEO, co-chaired the City of Kelowna's Journey Home Task Force on Homelessness.[30] The task force is the largest multisector community consultation process on homelessness conducted in Canada. Its five-year plan details how the city and its partners can prevent homelessness, which is experienced by over 2,000 people in Kelowna each year.

The company also demonstrates its spirit of service to communities through two very useful initiatives: the Urban Systems Foundation and Urban Matters Community Contribution Company (CCC). The Urban Systems Foundation, funded by Urban Systems' partners and employees, supports employee-driven initiatives that are inspired to positively enhance lives. The foundation's mission, vision, and guiding principles exemplify how companies can leverage their employees' talents to build vibrant communities.[31] The foundation undertakes projects designed by employee teams at each branch. Employees then volunteer their time and expertise to complete the projects, which range from helping the homeless to mentoring children and young adults to building a playground or a community garden. The foundation also responds to urgent needs locally or internationally that arise throughout the year, such as natural disasters or a family facing exceptional hardship, and participates in community events to help others.

Urban Matters CCC is a self-financed, nonprofit social enterprise set up to benefit communities by helping to make change happen.[32] Urban Matters partners with governments, community organizations, social entrepreneurs, and socially committed business leaders to convene and to consult on and create change that can address complex social issues. The goal is to support changemakers to improve their community. Trina Wamboldt, a community catalyst with Urban Matters, offers practical advice on the steps any organization that wants to engage its people in social innovation must take. Step one is to assess the innovation climate in your organization to determine its readiness to go down this path: "Find the people in your organization who are budding social entrepreneurs and figure out what gets them fired up."[33] In other words, harness the power and passion that already exists within your workforce.

## A Healthy Organization Model

As a guide for assessing the health of your company, worksite, or department, I offer a basic model of a healthy organization. This model generalizes from the examples just described and draws extensively on research evidence that shows the importance of work environments, employee experiences, culture, and leadership. The model also has been confirmed in practice through my consulting work with numerous organizations aspiring to move in this direction, and through conversations with numerous managers and employees across Canada and internationally.

Figure 1.1 identifies the basic building blocks of a healthy organization: a positive culture, an inclusive approach to leadership, and vibrant workplaces that inspire employees. Taking action to make your organization healthier requires a clear understanding of how the main components of the healthy organization model are interdependent.

**Figure 1.1** The Healthy Organization Model

Here is the underlying logic: The stage is set for a high quality of work-life and sustainable future performance by having three things in place: a strong culture grounded in people values; a commitment from top managers to improve the workplace as a way of achieving business results; and active encouragement for all employees to demonstrate leadership in their roles, especially by taking action to improve their work environment. Living these values is a hallmark of a healthy organization. One of its clearest expressions can be found in an organization's people policies, programs, and practices. How does the organization approach all human resource issues, from recruitment and development to retention, engagement, and health and safety? At the core of a healthy organization is a vibrant workplace designed to genuinely inspire employees.

A vibrant workplace is essential because it's the environment in which people work day in and day out. Vibrant workplaces do more than engage employees. They actually cultivate a sense of personal inspiration about the work in hand. An engaged employee is satisfied and loyal. An inspired employee is more than this, actively seeking out ways to develop and use their skills, knowledge, and abilities to further corporate goals. In today's knowledge-based economy, it is not enough for individuals to be skilled and well educated. In order for employees to apply their capabilities, they need relationships, resources, and systems that enable them to collaborate. When workers collaborate, the sum becomes greater than the parts: teams develop capabilities for performance, innovation, and creativity that far surpass what each individual member brings to their job and the organization, its customers, and society.

The components of a healthy organization are mutually reinforcing. The result is an upward spiral that further strengthens the culture, validates the importance of shared leadership, maintains vibrant workplace conditions, and continues to inspire employees. The more employees feel they are able to contribute to the organization's success, the more they feel empowered to further expand their capabilities in new ways. This process of learning and innovation also includes refinements to the work environment, continually adapting jobs, processes, structures, and systems in ways that maximize people's contributions. This leads to humanly sustainable success, which is how organizations can continue to benefit all stakeholders in the future. Again, wellness is not an end goal but a natural result of healthy processes for involving individuals in improving all aspects of the organization's operations.

Success is multidimensional. A healthy organization meets the needs of customers and other stakeholders, achieves financial results, and benefits the wider community. It also does more than promote personal health and wellness by providing a high quality of work-life for employees based on their total experience of their job and work environment. It also provides net benefits for communities by operating in socially, environmentally, and ethically responsible ways. In both business and human terms, these are the conditions for sustainable success.

I now will describe the components in figure 1.1 and their interconnections.

## Culture

Two building blocks of healthy organizations – culture and leadership – are closely intertwined. A positive culture exudes a high value placed on employees, customers, and society. Inclusive leadership practices these values, reflecting a mind-set that everyone in the organization has a responsibility to improve the workplace as the route to better business results – and a better society. Culture and leadership are well-documented enablers of healthier workplaces. A systematic review of successful wellness strategies identified a critical success factor as a corporate culture that encourages wellness to improve employees' lives, not just to reduce costs.[34] Also influential – and this speaks to the active engagement of employees – are corporate policies and practices and physical workspaces that encourage participation.

Deborah Connors was the inspiration behind the Health Work and Wellness Conference in Canada (renamed the Better Workplace Conference), which over seventeen years created an extensive community of practice.[35] This was not your run-of-the-mill workplace wellness conference. Deborah and her team pursued a bold mission for these annual events: "creating extraordinary workplaces by developing extraordinary people." Discussions at the conference shone a spotlight on the critical role that culture plays in successful efforts to make workplaces better. As someone who participated in a number of these conferences, I recall the diversity of approaches that can lead to a more positive and supportive culture.

An "emerging best practice" in the eyes of workplace health promotion researchers and practitioners is for employers to promote a "culture of health." This refers to integrating health into how the organization operates, thinks, and acts.[36] Doing so requires leadership commitment, a physically and socially supportive environment, and active employee involvement in health promotion. It also requires a robust employee communication strategy that continuously reinforces this corporate commitment, educates workers about all aspects of a healthy workplace, and enables them to make use of health-promoting resources. The concept of a culture of health will have a familiar ring if your organization already has developed a "safety culture." Just as with a safety culture, a culture of health contributes to positive outcomes for individual workers, improves organizational performance, demonstrates and reinforces corporate values, and contributes to CSR or sustainability goals. Creating and maintaining a healthy and safe culture is a shared responsibility that, as I explain in chapter 5, is at the core of inclusive leadership.

Managers set the tone for corporate culture. Writing in the *Harvard Business Review*, Emma Seppälä and Kim Cameron observe that many companies mistakenly attribute success to having a hard-driving, high-pressure culture. These two experts offer a useful corrective to this view: "A large and growing body of research on positive organizational psychology demonstrates that not only is a cut-throat environment harmful to productivity over time, but that a positive environment will lead to dramatic benefits for employers, employees, and the bottom line."[37] Employee well-being flows from a positive culture, not a hard-driving one. And managers can cultivate this culture by consistently doing four things: fostering social connections; showing empathy to employees; going out of the way to help employees; and encouraging employees to talk to them, especially about their problems.

## Leadership

Culture and leadership go hand in hand. The European Network for Workplace Health Promotion (ENWHP) has long recognized this connection. The ENWHP has been actively engaged for many years with Europe's largest public and private sector employers – along with national occupational health and safety, public health, and social insurance agencies – promoting healthy workplaces.[38] Its vision is to develop and promote "good workplace health practices" that will contribute to sustainable economic and social development. To achieve this vision, the ENWHP focuses on the following determinants of healthy work: the values and policies of decision-makers inside and outside the workplace; a culture of participation; leadership and management practices; how daily work is organized; job security; the quality of the work environment; and personal health practices. These are the features of a healthy and sustainable organization.

A Canadian retail chain with 1,500 people at multiple stores requested my assistance developing a healthy organization strategy. As the HR manager admitted at the outset: "We have been working on healthy workplace stuff for years." But as he emphasized, the time had come to consolidate these efforts and move on to the next level: crafting a healthy organization strategy. The company now had in place a solid foundation on which to build: an active healthy workplace advisory committee consisting of employees and managers; a revamped OHS approach with the introduction of a widely used safety management system; an online health risk assessment for employees; and a newly recruited manager of workplace health and safety keen to link OHS and wellness. The HR manager knew from exit interviews that the biggest cost of job stress cost was turnover. Acknowledging this progress, the executive team had just given its support to focus more strategically on organizational health.

For the company to get a handle on organizational health, several things had to fall into place. First, they had to develop the right language with clear definitions of what organizational health is and the outcomes the company was seeking from this approach. Second, they needed to describe their corporate culture and how it supported health, safety, and wellness, rather than tying these to separate value statements. Third, they needed to articulate what a meaningful and impactful healthy organization strategy looks like and how it would contribute to corporate performance, especially customer relations. Fourth, they wanted to take a fresh look at the results from their annual employee engagement survey using a healthy organization lens. And fifth, they agreed to work closely with their employee assistance program provider to make fuller use of available resources, especially in the area of mental health.

For all this to happen, it was critical to secure 100 percent support from executive team members. The evolving definition of a healthy organization the team was developing emphasized the vital role of healthy relationships and collaboration. Furthermore, culture was defined as the behaviors that everyone expects of each other, or as the executive team agreed, "how we treat each other, make decisions, and work together." These definitions helped executives to reflect on how they could work better together, which led to a discussion of how they could actively model healthy behaviors and lead required changes within their business units. The executive then clearly delineated the roles of the healthy workplace advisory committee, the joint employee–management OHS committee (required by law), the HR manager, and the new OHS manager in collaboratively advancing a healthy organization agenda. It took time, but the executive came to realize that a well-executed healthy organization strategy had the potential to increase employees' responsiveness to customers, which would improve customers' in-store experience and forge closer relationships with them – achieving a major corporate goal. And with this realization, the executive set the stage for shared responsibility for these goals right across the organization – what I call "inclusive leadership."

Jeffrey Pfeffer's analysis of how people's jobs and work environments can be bad for their health leads him to a powerful conclusion about what needs to change. He puts it bluntly: "Employers have a choice."[39] They can decide to implement practices that will enhance employees' health and overall well-being and at the same time reduce costs and productivity loss. Five things must happen if senior leaders are serious about making employee health and well-being a strategic priority: health and well-being need to be measured and reported, just as for pollution; companies with unhealthy or toxic workplaces need to be publicly identified as "social polluters"; the true costs of unhealthy practices must be passed on to employers; employers need to be made aware that improving employee health and well-being can also improve productivity and profitability; and employers and policy-makers must consistently give human sustainability much higher priority. As I document throughout this book, these five change enablers are slowly but steadily taking root. And more employers are, in Pfeffer's words, making the right choices.

## Vibrant Workplaces

A vibrant workplace is at the core of a healthy organization. As I've noted, many organizations today have policies, programs, and resources in place designed to keep their employees safe and healthy. Using these as a springboard, an organization can jump to the next level by addressing the job characteristics, relationships, work environment factors, and organizational supports known to shape positive employee experiences and develop performance capabilities.

Let's look more closely at the specific features of relationships, jobs, work environments, and organizational supports that define a vibrant workplace:

• *Jobs*: Employees have the autonomy to direct their own work, something that they find both challenging and meaningful. Employees have ample opportunity to learn and to develop and apply their skills and abilities on the job. They know how their role fits in and makes a difference. Compensation and other rewards are fair and at a decent level.

- *Relationships*: Mutual respect characterizes working relationships among coworkers and between employees and managers. People trust each other and are committed to a shared vision and mission and to shared values. Employees experience a sense of belonging because the workplace is a true community.
- *Environments*: The work environment is open, collaborative, and participatory. There is a premium on two-way communication throughout the organization. Employees have meaningful input into decisions affecting them. All employees' contributions are valued and recognized. Work is team based and cooperative.
- *Supports*: Supervisors support employees to succeed in their jobs, develop their talents, and have a balanced life. Coworkers are helpful and friendly. Employees have adequate facilities, equipment, tools, and other resources needed to do their job well. There are appropriate policies and programs in place to promote health, safety, and effective human resource management practices.

Notice that few of these ingredients specifically refer to health. Thus, a vibrant workplace is more than simply healthy or safe. It puts in place the organization-level drivers of well-being and performance. Job stress, burnout, and work–life imbalance are major workplace challenges today. These result from a range of unhealthy workplace conditions that undermine quality of work-life, performance, and sustainable, responsible business practices. Solutions must target the ingredients of a vibrant workplace – which is the reverse image of an unhealthy, dysfunctional, toxic, and unproductive workplace. The most effective solutions to stress, burnout, and imbalance involve finding the right mix of job autonomy, decision input, support, resources, and flexibility to offset job demands. Thus, by taking actions that address the root causes of these problems, managers and HR professionals will reduce workplace risks to employee well-being and performance.

## Inspired Employees

Vibrant workplaces are the contexts in which employees are able to thrive at work. A vibrant workplace inspires employees to continually develop and apply their capabilities to deliver excellent results and experience personal fulfillment through this. Employees not only achieve their personal health and wellness goals – most of all, being highly satisfied with their jobs and employer – but they also learn and collaborate, two activities essential for an organization to fully tap its human capabilities.

Workers who feel inspired actively learn, share their knowledge, and apply and further develop their capabilities. They collaborate effectively with coworkers, customers, and partners to ensure the highest quality of services or products. And they are able to adapt to changes in the business environment, in customers' needs and preferences, and within the organization. They look forward to coming to work each day because they know they can make a difference, grow personally, and feel the pride of meaningful accomplishments. They do so within a web of supportive relationships, comprising coworkers, their immediate supervisor, and the management group to whom they or their team reports, informal networks of colleagues inside and outside the organization, and their clients or customers. Experiencing work in this way leaves an employee feeling more than engaged in their job.

Let's consider a definition of engagement that reflects what managers want employees to experience in their work: "Engagement is above and beyond simple satisfaction with the employment arrangement or basic loyalty to the employer – characteristics that most companies have measured for many years. Engagement, in contrast, is about passion and commitment – the willingness to invest oneself and expend one's discretionary effort to help the employer succeed."[40]

However, employers today need more than just extra effort. Rather, they need employees who can be creative and innovative, think and act proactively, and find ways to exceed customers' or clients' expectations. Inspired employees channel the sense of purpose they derive from work to acquire new skills and knowledge and apply these for the benefit of the organization and its stakeholders. Inspired employees set high standards for themselves and their team, actively anticipating and responding to internal and external challenges. This is a virtuous circle. The positive experiences of learning, teamwork, achieving job and career goals, and contributing to organizational success deepen that psychological state of feeling inspired.

Yet many employees are languishing at the opposite end of the continuum from being engaged, never mind inspired. According to Gallup research, organizations are facing an employee burnout crisis.[41] A recent Gallup study of nearly 7,500 full-time employees found that 23 percent of employees reported feeling burned out at work very often or always, while an additional 44 percent reported feeling burned out sometimes. That means about two-thirds of full-time workers experience burnout on the job, resulting in increased absenteeism, work–life conflict, healthcare utilization, and turnover – and disengagement. So it is no coincidence that in 2019, the WHO recognized burnout in its International Classification of Diseases as an "occupational phenomenon" that results in exhaustion, mental detachment from one's job, cynicism, and reduced professional efficacy.[42]

One explanation of why employers do not achieve the engagement goals they seek is the confusion between engagement as an outcome and the actions, processes, and conditions that lead to this outcome. Basically, this comes down to the difference between using the word as a noun or a verb. Employee engagement surveys typically measure working conditions that lead employees to contribute to the performance of their work unit or larger corporate goals. The actual dynamics of being engaged remain opaque. So I encourage HR and wellness professionals to actively employ the concept of engagement. This will focus management's attention on how to involve (i.e., engage) employees in decisions, initiatives, and changes that build more vibrant workplaces. Not only will this inspire them in their work; it is also likely to increase their participation in existing wellness programs.[43]

Inspired employees work collaboratively and help each other out. By collaborating, individual employees and teams collectively generate and apply new knowledge and skills. This is what generates innovation. Management guru Peter Drucker observes that knowledge workers teach each other and learn together.[44] Innovation flows from this shared teaching and learning, keeping an organization ahead of the competition or able to provide even better services or products at lower costs. Practical insights and potential solutions are transmitted through interpersonal communication, a basic point that has given new relevance to what social scientists call "social capital" and "social networks."

At a telecommunications company's call center, where I was conducting research on job stress, hundreds of customer service representatives stayed on top of a steady stream of new products and services by doing just what Peter Drucker advises. The company's knowledge management system, which customer service reps accessed online, was unable to keep up with all these changes. So the call center workers invented informal ways to share their knowledge and to support each other. Recognizing that nobody could know everything about each of the new products and services, employees regularly shared their solutions and helped each other during customer calls. This innovation in teamwork may seem small, but in a business where customer satisfaction drives revenues, every improvement in service counts. For the employees, being able to devise and share their own solutions to customer problems boosted morale, instilled pride, and helped them manage job demands. And they also experienced less stress and achieved higher call quality ratings than the company's other call centers.

This example shows how vibrant workplaces encourage individual and group learning. Indeed, a healthy organization is by its very nature a learning organization. In learning organizations, individuals and teams generate and share knowledge, engage in critical thinking that is system focused, and are supported by a culture that values experimentation.[45] Performance improves as employees' capabilities expand and they discover new work methods, services, or products. Learning also helps workers to reproduce successes and avoid repeating mistakes. Harvard University's David Garvin uses the term "learning facilitators" to describe organizational features that support the learning process. According to Garvin, employees throughout a learning organization are encouraged to acquire, interpret, and apply new knowledge or ideas. Learning facilitators include key attributes of what I call a vibrant workplace: openly sharing and debating different perspectives; constructive feedback; time and space for learning; and a sense of psychological safety.[46] These dynamics of a healthy organization enable it to avoid what Peter Senge calls learning disabilities, which arise when work design and management practices discourage active learning.[47]

Another barrier to active learning could be the attitudes executives have about their employees' ability to learn and adapt. A project on managing the future of work undertaken by Harvard Business School and the BCG Henderson Institute discovered that executives were pessimistic about their employees' ability to adapt to future challenges. In contrast, employees saw change as a positive, especially if it opened up opportunities to learn new skills.[48] This speaks to the importance of directly involving employees in ongoing learning and making them part of any change initiative. This is what office-furniture manufacturer Steelcase has done. It established a Strategic Workforce Architecture and Transformation (SWAT) team, which experiments with different ways to respond to emerging business opportunities. The team created an internal platform, called Loop, which invited employees to volunteer to work on projects outside their area. According to Jill Dark, the director of the

SWAT team: "If you give people the opportunity to learn something new or to show their craft, they will give you their best work. The magic is in providing the opportunity."[49]

Learning and collaboration go hand in hand. Today's version of the learning organization can be called the collaborative organization. The twinning of learning and collaboration reflects the realities of the twenty-first-century knowledge-based economy, which places a premium on creatively applying knowledge. The project teams, business networks, and global supply chains of today's successful corporations require effective ways for workers to anticipate challenges and create solutions. The emerging form of work organization in this century is post-bureaucratic. It is fluid, flexible, and ceaselessly recombining knowledge into business solutions. Some experts refer to the knowledge-based, flexible organization as a collaborative community, grounded in a shared ethic of interdependent contributions. Trust in working relationships becomes critical for the level of collaboration that successful businesses require – a point I will elaborate on in chapter 4. The flexible organization takes many forms, such as short-term projects, supply chains, business alliances and partnerships, virtual networks, and outsourcing arrangements. All rest upon working relationships that foster learning and collaboration.

Consider two cases from very different sectors: construction and healthcare. The industrial construction sector makes airports, hydro dams, tunnels, refineries, and other large facilities. Stakeholder relationships more often than not have been adversarial, and the industry lags behind others in its HR practices. The sector is engineering dominated. Project management has been viewed as a way to limit project costs and efficiently marshal resources. But there is growing recognition that more cooperation, communication, and trust are needed as a basis for project success. A construction project is a complex web of short-term relationships involving different members with diverse skills. Project success depends on the strength and quality of these relationships. According to construction project management experts, "a cooperative approach between construction organizations would bring about trust and commitment-induced efficiency, and better resource allocation and utilization which leads to increased industry performance."[50] Thus, the willingness and ability of project stakeholders to collaborate is what leads to projects being completed on time, on budget, and to high technical standards.

The Mayo Clinic is an outstanding example of healthcare teamwork. Len Berry, a Texas A&M University professor and a senior fellow at the Institute for Healthcare Improvement, calls it a "collaborative organization," based on months he spent observing how the Mayo's teams serve patients.[51] The clinic enjoys an enviable global brand and can attract leading talent because it follows a basic philosophy – pursuing the ideals of service ahead of profits, sincere concern for the welfare of each patient, and continual interest among staff in each other's professional development. Collaboration is grounded in this philosophy. At the Mayo, it takes a team to care for a patient. Collaborative patient care is supported through recruitment, leadership development and training, and appropriately designed infrastructure from information technology systems to physical workspaces. And collaboration infuses the culture. When the Mayo conducted focus groups with patients, their families, staff, and volunteers to document the common themes in their experiences at the clinic, the dominant image that emerged was of people holding hands.

In sum, a common feature of a healthy organization is that all of its people are inspired by opportunities to learn, collaborate, and contribute. Through these activities, employees and managers become resilient as well as innovative in the face of change. Indeed, they will have the agility to anticipate and adapt to change. This future orientation is also part and parcel of what makes an organization humanly sustainable.

## Sustainable Success

No organization can last long if it burns out employees, exhausts credit lines, alienates customers, acts unethically, damages the environment, or imposes other costs on society. By contrast, organizations that thrive constantly regenerate their resources. This requires long-term and holistic thinking, exactly as we have come to view the challenges facing the natural environment. Organizations, too, are fragile ecosystems. Future success depends on renewing the fine balance needed between people, systems, structures, and leadership. Organizations like the World Bank, SAS Institute, and Urban Systems point the way.

I use the term "sustainable success" to link financial, worker, environmental, and societal goals. Organizations need to renew the capabilities of their workforce, renew their relationships with customers and communities, and not have a negative impact on the environment. The links between people and performance also benefit communities. Employees' pride comes from contributing to excellent products or services and from being part of an organization that "gives back" and intentionally makes a positive contribution to communities and the natural environment in which it operates. We will explore these points in chapter 7. For now, consider how local and national community-based nonprofit organizations and charities are forming closer partnerships with businesses. Such partnerships demonstrate a corporate commitment to social and environmental responsibility. But none of this is possible, of course, without success in basic business terms. That is precisely why the vibrant workplace is central to my healthy organization model: this type of workplace generates both economic and social performance.

Research shows that a cluster of working conditions and management practices that are similar to what I call a vibrant workplace encourages employees to achieve higher levels of job performance. A *Journal of Applied Psychology* article used Gallup data from 198,514 employees in 7,939 business units in thirty-six companies to test the relationship between employees' overall job satisfaction and the performance of their business unit.[52] Business performance was measured by customer satisfaction, profitability, revenues, turnover, and safety (lost-time work injuries). The conclusion: business units performed better when employees were satisfied and had managers and working conditions that engaged them. However, this study and others like it do not address two main ingredients of sustainable success. First, they do not illuminate how workplace conditions leading to greater job performance contribute to employees' overall health and wellness. Second, there is no community connection. The advantage of the healthy organization model is that economic performance, well-being, and benefits for society are interwoven.

Healthy organizations benefit society. They have figured out how to integrate external CSR commitments with their internal people practices. As critics have noted, CSR without HR is PR. To avoid falling into this trap, the World Bank, SAS Institute, Urban Systems, and many similar organizations apply the same sustainability principles internally as they do externally. For example, healthier employees are less likely to use healthcare services. This has important implications for publicly funded health services and for employer-provided health benefit costs. The supportive work environment of a healthy organization helps employees to enjoy a fulfilling personal, family, and community life. Employees have more time and energy to contribute to raising their children, assisting their aging parents, and volunteering in community activities that matter to them. The philosophy of a healthy organization is, above all, people focused. So there is consistency between treating employees and customers well and being a responsible corporate citizen.

Green buildings are an emerging trend to watch because of their potential to mutually benefit employees and society. One way that companies are reducing their carbon footprint is by improving the physical design of workplaces. Research by the U.S. Green Building

Council concludes that employees who work in green buildings that are LEED (Leadership in Energy and Environmental Design) certified are "happier, healthier and more productive" than those in conventional and non-LEED buildings.[53] The WELL Building Standard of the International WELL Building Institute (IWBI) has become the leading method for advancing health and well-being in buildings.[54] The WELL v2 Building Standard is an evidence-based approach to designing, building, and maintaining buildings with the goal of improving people's health and well-being. For example, there is a trend in real estate development and workspace design in the United Kingdom to boost workers' physical activity and improve mental health. Simple things, like having a single location for a coffee machine and drinks, encourage staff to move around and socialize. The incorporation of natural and tactile materials (such as wood, natural fibers, exposed brick, etc.) into a space supports workplace mental well-being by encouraging workers to interact with their physical environment. By considering all aspects of a building's design, the IWBI encourages companies to think beyond just adding a fitness center as they look for better ways to support employee health, wellness, and productivity.

Companies with a strong commitment to sustainability also have an edge when it comes to recruiting and retaining talent. The First Tech Credit Union office in Hillsboro, Oregon, recently became America's largest mass timber building (using engineered wood in place of steel and concrete).[55] A key design principle shared by the building's owners, architects, engineers, and builders is "people first": "It needed to be a place that would encourage the health and well-being of employees, help to attract and retain talented people and reflect Pacific Northwest values."[56] I learned about this project from Hardy Wentzel, CEO of Structurlam, the British Columbia-based company that designed and produced the mass timber used in construction. Hardy described the positive reactions of managers and employees after they relocated to the new office. More broadly, research confirms that green buildings promote well-being by providing a healthy environment and sense of community, resulting in greater employee productivity and job satisfaction.[57]

## Making Well-Being a Priority

To recap, a healthy organization cultivates vibrant workplaces – supported by strong people-focused values and leadership – that truly inspire people. This reflects a dynamic, ongoing process in which workers and managers at all levels continually develop and apply their capabilities in pursuit of organizational goals. The criteria for success will vary, or course, depending on the size, sector, and location of the organization. But what matters most of all is that success is humanly sustainable. There are no cracks in the foundation or other signs of weakness that could seriously impair the organization's future. Benefits will continue to flow to workers, to customers or clients, to owners, and to the larger community in which the business operates. In short, healthy organizations can achieve a multiple win.

For employees, benefits can be measured in terms of overall well-being, work–life balance, professional development and personal growth, and a generally high quality of work-life. For the organization, success includes financial performance, operating efficiency, reduced human capital risks and costs, and positive social and environmental impacts – all of which add up to future sustainability. There are also community benefits. The people-focused values of a healthy organization are expressed in a range of socially and environmentally responsible actions. These include, but are far from limited to, partnering with non-governmental organizations (NGOs) on projects that benefit society, making charitable contributions, supporting employee volunteering, and reducing the organization's carbon footprint. And by contributing to a healthy and skilled workforce, the organization is reducing the burden on publicly funded healthcare and building capabilities that individual employees can carry into their personal, family, and community activities.

I also have emphasized that the healthy organization model invites us to take a holistic, long-term view of workplaces. The model invites you to look for – and talk with colleagues about – opportunities in your organization to connect internal people practices and values with how the organization operates within its communities. Think about ways that multiple internal and external stakeholders can contribute to and benefit from the organization's activities. A healthy organization is responsive to the needs of its customers or clients, employees, and social and physical environment. Above all, it strives to improve the well-being of all stakeholders. As chapter 2 will show, the very idea of a healthy organization has its roots in workplace health promotion. Indeed, the limits of the workplace health promotion paradigm are what led me to the expanded view of well-being and performance captured in the vision of a healthy organization presented in this book. That's what we will examine next.

## CHAPTER 2

# Beyond Workplace Health Promotion

I opened this chapter in the first edition of *Creating Healthy Organizations* with a description of Singapore's promotion of healthy employees in healthy workplaces through its HEALTH Awards, which I attended as a speaker and workshop leader in 2008.[1] Singapore's government and business communities have done many innovative things to build an economic powerhouse. One of the country's success factors is the active promotion of a healthy population. The HEALTH Awards, which stand for "Helping Employees Achieve Life-Time Health," are sponsored by the government's Health Promotion Board. The goal is a healthier workforce and ultimately greater economic productivity and living standards. What motivates employers and employees to participate in the HEALTH Awards is the useful feedback they receive, public recognition from being an award winner, and recruitment and retention benefits.

The Singapore HEALTH Awards illustrate that the next step for employers that have implemented wellness programs is to expand their focus to encompass the organizational factors influencing employee well-being. Listening to the stories of some of the 358 companies and public sector organizations that received an award in 2008, I was struck by how many were progressing toward their own vision of a healthy organization. A decade later, Singapore's national Workplace Health Strategy, managed by the government's

Health Promotion Board, provides more resources for employers and workplace health champions. This includes the *Essential Guide to Workplace Health Promotion*, containing best practice guidelines for how to plan, implement, and evaluate a workplace health promotion program.[2] And there are more resources addressing workplace mental health, such as training to equip managers and HR staff with knowledge and skills on self-care, including stress management, and how to support workers with mental health problems.

However, despite Singapore's efforts to expand the reach and impact of workplace health promotion programs, more needs to be done. According to Willis Towers Watson's 2017 *Benefits Trends Survey*, 44 percent of Singapore employers identified stress as the top health issue they faced, and 60 percent of employees reported having above-average or high levels of stress.[3] Yet only 27 percent of employers surveyed were taking action to reduce work-related stress. A survey by Roffey Park, a leadership institute based in Singapore and the UK, echoes these findings.[4] Its *Working in Asia* survey found that Singapore workers spent more hours at work compared with their peers in Hong Kong and China, and that 52 percent reported rising stress levels. And more than two-fifths of Singapore respondents to the survey reported working more than fifty hours a week, with 16 percent putting in more than sixty hours. Workload, lack of support, and organizational politics were identified as leading causes of workplace stress, resulting in what the Roffey Park report calls "a burnout culture."

Generally speaking, Singapore's workplaces mirror trends elsewhere. Over the past decade, many other countries and regions have introduced publicly accessible workplace wellness resources and programs to recognize organizations for making progress on this front. Yet despite growing evidence that workplace stress is a serious problem, most employers have not addressed the root causes of stress, burnout, work–life conflict, harassment, toxic work environments, and other contributors to reduced employee well-being. Yet it is easier now to take the necessary actions, given the wide range of free workplace health promotion resources and a greater awareness about workplace mental health issues. Compared to a decade ago, we are far better equipped to create supportive organizational contexts that enable workers to thrive both physically and psychologically.

In this chapter, I provide a call to action, presenting the evidence, ideas, and actions that you and other change agents will need to plan and successfully implement workplace changes that will

1 build on your existing health, safety, and wellness initiatives, moving them to the next level by focusing on organizational factors that promote overall employee well-being;
2 expand health promotion by creating the organizational conditions and individual resources that enable employees to physically and psychologically thrive;
3 provide an evidence-based, integrated, and comprehensive approach to making workplaces healthier and safer as a way to enhance workers' well-being and organizational performance;
4 address the organizational causes of psychologically unhealthy work environments, particularly stress, burnout, and work–life conflict; and
5 integrate the actions required to make your workplace psychologically healthy and safe into existing wellness and occupational health and safety programs, policies, and plans.

## Expanding Our Focus on Well-Being

The terms "health," "wellness," and "well-being" often are used interchangeably. Their meanings overlap, which blunts the educational and communication potential of the terms. Yet as the language of health evolves, workplace policies and programs have shifted from a narrow focus on individual workers' physical health to a more encompassing concern with their overall well-being. And with that shift comes progress toward truly healthy organizations.

Wellness expands our understanding of health beyond physical health by emphasizing the lifelong process of living a fulfilling life. "Wellness" refers to an active and ongoing process of individuals becoming aware of and making choices that will improve their quality of life. "Wellness" is also used as a generic label for employer-sponsored programs that provide the resources individuals need to adopt healthy attitudes and behaviors.[5] Wellness programs are based on self-responsibility, encouraging individuals to make healthy lifestyle choices.

The latest addition to the healthy workplace lexicon is "well-being." A positive state of well-being is the ultimate goal of a truly healthy organization. Well-being encompasses major life domains: work, finances, emotional health, physical health, behavioral risks, quality of social connections, and community.[6] The word variously describes a person's or population's quality of life, overall health, or happiness. Above all, well-being is based on a worker's subjective assessment of their job and work environment, which reveals to what extent they have what they need to thrive. As we will see, you can leverage your existing approach to employee health, safety, and wellness to make employee well-being an organizational goal. By doing so, you will be opening up possibilities for addressing psychological health and safety, resilience, stress, burnout, and work–life balance. Furthermore, you also will be increasing your organization's human capacity for sustainable success.

## Taking a Holistic Approach to Healthier Organizations

Workplace health interventions span a wide continuum in their scope and effectiveness. As one group of experts aptly observes, there is a huge difference between comprehensive workplace health promotion and "random acts of wellness."[7] Examples of the latter include programs that do one thing only, such as referring employees to a website for healthy lifestyle tips, holding occasional educational sessions on healthy living, offering health risk assessments without any program follow-up and support, or introducing an off-the-shelf mental health program without first confirming your workforce's needs in this regard or investigating the efficacy of the program. On their own, these types of interventions have limited impact.

The benefits of comprehensive worksite wellness programs are firmly established. Many studies show that the most successful workplace interventions provide individualized risk reduction and disease management within a comprehensive program design that includes a range of individual and organizational resources.[8] The question for management is not whether to introduce wellness programs, but how to design, implement, and evaluate programs to achieve the best outcomes – topics I cover throughout this book.[9] Still, most workplace wellness programs target the health behaviors of individual employees. Typically, these programs focus on reducing health risks by encouraging physical activity, healthy eating, and smoking cessation.

Despite growing awareness over the past decade of workplace mental health issues, employers have done far less to target the psychosocial work environment, which encompasses how work is organized, the design of jobs, the psychological experience of work, and workplace relationships. These organizational, social, and psychological features of work profoundly influence employee well-being and job performance. Embedded in the psychosocial environment are the root causes of today's leading workplace health risks, notably stress and burnout. In a healthy organization, every effort is made to improve the psychosocial environment.

As I outline in this chapter, targeting job design and workplace practices and relationships reflects a growing expert consensus that this is the best pathway to a healthier organization. The most significant advance in this direction is the Total Worker Health (TWH) program of the US National Institute for Occupational Safety and Health (NIOSH). NIOSH partnered with the Rand Corporation to review relevant research on well-being and came up with a practical framework for defining and measuring worker well-being.[10] Basically, well-being serves as a positive and unifying goal that captures the multitude of influences on workers' health and quality of life.[11] More specifically, the TWH framework guides actions in five interrelated areas:

- workplace physical environment and safety climate (workers' perceptions of workplace safety);
- workplace policies and culture;
- workers' physical and mental health status;
- individuals' work experiences and evaluations of their overall quality of work-life; and
- external factors in the home, community, and society that can influence worker well-being.

Compared with traditional approaches to occupational health and safety or workplace health promotion, the TWH framework is far more integrative. The framework combines prevention and promotion efforts, addresses work and non-work factors necessary for workers to thrive and achieve their full potential, and tracks results using both objective (individuals' working and living conditions) and subjective (individuals' perceptions and beliefs) measures.

NIOSH isn't alone in recommending this new approach. The SafeWell model and accompanying resources were developed by the Center for Work, Health and Wellbeing at Harvard University.[12] SafeWell advocates the integration of organizational programs, policies, and practices that address occupational health and safety (OHS), employee health promotion, and the psychosocial work environment at the organizational and individual levels. SafeWell also encourages the active participation of employees and managers across the organization, which is essential for developing organizational capabilities and expertise to continuously improve the work environment. Also consistent with the TWH approach is California's Commission on Health and Safety and Workers' Compensation's ten principles that employers can follow to integrate their wellness and OHS programs.[13]

There's also untapped potential for an integrated approach to employee well-being in corporate human resource strategies. Fostering a highly engaged workforce is a priority for many employers. This goal can more readily be achieved by recognizing that healthy and safe employees are also more engaged at work. A psychologically healthy and safe workplace fosters a high level of employee engagement. Engaged employees have high levels of job autonomy and have supportive coworkers and supervisors – all critical for reducing workplace stress. Employee morale also influences participation in workplace health promotion programs.[14] Workplace wellness and OHS programs can increase employees' buy-in through their involvement in planning, implementing, monitoring, and improving health and safety outcomes. In short, increased workforce engagement and well-being are complementary goals. More on this in chapter 3, where I outline vibrant workplace ingredients.

What I've just described is a strategy for reducing a wide range of employee health and safety risks by designing the work environment to actively promote well-being. This organizational health perspective makes it easier to find synergies between wellness initiatives and human resources, occupational health and safety, and corporate social responsibility policies, practices, and goals. It also advances beyond individuals' health attitudes and behavior to get at underlying workplace factors that affect employee health and well-being. That's how employee well-being becomes a performance driver. Moving in this direction should not be a huge leap for organizations that already have an OHS management system and a wellness program.

While the TWH approach originated in the US, there are similar efforts to integrate health and safety in other countries. In Europe, the European Network for Workplace Health Promotion (ENWHP) provides numerous case studies of best practices. The network identified and evaluated fifty "models of good practice" from eighteen countries, showing that effective interventions already exist for promoting mental health and helping employees who are experiencing mental ill health. An instructive example is Deutsch Post DHL, which has 167,000 employees in Germany and about 500,000 worldwide.[15] Its corporate health policy integrates occupational health and safety with health promotion, including mental health, and is founded on the company's philosophy – respect and results – which refers to mutual respect and support for all employees to be leaders. The company's health promotion "toolbox" includes resources, mostly focused on prevention, in sixteen areas, including stress and mental health.

## Connecting Worker Health and Safety

In this section, I provide an overview of how evidence and practical resources are converging around the need for the holistic, system-wide approach just advocated. Studies in a wide range of disciplines support an integrated and comprehensive approach to health, safety, and well-being. There are also practical online resources available in Canada and other countries that change agents can use to improve their workplaces with the goal of promoting worker well-being.

Experts have long argued that employers have much to gain by integrating health and safety promotion, prevention, and protection programs.[16] As the frontier of workplace safety research advances, we are learning more about the organic connections between safe and healthy psychosocial work environments, and what typically have been HR concerns – job satisfaction and turnover. OHS professionals will be interested to know that work stress has a bearing on workers' safety behavior. When workers experience high levels of role conflict, lack clear job goals, are concerned about their job security, and use avoidance tactics to cope with workplace problems, they are less compliant with safety policies and practices.[17] Another survey of over 16,000 US workers concluded that stressful working conditions – specifically job insecurity, work–family imbalance, and a hostile work environment – each were associated with increased work-related injuries.[18] Findings like these place psychosocial factors squarely within the domain of OHS risk assessment. What's more, there's new evidence connecting safety with HR goals. A strong safety climate positively contributes to job satisfaction and reduces turnover.[19]

In short, workers' physical and mental health can't be separated. Physical health problems can lead over time to mental health problems, and vice versa. This is what researchers call "comorbidity," and it provides another strong argument for taking an integrated approach to workplace health and safety. Digging right into the research, here is a sampling of studies that amplify this point.

Back pain is a common physical health problem within the working-age population. It can also lead to common mental disorders.[20] Individuals who experience chronic workplace stress (high job demands and low control over these demands, or what is called "job strain") have a 30 percent excess risk of developing coronary heart disease (CHD).[21] A Finnish study found that over a five- to seven-year period, workers performing repetitive movements and who had repeated exposure to awkward postures and back rotation were at greater risk of common mental disorders.[22] In France, a national study calculated that between 8.8 percent and 10.2 percent of CHD morbidity and 9.4 percent to 11.2 percent of CHD mortality are attributable to job strain, which can be prevented through work redesign.[23] Furthermore, individuals working long hours are not only at higher risk of experiencing stress, but are also at increased risk of stroke.[24] Workplace physical activity programs can help to improve participants' mental health.[25] More specifically, yoga not only can alleviate lower back pain; it also has positive mental health effects.[26] Workers who suffer physical injuries on the job and receive workers' compensation can experience difficulties returning to work because of mental health problems developed while recovering from the physical injury.[27] Furthermore, injured workers who successfully return to work experience beneficial effects on their mental health. These studies, and many others like them, highlight the advantages of an integrated approach to workplace health promotion and illness and injury prevention, based on the understanding that physical and mental health are closely intertwined.

## Benefits of a Healthy Organization

Let's now connect the evidence dots in a different direction, looking at studies showing a strong link between the quality of the work environment (what I'm calling a "vibrant" workplace), healthy and safe employees, and business performance.

We can gain useful insights in this regard from US companies that have received the annual C. Everett Koop National Health Awards, conferred by a nonprofit organization called the Health Project to recognize significant cost-effective improvements in workers' health by employers and a culture of health.[28] Between 2000 and 2014, Koop Award winners' stock value appreciated by 325 percent, compared to an average market appreciation of 105 percent for other companies comprising the S&P 500 Index. The award-winning companies were a diverse group, from Prudential and Pfizer to Volvo, IBM, and Union Pacific Railroad. These companies view their workplace health and safety programs as reflecting their commitment to corporate social responsibility. Their experience shows that effectively promoting employees' health and safety requires ongoing effort and investments over the long term.

Another study concluded that adopting workplace health promotion best practices is an essential component of an effective business strategy.[29] Researchers used the HERO Scorecard (mentioned in chapter 1) to document workplace health promotion best practices. They then created a stock portfolio of high-scoring workplace health promotion companies, comparing the portfolio to the S&P 500 Index. During the six-year period of the study, companies in the high-scoring HERO portfolio substantially outperformed those in the S&P 500 Index. Coordination of workplace health promotion with other programs, including occupational health and safety, is a criterion under HERO's program management practices. The study concluded that "investment in workforce health and well-being is one facet of high-performing, well-managed companies."[30]

At a Fortune 100 company, researchers discovered that employee well-being predicted future business performance and employee-related costs.[31] These costs included employee healthcare utilization, productivity (absenteeism, short-term disability, presenteeism, and job performance), and retention. The study used a broad definition of well-being based on six dimensions: appraisal of one's present and future life situation; daily positive or negative emotional experiences; physical health risks; health behaviors (e.g., diet, exercise, smoking); satisfaction with one's work environment; and access to resources needed to be safe and healthy. The practical insight for employers is that key aspects of well-being can be measured in an employee survey and used to predict future human capital costs and risks.

Other studies show that employees are more creative and are able to achieve higher levels of job performance when they are in a healthy psychosocial work environment. A meta-analysis (a "study of studies") that pooled results from fifty-seven studies in this area confirmed that the quality of an employee's relationship with their supervisor, a sense of psychological empowerment, and a supportive culture and leadership contribute positively to job performance.[32] Furthermore, reducing job stress will create a more productive work environment, according to another meta-analysis that examined results from 169 job stress studies.[33] An employee with challenging job demands but who has the autonomy to make decisions, appropriate job resources, and support from their coworkers and supervisor to manage these demands not only will experience higher levels of well-being and engagement; they also will be better able to achieve company goals.

The bottom line: healthy, happy, and safe employees are more productive and have the energy and commitment for consistently good job performance. That benefits the workers themselves, their employer, the economy, and society.[34] I like to think of these outcomes as a positive upward spiral between well-being and sustainable business success.

## The Long Arm of Job Stress

Stressful working conditions are probably the greatest health and safety challenge for today's workers. Most employers are doing a commendable job of complying with occupational health and safety regulations and legislation. In Canada, the US, Europe, Australia, and other advanced industrial countries, lost-time injury rates have steadily declined over the past several decades. Yet despite the spread of workplace health promotion programs, the problems of stress and burnout persist and, if anything, are getting worse.[35] These work problems detract from a person's quality of life, measured by job satisfaction and by overall life satisfaction, which is a widely used indicator of well-being. Unless these job quality trends are reversed, employers will face mounting costs in terms of health benefits, absenteeism, presenteeism, disengagement, and turnover.

As we will see in this section, the long arm of work stress reaches outside of the workplace to undermine employees' quality of life. The 2015 Rethinking Work survey, conducted by EKOS Research Associates in partnership with the Graham Lowe Group, asked a representative sample of Canadians about their work experiences. The results, presented below, clearly illustrate how job stress is related to well-being.

Work–life balance and job stress are close cousins. More workers are finding it harder to achieve work–life balance, often due to job stress.[36] Work–family conflict negatively affects employees' mental health and reduces their subjective well-being.[37] This conflict can contribute to psychosomatic symptoms, depression and psychological distress, use of medication, alcohol consumption, substance abuse, clinical mood disorders, clinical anxiety disorders, and emotional exhaustion.[38] Work–family conflict costs employers through turnover, low morale, and increased absenteeism. Equipping supervisors with the people skills they need to support employees' work–life balance and providing flexible work arrangements are two effective interventions.

The Rethinking Work survey shows how work spills over into people's personal lives. Consider that more than two-thirds of survey respondents who found it harder to balance work with their personal and family life also frequently experienced job stress (see figure 2.1). By contrast, among workers who found work–life balance getting easier, about two-thirds reported having what can be considered manageable job stress.

Job stress is also associated with reduced work engagement and well-being. As figure 2.2 reveals, Rethinking Work survey respondents who often or always experienced job stress in the prior twelve months were significantly less likely to look forward to work – a

**Figure 2.1** Relationship between Work–Life Balance and Job Stress

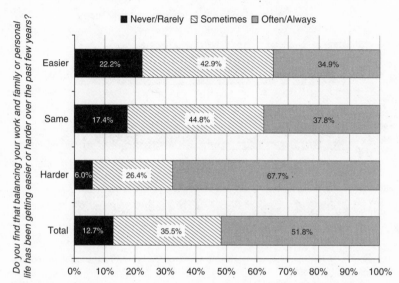

*In the past 12 months, how often did you experience stress in your job?*

Differences between the 3 work-life balance groups are statistically significant.
Chi-square test, p < .001.
Source: *Rethinking Work*, EKOS Research Associates & Graham Lowe Group, Canadian workforce survey, December 2015. Base n=6,948

good indicator of how motivated and engaged individuals are in their work. This group of workers also had considerably lower job satisfaction and life satisfaction. Note that we measured the latter with a widely used global indicator of a person's well-being, asking respondents to rate their overall satisfaction with life using a 1 to 10 rating scale, where 1 is very dissatisfied and 10 is very satisfied. Most striking about the results in figure 2.2 is that more than three-quarters of those workers who experienced manageable job stress (i.e., never, rarely, or sometimes in the past twelve months) looked forward to work and were satisfied with their job and their life.

The practical implication of these Rethinking Work findings is that employers can improve engagement, job satisfaction, and

**Figure 2.2** Relationship between Job Stress and Key Well-Being Outcomes

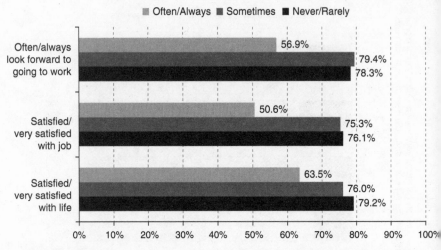

*In the past 12 months, how often did you experience stress in your job?*

■ Often/Always ■ Sometimes ■ Never/Rarely

Often/always look forward to going to work: 56.9%, 79.4%, 78.3%

Satisfied/very satisfied with job: 50.6%, 75.3%, 76.1%

Satisfied/very satisfied with life: 63.5%, 76.0%, 79.2%

Differences between the 3 job stress groups are statistically significant for all outcomes. Chi-square test, p < .001.
Source: *Rethinking Work*, EKOS Research Associates & Graham Lowe Group, Canadian workforce survey, December 2015. Base n=6,968

well-being by targeting work groups experiencing high levels of stress. An employee survey can help to identify these at-risk workers. As a start, let's look at the demographics of Rethinking Work respondents who experience high stress and increased difficulty with work–life balance. Workers facing these problems are more likely to be female, between the ages of 35 and 54, university educated, a member of a professional association, and with above average pay. In short, this at-risk group is made up of knowledge workers in their prime working years who likely have caregiving responsibilities. To amplify this point, I turn to one of the largest-ever work–life balance studies, conducted by Linda Duxbury and Chris Higgins.[39] These researchers found high levels of role overload, stemming from work demands combined with caregiving demands, to be pervasive and systemic in the large Canadian organizations they studied. Yet few employers provided any form of support to help workers balance their work and caregiving roles. As a start, Duxbury and Higgins encourage employers to recognize caregiving as a legitimate work issue.

## How Well-Being Is Distributed in the Workforce

This profile of stress and work–life balance gives only a partial picture of how the quality of work and the quality of life are experienced by different groups of workers. What's missing from most studies of these issues, as well as studies looking at workplace health and safety, is a full consideration of all groups in the labor market today. Such an analysis is especially important, given the rise of precarious work. Workers in contract or temporary positions – hallmarks of the "gig" economy, which is powered by new digital technology platforms such as Uber and TaskRabbit – often get left out.[40] And while these freelancers may have short gigs with corporations who treat their permanent employees well, precarious workers' tenuous position precludes them from accessing corporate programs or benefits. Simply put, they are on their own when it comes to health and safety.

According to the International Labour Organization (ILO), precarious or "non-standard" forms of work – which include temporary work, part-time and on-call work, subcontracting, self-employment, and other forms of work that fall outside of standard employment relationships – are becoming more common globally.[41] Precarious work is both temporary and insecure, the opposite of what full-time employees in a continuing employment contract have with one employer. However, it can cut two ways. On the upside, it has the potential to offer workers more autonomy and flexibility; they can be their own boss. But on the downside, it makes them vulnerable to the negative health effects of economic insecurity, no health benefits, and often a lack of protection from legislated standards for employment or occupational health and safety.

This should concern policy-makers looking for ways to give all workers access to the opportunities of the digital, knowledge-based economy. As we can see from figure 2.3, there is considerable variation in how workers in different labor market locations experience well-being. Surprisingly, what stands out is the overall high well-being experienced by self-employed individuals. However,

**Figure 2.3** Key Well-Being Outcomes by Job Type

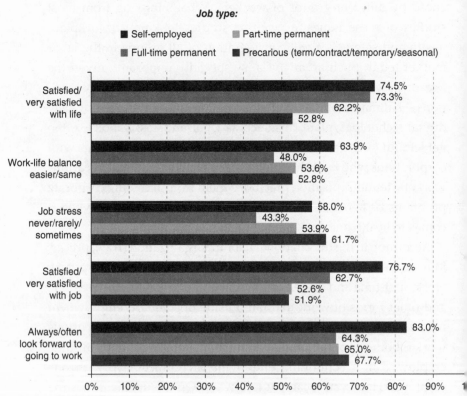

Differences between job types are statistically significant for all outcomes.
Chi-square test, p < .001.
Source: *Rethinking Work*, EKOS Research Associates & Graham Lowe Group, Canadian workforce survey, December 2015. Base n=6,850

there are several explanations for this group's relatively high levels of job and life satisfaction, work–life balance, and work engagement. Two stand out: the rapid increase in self-employment among older workers at the tail end of their working careers; and the presence of many well-educated professionals (such as lawyers, doctors, accountants, and business consultants) among the self-employed. Unlike many employees, these workers have the work rewards, job control, and flexibility that contribute to positive work experiences.

Full-time continuing employment has long been considered the gold standard for a "good" job. However, that is only partially true now. Full-time employees are second only to the self-employed in their job and life satisfaction. However, they experience more job stress than any other labor market group and have similar levels of work engagement to their counterparts in part-time or precarious jobs.

Precarious workers present a somewhat contradictory picture. Just over half are satisfied with their job or their life. However, they are slightly more motivated than full-time employees to go to work each day, a finding that should raise a red flag for employers. And precarious workers also experience less job stress than other workers. This suggests a big trade-off, because manageable stress certainly does not compensate for an absence of other positive job features, notably economic security.

To expand this discussion, the Rethinking Work survey also asked respondents if they agreed or disagreed with the statement "I feel I have lost all control over my economic future." Over a third of workers in precarious situations agreed or strongly agreed with the statement. Furthermore, half of precarious workers also saw a good chance that they would lose their job in the near future. It would seem, then, that economic insecurity plays a part in reducing the well-being of workers in precarious jobs. As the ILO observes, governments can't force employers to treat contract or temporary workers the same as full-time employees. Nonetheless, there are policy levers governments can use, especially strengthening and expanding the coverage of employment and health and safety standards, to extend better protections to these vulnerable workers. This is precisely what groundbreaking legislation in California will do by classifying contract workers for app-based companies, such as Uber and Lyft, as employees.[42]

## An Organizational Approach to Reducing Job Stress

We know a lot about what causes job stress and how to reduce it. The bottom line: stress is caused by workplace structures, processes, and relationships. Hundreds of studies confirm that people feel under stress when their job demands exceed their resources to respond to these demands.[43] High job demands – urgent deadlines, too much work, unclear roles, excessive work hours, competing or conflicting goals – and a low level of control over these demands increase a person's exposure to what researchers call job strain – which is the main cause of work stress. Furthermore, workers who perceive a negative imbalance between the amount of effort they put into their job and the economic and psychological rewards they receive are likely to experience stress. So too will workers who feel they are being unfairly treated by management – a perception that's examined by the organizational justice perspective on stress.

Job strain is bad for workers' health and costly for employers.[44] Stressed-out employees report more fatigue, cynicism, inefficiency, depression, low motivation, headaches or stomach problems, and unhealthy coping behaviors such as increased smoking and alcohol consumption, and poor diet. They experience higher rates of turnover, absenteeism, and presenteeism (going to work but not being well enough to fully contribute).[45] The chronic experience of job strain has been linked to degenerative disease processes, such as heart disease, as well as depression, diabetes, asthma, migraines,

and ulcers. Severe job strain can also lead to burnout, a psychological state that is the opposite of being inspired by one's work.[46]

## Making Workplaces Mentally Healthy and Safe

Most interventions to reduce stress target individuals. The message to employees is they should become more resilient, cope
better with the realities of their job, and manage their work more
efficiently. A systematic review of published research on stress
management programs concluded that there is no standardized
framework or common set of measures for assessing the implementation or impact of these interventions.[47] However, there is
some recent evidence that in-person (i.e., face-to-face) and computer-based (Internet- and mobile-based) stress management programs can be effective in reducing stress in employees.[48] While it
is difficult to draw definitive conclusions about what works and
what doesn't, neither can we dismiss stress management interventions as unhelpful. They can be one useful component of a broader
workplace mental health strategy.

The field of positive psychology has spawned resilience research
and practice, which emphasize that positively oriented psychological
strengths and capacities can be developed and measured in a workforce. Among these strengths is an individual's capacity to cope
with stress. The goal is to help organizations and their members
flourish and thrive. There is some evidence that resilience training contributes to these goals, although we do not yet know which
training format or content is most effective.[49] The biggest benefit of
resilience training seems to be developing individuals' capabilities
and resources as protective factors for mental well-being.[50]

Looking beyond job stress to common workplace mental health
issues, depression stands out. The Institute for Work and Health
(IWH), which has extensively researched physical safety on the

job, has expanded its focus to include workplace mental health. The IWH's *Evidence-Informed Guide to Supporting People with Depression in the Workplace* offers tips and suggestions intended to help people with depression cope with symptoms while working or returning to work after an episode of depression. It is also a useful guide for managers, coworkers, human resources staff, union representatives, and other worker representatives. As the IWH states: "When it comes to supporting workers with depression, everyone can help."[51]

Other studies also confirm the benefits of specific workplace mental health interventions. A review of randomized controlled trials (RCTs) of workplace interventions to reduce depression found promising results.[52] Various therapeutic approaches were studied, with cognitive behavioral therapy the most frequently used. Most of the RCTs found reduced depression symptoms for participating employees. The Work Outcomes Research Cost-Benefit (WORC) project, in Australia, addressed the high costs of presenteeism (work-related productivity lost due to ill health) associated with psychological distress.[53] Project participants received ongoing telephone-based support from a psychologist over a twelve-month period. This study group showed net gains in work productivity through decreased presenteeism that more than offset the costs of the WORC program intervention.

But to emphasize, interventions targeting individuals do not change the underling organizational causes of psychological distress. Organizational-level solutions to job stress require giving workers the autonomy, resources, and support to manage these demands. As I discuss in the next chapter, these are basic ingredients of a vibrant workplace. Corporate leaders are now being advised to take action to reduce job stress at the organizational level.

Workplace bullying, harassment, and discrimination also pose mental and physical health risks. Research in this area highlights the need for employers to prevent these negative behaviors and provide support to those workers who are exposed to them.[54] Recently, the #MeToo movement has heightened employers' awareness of their legal and ethical responsibility to prevent workplace sexual harassment.[55] In Canada, legislation requires employers to take proactive steps to build a safe and respectful environment free from violence and harassment. In 2004, Quebec was the first North American jurisdiction to provide legal protection against the psychological harassment of employees. The federal government and several provinces now have workplace violence and harassment prevention legislation. In response, employers are developing anti-harassment policies, completing risk assessments, and providing managers and employees with appropriate training.

Tony Schwartz and Catherine McCarthy, writing in the *Harvard Business Review*, point out the futility of working longer hours to keep up with ever-rising workloads – a huge source of stress. Swartz and McCarthy work with large corporations, such as Watchovia, Sony, and E&Y, providing training and coaching on how managers and employees can expand and renew their energy in four areas: body, emotions, mind, and spirit. But it's not just energy management training that's needed, they argue. According to Schwartz and McCarthy, employers also need to consider changes in corporate policies, practices, and culture. As they explain: "To effectively reenergize their workforces, organizations need to shift their emphasis from getting more out of people to investing more in them, so they are motivated – and able – to bring more of themselves to work every day."[56] This is a fundamental shift in thinking for many corporate leaders.

So what will it take for organizational decision-makers to follow the advice of Schwartz, McCarthy, and other experts? As I outline in chapter 6, there are ways to change corporate policies, practices, and culture that give greater priority to improving employee well-being as a route to more sustainable organizations. As a prelude to that discussion, it is helpful to become better acquainted with the wide range of publicly available resources that change agents can use to make their workplaces psychologically healthier and safer.

## Progress on Workplace Mental Health in Canada

Reflecting back on over more than a decade of efforts to improve workplace mental health in Canada provides valuable lessons about how to design initiatives that extend beyond physical health, enabling more workers to psychologically flourish in their jobs.[57] In this expanded approach to workplace health and safety, employers and employees now are far more aware of how stress, burnout, toxic work environments, and depression and other mental health problems affect workers. The workplace has slowly become a key venue for mental health promotion. Canadian employers, managers, workers, and health, safety, and HR personnel now have access to a well-equipped workplace mental health toolkit, thanks to significant public and private sector initiatives.

Let's briefly consider three early milestones in Canada. In 2007 the federal government established the Mental Health Commission of Canada (MHCC), tasked with developing a national mental health strategy. As already noted, the MHCC has provided a stream of influential research, resources, and advocacy on mental health issues.[58] Around the same time, the Great-West Life Assurance Company showed corporate leadership by launching the Great-West Life Centre for Mental Health in the Workplace, along with extensive online resources.[59] And Bell Canada, a large telecommunications company, launched in 2010 the national Bell Let's Talk campaign to remove the stigma associated with mental illness.[60] Now many employers use the annual Bell Let's Talk day as an opportunity to raise awareness of and provide education on workplace mental health.

These national efforts have promoted greater corporate awareness that continues to generate action. There now is good momentum on which to build and free resources to keep up that momentum.

Indeed, the MHCC has made a strong case for employer action to address mental health. According to the MHCC, mental health issues impose significant costs on Canadian employers annually, accounting for 20 percent of sick leaves and 30 percent of disability claims.[61] Yet, as the MHCC points out, 60 percent of people with a mental health problem or illness won't seek help for fear of being stigmatized. The MHCC's anti-stigma campaign has helped to break down the stigma that makes it difficult for individuals to seek help for mental health difficulties.

I've already noted the MHCC's partnership with the Canadian Standards Association and the Bureau de normalisation du Québec to launch the National Standard of Canada for Psychological Health and Safety in the Workplace (the Standard).[62] This consensus-based voluntary standard for psychological health and safety is widely recognized as a breakthrough in workplace mental health promotion. The Standard supports action along two complementary paths: providing accessible resources and reducing the stigma attached to mental illness so that workers who are experiencing mental health problems can get the help they need; and supporting actions to make workplaces psychologically healthy and safe.

The Standard provides a framework and resources for identifying, assessing, and reducing psychological health risks in the workplace.[63] The Standard consistently uses the concept of "psychological health and safety," which is more positive and inclusive language than the medicalized term "mental health." Workplaces are psychologically healthy and safe when harassment, discrimination, verbal abuse, unfairness, and disrespect are not permitted and when employees have meaningful influence over their daily work. A psychologically healthy and safe workplace fosters workers' psychological well-being and enhances organizational performance – the twin goals of a healthy organization.

The Standard is attracting growing attention not only from workplace health advocates, but also from the OHS community. It is designed to be incorporated into the occupational health and safety management systems many employers already have in place.[64] Its approach to leadership support, participation, risk and needs assessment, planning, implementation, evaluation, and continuous improvement is familiar to OHS professionals. In these ways, the Standard can be viewed as a useful expansion of OHS management systems rather than something entirely new. In addition to an implementation guide, the Standard is supported by Guarding Minds @ Work, a free and easy-to-use online psychosocial risk assessment and set of organizational audit tools.[65]

In my view, the centerpiece of the Standard is its focus on thirteen workplace factors that contribute to psychological health and safety (see box 2.1). These factors must be addressed in any successful effort

---

**Box 2.1 Workplace Factors Contributing to Workplace Psychological Health and Safety**

1  Psychological and social support
2  Organizational culture
3  Clear leadership and expectations
4  Civility and respect
5  Psychological job demands
6  Growth and development
7  Recognition and reward
8  Involvement and influence
9  Workload management
10  Engagement
11  Work–life balance
12  Protection from violence, bullying, and harassment
13  Physical safety

Source: Canadian Standards Association. (2013). *National standard of Canada for psychological health and safety in the workplace.*

to reduce job stress and burnout. The thirteen factors can be assessed using the Guarding Minds @ Work tools. The assessment process may identify other psychological risk factors that can be added to this list.

Legal experts expect that courts, tribunals, and arbitrators will take the Standard into account when determining an employer's responsibility to provide a psychologically healthy and safe workplace. In other words, the Standard raises the bar for an employer's duty of care by including psychological well-being. There's a growing expert consensus that effectively addressing workplace mental health requires an evidence-based, integrated, and comprehensive approach incorporating prevention, intervention, and accommodation. This combines the reduction of workplace psychosocial risks to mental health, developing workers' capabilities to achieve mental well-being, and addressing mental health problems among workers regardless of the cause.[66] This is what the Standard helps employers to do.

## Lessons from the Standard

The Standard was the first of its kind anywhere, so it has become the instrument of choice in Canada for dealing with workplace mental health issues. A systematic review of twenty English-language guidelines developed specifically for employers to detect, prevent, and manage mental health problems in workplaces assessed their quality and comprehensiveness.[67] These guidelines were rated on a scale of 0 to 100. The highest-scoring guidelines included these features: recommendations for primary, secondary, and tertiary interventions; recommendations that target both individual and organizational levels; advice on how to minimize risk factors and promote positive factors; and extensive tools for the implementation of these recommendations. Guidelines receiving a low score lacked practical tools, implementation guidelines, and a preventative approach that targets both the individual and organizational levels.

Of all twenty guidelines, the Standard ranked highest with an overall score of 91 percent. The next two highest rated were the Psychosocial Risk Management Excellence Framework from the PRIMA-EF Consortium in Europe, and *Heads Up: A Guide for Employers and Employees*, by Australia's Mentally Healthy Workplace Alliance. The researchers recommend that many of the guidelines need more consistent terminology. For example, some use "mental health," "psychological health," and "mental illness" interchangeably. In contrast, the Standard consistently uses a clear definition of psychological health and safety.

Within Canada, the Standard's implementation process has come under the microscope. One team of experts concluded that the Standard's wide scope and complexity, despite guidebooks and other tools being readily available, are barriers to implementation. As they suggest: "Simplified engagement and implementation strategies may be needed along with a tailoring of the Standard to nuanced differences between types and sizes of industries."[68] My observation is that a good number of employers have addressed this concern by adapting the Standard to fit their unique context, rather than full-scale adoption. Another study of employers' awareness and implementation of the Standard, published in the *Canadian Journal of Psychiatry*, surveyed a cross section of Canadian employers.[69] Of the 1,010 companies in the study, very few (1.7 percent) had implemented the entire Standard. Another 20.3 percent reported that their organizations had implemented elements of the Standard, and 17.0 percent reported that they were aware of the Standard but had not taken any action. Just over 70 percent expected that some elements of the Standard would be implemented within the next year. Employers' perceived benefits associated with implementation of the Standard included increased job satisfaction and employee retention. The biggest barrier to implementation is the belief that psychological health and safety are not relevant in workplaces.

Clearly, more work needs to be done to convince employers that mutual benefits will flow to organizations and their workforces by systematically addressing psychological health and safety. Helpful in this regard is the MHCC-sponsored research documenting the implementation of the Standard in forty organizations.[70] These case studies, involving organizations of different sizes and in a variety of industries, show how improvements can be made in the psychosocial work environment by meeting the Standard's requirements. The case studies offer valuable lessons for future workplace mental health initiatives. Interestingly, most implemented the Standard primarily for ethical reasons. Box 2.2 summarizes seven practical insights.

**Box 2.2 Seven Practical Insights for How to Implement the National Standard of Canada for Psychological Health and Safety in the Workplace**

1 Define your organization's unique business case for improving mental health, including the investments it is prepared to make and the expected benefits, which can go beyond the financial to include alignment with mission and values, staff engagement and well-being, and social responsibility.
2 Adapt resources, such as those provided by the Standard, to your organization's unique needs and existing programs, policies, and practices. A customized approach to workplace mental health promotion works best.
3 Greater success in implementing the Standard and other psychological health and safety initiatives results when you embed psychological health and safety within your organization's culture. The absence of a culture of health is a major barrier to progress – a point I explore in chapter 4.

4 Even so, don't wait to have the perfect plan to start. Adapting parts of the Standard or using some of its tools can jump-start change, as long as there is a long-term vision of what the organization wants to achieve and a commitment to continuous improvement in pursuit of that vision.

5 Leadership commitment to improvement goals is an essential prerequisite for success, but so too are high levels of commitment at all levels of the organization. A lack of commitment, especially by senior leaders, is a significant barrier to progress.

6 Dedicated resources also are essential if mental health initiatives are to have a measureable impact on staff well-being. The lack of adequate resources is another significant barrier to progress.

7 After identifying the priority actions for your organization, set clear improvement goals and systematically measure improvements, reporting progress widely and engaging management and employees in ongoing psychological health and safety improvements.

## Tracking Progress in Other Countries

Outside of Canada, one of the best-known and most widely used resources to combat workplace stress is Great Britain's management standards for reducing and preventing work-related stress, established by the Health and Safety Executive (HSE, the national occupational health and safety agency). According to the HSE, work-related stress results in 11 million lost work days annually.[71] Employers are required by law to assess the risk of stress-related ill health arising from work activities and take action to control that risk. The HSE provides assessment tools, including a workplace survey, and other resources and guidance to employers on how to assess and reduce workplace stress. A team of researchers examined the barriers to successful implementation of these management standards.[72] Based on an analysis of 100 public sector organizations, a supportive context for successful implementation of the management standards had these features: active and visible support from senior management, line managers, and human resource departments; regular communications on progress reducing stress; adequate organizational resources, expertise, and other capabilities; assessments carried out at the organizational level as well as at the departmental/team level; and the active involvement of employees and their unions. The main barriers to progress on workplace stress reduction were ongoing organizational change, a lack of organizational capability, and the significant time and resource requirements for conducting assessments using focus groups and a stress survey.

In addition to the HSE's management standards for work-related stress, three other European models have been developed for its assessment and management: START (Germany); Screening, Observation, Analysis, Expertise (SOBANE) (Belgium); and the model of the National Institute for Prevention and Safety at Work (INAIL-ISPESL) (Italy). These European models take a participatory approach, encouraging the active involvement of workers. A close examination of these models led researchers to identify limitations, particularly a lack of clarity on preventive interventions and the absence of standardized risk evaluation tools.[73] As the researchers conclude, while progress is being made in Europe addressing workplace mental health issues, a large gap remains between policy and practice. Implementation challenges are getting in the way of the positive impact expected by policy-makers and experts.

My intent here is not to provide an exhaustive review of all the resources now available to address workplace well-being. You can expect more to come on stream in the near future. Still, it is helpful to examine several more examples of significant steps that have been taken in other countries. Consider actions in Australia to advance the goal of mental well-being in the workforce. Specifically, the New South Wales state government in Australia gave $55 million in 2018 for workplace mental health, the largest investment of its kind in the country to date.[74] The Australian state of Queensland developed a suite of online resources, People at Work, intended to help organizations assess and reduce psychological health risks. Resources include a reliable and valid psychosocial risk assessment survey and guidelines for implementing psychosocial risk management.[75] The state of Queensland's Work Health and Safety Act 2011 requires employers to provide and maintain a working environment that is safe and without risks to health, including psychological health.[76] At the national level, the government's Mental Health Commission established in 2012 the collaborative Mentally Healthy Workplace Alliance, which offers a range of resources to improve workplace mental health.[77] And Safe Work Australia coordinates OHS policies and practices across the country's states and territories, with a focus on psychological safety.[78]

## How You Can Move Beyond Workplace Health Promotion

I recognize that employers are at different stages in their journey to creating healthier workplaces. Regardless, your existing workplace health promotion and OHS initiatives can be leveraged to achieve greater improvements in employee well-being and business success. Employers who integrate health, safety, and well-being, along with human resource and corporate social responsibility goals, reap productivity and reputational advantages, a healthier and more engaged workforce, and cost savings. Most important, when planning your next steps, think how you can expand your approach to be more holistic, integrated, and comprehensive. Challenge your colleagues to think big. Having this expanded mind-set will help you to envision your future workplace as a healthy organization. Don't wait for the perfect plan to take your next step, as long as you have that vision as a guide.

For employers who already have successful healthy workplace initiatives, the next step involves expanding the reach to get at the full range of workplace determinants of health, well-being, and performance. Employers considering the introduction of their first wellness initiative will achieve greater gains by following the above advice for a holistic approach that addresses what NIOSH calls total worker health.

I have detected informal signs that a critical mass of employers is embracing the approach outlined in this chapter. At various national and international conferences and workshops I have participated in, OHS professionals have shown a keen interest in learning about psychological health and safety. While a decade ago, I was speaking almost exclusively at workplace wellness conferences, now I am invited to take the message in this chapter to occupational health and safety and HR conferences. There is no question that workplace mental health is on the agenda of many employers, especially larger ones. In my discussions with managers, many realize that the changes these new approaches require must involve people at all levels of the organization. More corporate executives understand that protecting and promoting the health, safety, and well-being of their employees is both a legal and an ethical responsibility. As an executive at an airline with over 100,000 employees told a duty of care conference: "We feel a responsibility for their well-being." At the same time, it is also clear from numerous discussions I have had with managers and corporate leaders that they are still figuring out how to do this. That's what subsequent chapters will help you to do.

## CHAPTER 3

# How Vibrant Workplaces Inspire Employees

What does a healthy organization look and feel like? The most accurate way to answer this question is to ask your coworkers or employees. Most employees and managers I have posed this question to have answered with their own shortlist of what defines a healthy workplace and why achieving this vision is important for them, their employer, customers or clients, and society as a whole. Usually, the discussion also revolves around what makes people look forward to coming to work each day. What I have learned from these conversations about positive work experiences is that there is no difference between what really inspires them about their jobs and what makes the office, hospital, factory, store, or other setting in which they spend their day a healthy and safe work environment.

This chapter looks at healthy organizations through the eyes of employees. I focus on individuals' personal work experiences to describe what makes a workplace more than just healthy and how these factors do more than just engage employees. I believe that the aspirations people carry into workplaces provide a common vision of a vibrant workplace. The defining feature of a vibrant workplace is a seamless connection between workers' well-being and organizational performance, with greater benefits than can be achieved by stand-alone health promotion or HR programs.

While meeting the aspirations of workers may be a desirable end in itself, it falls short of a business case for investing in an organization's people. We also need a more detailed answer to the question about what a healthy organization looks and feels like. By taking action to address employees' aspirations for vibrant, inspiring work environments, change agents are putting in place a cornerstone of healthy organizations. A vibrant workplace energizes the entire organization by enabling employees to continually find better ways to meet customers' or clients' needs. The result is a talented, motivated, and healthy workforce able to sustain higher levels of performance. The healthy organization ideal is an integrating framework that helps to connect the dots of well-being, workforce capabilities, and performance.

My objective in this chapter is to encourage readers to think about using employees' day-to-day work experiences as the starting point for designing a work environment that is healthy, safe, and inspiring. Here are the main action insights the chapter offers:

1 Just as companies focus on enhancing their customers' experience, they also must find ways to improve their employees' experience, because these goals are closely connected.
2 By understanding what truly inspires employees, you can identify how a vibrant workplace develops employees' capabilities and promotes well-being.
3 Involving employees in crafting a vision of the kind of workplace they want provides a blueprint for improving the drivers of well-being and performance.
4 A vibrant workplace vision can also help you find solutions to human resource challenges, particularly retention, recruitment, engagement, and development.
5 Employees' assessment of whether they have a healthy workplace also gauges how well an organization is developing the capabilities it will need for sustainable future success.

I invite you to use the ideas in this chapter to stimulate discussions in your team, unit, OHS or wellness committee, department, or organization about a shared vision of a vibrant workplace. Once this conversation begins, you soon will be talking about what really motivates people to do their best work. That is how you can advance further down the path to building a healthier organization.

## Focusing on Workers' Experiences

Employers ignore at their peril employees' perceptions, just as it is a mistake for businesses to ignore their customers' feedback about their products or services. Employees' experiences of their job and work environment have an enormous impact on their work attitudes and behaviors, their overall well-being, and their job performance. An accurate way to gauge what makes employees feel satisfied and committed – or better yet, inspired – is to ask them to describe the ideal workplace. Taking this positive approach, rather than starting with workplace problem-solving, mobilizes employees and managers around a shared vision of a vibrant workplace. The result is a collective aspiration that can be a powerful energizer for change and improvement.

Employees' experiences are reflected in their assessments of many aspects of their work situation, including choices, trade-offs, and preferences. Such personal calculations are filtered through what each individual or group considers most important. In this way, values and perceptions shape our individual and collective definitions of a healthy organization. What I am proposing is an employee-centered perspective on organizational success. The best route to excellent customer or client experiences is through excellent employee experiences. Here's the basic logic I expand upon in this chapter: vibrant workplaces = inspired employees = sustainable success.

Improving organizational performance by putting employee well-being first may sound counterintuitive. But it works. This point is emphasized by Isadore Sharp, who founded the Four Seasons luxury hotel business in 1961 and served for many years as its CEO.[1] Sharp describes how every Four Seasons employee focuses on one priority – pleasing customers – because every manager focuses on pleasing employees. Four Seasons' management trusts and empowers staff to do what is best for customers. As a result, employees are passionate about providing a quality of guest experience far superior to what is available in other hotels. When Four Seasons opened a hotel in New York, 15,000 people were interviewed for 400 positions. It has the lowest turnover rate in the industry. Four Seasons' success comes down to a strong corporate philosophy based on the Golden Rule: "Treat others as we would have them treat us." That includes providing all hotel employees complimentary stays at any Four Seasons so they can experience the hotels "like guests do."[2] Four Seasons is but one example of how employee and customer experiences converge.

## Envisioning Vibrant Workplaces

I like to begin a workshop on creating healthy workplaces by inviting participants to think about what the ideal healthy workplace looks and feels like for them. I ask participants to spend a few minutes writing down their personal vision of a healthy workplace, one in which they can imagine experiencing an excellent quality of work-life. Sitting in small groups at round tables, they are then asked to share their personal visions with others at the table. It takes about fifteen or twenty minutes for people at each table to agree on the ingredients of a healthy workplace. And when the table visions are presented to others, it is remarkable how much convergence there is around what people consider most important in the ideal workplace – and how far beyond health these visions move the discussion.

Indeed, absent from how employees and managers envision the ideal healthy workplace is an emphasis on individual health promotion or wellness programs. That is because in the minds of employees the fundamentals of a healthy workplace transcend personal health and wellness activities. This insight is important for managers, workplace health and wellness professionals, and wellness committee members, many of whom still operate within the health promotion mind-set described earlier.

This is a recurring theme in consultations I have conducted with frontline employees, professionals, and managers from a variety of organizations. A group of employees at an industrial facility stated that a healthy workplace means much more than "management giving us gym passes or fitness programs." It wasn't that they opposed what they called "lifestyle programs." They wanted to see fundamental changes in the workplace. These workers went on to talk about the things that needed fixing, such as cleaning up dirty and cluttered workspaces, supervisors using respectful language when talking to their employees, and a variety of small changes that would give production workers a greater sense of dignity in their jobs. Later discussions with managers and workplace health and wellness staff in the same company acknowledged that launching a wellness program that did not address unhealthy working conditions would be a waste of time and money.

Employees' visions of healthy workplaces go directly to the levers that managers are trying to pull to improve retention, engagement, and performance. These actions build an organization's reputation as an exemplary employer, sought out by talented job seekers and fostering employee pride and loyalty. A compelling vision will achieve these goals.

Managers with a bottom-line focus may be asking, "So what?" Skepticism about how employees and managers view a healthy workplace should evaporate once the connection with improving employee engagement is clear. In my experience, employees and managers see an engaging work environment and a healthy one as part of the same organizational fabric. Indeed, when asked to envision the ideal future workplace, what most often comes up raises the bar much higher for employee well-being, performance, and passion about work.

A natural resources organization I worked with wanted to create a culture of engagement. To senior management, this meant a workplace that personally involved each and every employee in providing consistently excellent service. A team of professional employees was brought together from across the organization and asked by senior management to create a vision and an action plan for increasing engagement. At a workshop, the team came up with an engagement vision. By creating its own vision of engagement, the team realized where shifts in the corporate culture were required. Higher levels of engagement depended on a work environment having four main attributes:

- Everyone feels like they belong to one big team with common objectives, and everyone understands how their job contributes to these objectives.
- All interactions are meaningful and positive. Communication is open and based on trust. Knowledge is gained and shared effectively.
- Employees feel empowered to be innovative and take risks. Managers support employees, bring out the best in them, and recognize their contributions.
- Employees are motivated to do better and embrace change. Employees achieve a sense of accomplishment, work–life balance, and well-being.

You can use this vision summary to help identify improvements needed in your work environment and the expected benefits for coworkers or your employees. With this focus, you will move beyond individual wellness to addressing the ingredients of a healthy organization.

## The Big Picture: Why Some Workplaces Are Healthier and Safer than Others

There are some indications that Canadian workplaces, like those in many advanced economies, are becoming healthier and safer. Workplace injuries and fatalities are declining. More employers are promoting employee wellness, addressing workplace mental health issues, and providing employee assistance programs. For example, the Association of Workers' Compensation Boards of Canada reports that lost-time injury claims have declined nationally every year since 2000.[3] A Conference Board of Canada study found that, in 2017, one-third of employers had a formal wellness strategy, a substantial increase since 2009.[4] And as noted, workplace mental health promotion is now supported by new policies, resources, and practices.[5]

These broad trends suggest that the overall quality of Canadians' work-life should be improving. However, there is surprisingly little information on how workers assess the safety and health of their workplaces. To fill this gap, I partnered with EKOS Research Associates to survey a representative sample of Canadian workers, asking for their assessments of key aspects of workplace health and safety.[6] The 2018 Rethinking Work survey focuses on workplace climate. Central to theories of organizational behavior are employees' perceptions of their work environment, or what's called organizational climate.[7] Most workplace surveys are in fact climate surveys because they document how workers experience their immediate work environment. A better understanding of workplace climate can guide improvements in people policies and practices, leading to a more vibrant workplace.[8]

## Perceptions of a Healthy and Safe Work Environment

Looking at survey respondents' overall assessments of workplace health and safety, these workers were far more likely to report a safe work environment than a healthy one. Indeed, four out of five workers surveyed considered their work environment to be safe (i.e., they agreed or strongly agreed with the statement), compared with two in three who considered it to be healthy. These assessments are consistent with the national decline in lost-time work injuries, noted earlier, as well as the shift to a service-based economy with fewer physically demanding jobs. They also are related, but not in a symmetrical way. Almost all (95 percent) of respondents reporting a healthy environment also considered it to be safe. In contrast, 75 percent of those reporting a safe environment also assessed it as healthy. In other words, healthy workplaces are also safe, but safe workplaces are not necessarily healthy.

As discussed in chapter 2, experts recommend that employers take an integrated approach to health, safety, and wellness.[9] The occupational health and safety systems that many employers have introduced give greater priority to safety, particularly physical safety, than health. As a result, workers typically view safety through the lens of physical hazards and risks. So it is not surprising that 80 percent of the workers we surveyed considered their workplace to be safe. Furthermore, workplace psychological safety is still a fairly new concept. Recall from chapter 2 that Canadian employers have had the guidance of the voluntary National Standard of Canada for Psychological Health and Safety in the Workplace only since 2013.

To better understand how workplace health and safety are connected, I cross-tabulated responses to the two survey questions ("The work environment is healthy"; "The work environment is safe") and came up with important insights. First, about two-thirds of respondents agreed or strongly agreed with both statements. This suggests that a majority of employers have been taking a more integrated and comprehensive approach to promoting both health and safety. And second, 16 percent of survey respondents disagreed with both statements. In other words, one in six workers could be exposed to significant workplace health and safety hazards.

Workers' overall assessments of health and safety are related to specific workplace factors that a healthy organization requires. Figure 3.1 compares how two groups assessed these enabling workplace factors: those who agreed or strongly agreed that their workplace is both healthy and safe, and all others who did not provide these two positive assessments.

Echoing a central recommendation from many experts, leadership support is a critical enabler of making workplaces healthier and safer. For example, 83 percent of respondents with a healthy and

**Figure 3.1** Assessment of a Healthy and Safe Work Environment by Selected Organizational Characteristics

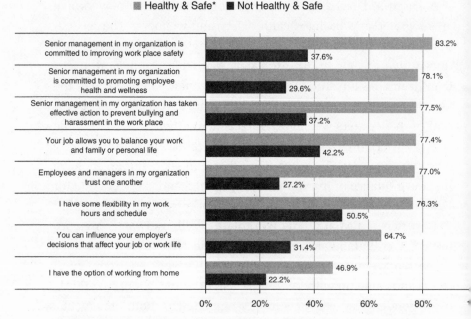

EKOS Research Associates' survey of Canadians in the workforce. October 2018. Base n=1,388
* Respondents who strongly agree or agree that their work environment is both healthy and safe. Between group differences statistically significant (p < .001).

safe work environment have senior managers who champion safety. This compares with 38 percent of the group who didn't provide this positive assessment of their work environment. The same pattern can be seen regarding senior managers' actions to promote health and wellness or prevent bullying and harassment. Also important, healthy and safe workplaces have higher levels of trust, provide workers more flexibility and say, and support work–life balance.

While we can't say definitively that the factors listed in figure 3.1 are the direct causes of positive perceptions of a healthy and safe workplace climate, the consistency of these findings do support this logic.

## Who Has the Healthiest and Safest Workplaces?

Which groups of workers have the healthiest and safest workplaces? Answering this question sheds light on how one of the central dimensions of job quality – a healthy and safe work environment – is distributed within the labor market.

There were no statistically significant demographic group differences by gender, marital status, spouse or partner employment status, household income, equity group (i.e., visible minority, Aboriginal, disabled), or immigrant status. However, health and safety assessment scores varied by nine workforce characteristics. Individuals with the most positive assessments of workplace health and safety tend to work in knowledge-based jobs, be self-employed or in part-time jobs, have a university education, work in the private or nonprofit sector and in smaller organizations, belong to a professional association, be age sixty-five or older, earn high incomes, and describe their household socioeconomic status as "upper class." Some of these characteristics are closely related; educated, older, professional, and more affluent workers have better access to these crucial features of a high-quality workplace than do other workers.

Three specific findings deserve our attention. First, smaller organizations are healthier and safer than larger ones. At first glance, this seems counterintuitive given that large organizations are more likely to have implemented health and safety management systems and wellness programs. However, the survey taps into workers' perceptions of how these systems and programs affect their day-to-day work-life. In this regard, it is telling that perceptions of trust are inversely related to organization size and therefore are much greater in small workplaces. So too are having a say and having flexible hours and schedules. Trust, input, and flexibility are essential ingredients that reflect the value an organization's culture places on workers' health and safety.

Second, self-employed individuals rate the health and safety of their work environments significantly higher than do full-time employees or workers in precarious jobs (e.g., temporary, seasonal, or contract positions). This effect also shows up in the higher ratings given by survey respondents working in the private sector, compared to the public sector, where large bureaucratic organizations predominate. And third, a respondent's age is the only personal characteristic associated with perceptions of workplace health and safety. Specifically, workers age sixty-five and older give the most positive health and safety assessments. Gender, marital status, being a member of a visible minority, an Aboriginal person, or a person with a disability, or being an immigrant are not related to these climate assessments. The likely explanation is that many older workers have remained in the workforce voluntarily, having the opportunity to choose a decent workplace or to become self-employed.

## Linking Worker Well-Being to Workplace Health and Safety

Workers' assessments of workplace health and safety are closely related to four critical measures of their well-being: job stress, job satisfaction, life satisfaction, and self-reported overall health.

I again compared two groups of workers: those agreeing that their work environment is both healthy and safe, and those who do not agree with both statements. Workers who rate their workplace as both healthy and safe are more satisfied with their job and their life as a whole, experience less job stress, and have better overall health compared with workers whose work environments do not meet the criteria of being both healthy and safe. These outcomes confirm that healthy and safe work environments – or more accurately, workers' perceptions of these features – enhance workers' well-being.

Thus, when a workplace is both healthy and safe, workers are more likely to experience less stress, higher job and life satisfaction, and better overall health. These are preconditions for a truly vibrant work environment that inspires workers to fully contribute their talents to achieve organizational goals. The global measures of health and safety climate used in the Rethinking Work survey could easily be added to your existing employee survey as an efficient way to track improvements. Basically, when workplaces are considered to be healthy and safe by those who work there, we can expect these workers to experience higher levels of overall well-being. In short, they flourish.

This evidence encourages an integrated approach to promoting workplace health and safety. This is best accomplished by focusing on improving worker well-being. This holistic goal ties together mental and physical health, safety, and quality of life.[10] Any actions in this regard must also be inclusive, so that the benefits of a healthy and safe work environment are available to all workers – not just educated professionals and other knowledge workers in decent-quality jobs.

When setting health and safety priorities, employers must recognize that from a worker's perspective, a healthy workplace is also safe. Given that many occupational health and safety programs emphasize safety, particular injury prevention, employers must realize that they can also achieve safety goals by giving equal emphasis to improving worker health. Senior management support for creating workplaces that are safe, health promoting, and free of bullying and harassment is a critical enabler of success. However, the relatively low levels of trust we have documented – especially in larger organizations – can be a roadblock to effective action in these important areas. The goal of trust-building must be explicitly incorporated into workplace safety, wellness, and HR strategies. Chapter 4 expands upon this key point.

## Engagement and Well-Being

Work engagement is a core feature of a healthy organization. That's why the Standard (discussed in chapter 2) lists engagement as one of the essential workplace factors that promotes workers' psychological health and safety. Ideally, employers want a workforce that is healthy, safe, present, and engaged. An organization may benefit more from a robust engagement strategy that encompasses employee well-being as one of its goals – especially in terms of lower absenteeism, presenteeism, stress, and turnover – than from a stand-alone workplace health promotion program.[11]

Researchers at University of Michigan's Center for Positive Organizational Scholarship describe fully engaged employees as thriving. They explain: "We think of a thriving workforce as one in which employees are not just satisfied and productive but also engaged in creating the future – the company's and their own."[12] Or in other words, thriving employees are inspired in their work. Successful companies such as Costco, Quik-Trips, and Trader Joe's understand that low costs, excellent customer satisfaction, and strong financial performance depend on these sorts of positive employee work experiences.[13] And they know how to avoid employee stress and burnout.

Employees thrive in jobs that give them a sense of purpose and room to develop their potential. If employees are disengaged and dissatisfied, experts recommend rallying them around a greater sense of purpose, so that they clearly understand how they can make a meaningful difference.[14] This opens the way for workers to feel more energized, committed, and innovative in their jobs. This happens all the more readily if a company has genuinely embraced a sustainability strategy that incorporates employee well-being as one of its goals.

There's good evidence that well-being is positively contagious. In a team setting, the well-being of each employee can enhance, or reduce, their fellow team members' sense of well-being. This is a two-way relationship, with each team member's well-being dependent on how other team members are feeling on any given day.[15] When collective well-being is strong in a workplace, so is productivity, loyalty, and employee health. As the Gallup Organization's extensive workplace studies reveal, when workers experience well-being in their jobs, they also "see their workplace as positive, productive, and engaging. Conversely, if they are struggling or suffering, it rubs off on the workplace and the team."[16] And to emphasize, this is not just an individual phenomenon; it can be cultivated within a team or an entire workforce.

## Individual and Organizational Resilience

Resilience is an old concept that is finding new resonance today among healthy workplace advocates. Decades ago, psychologists studied the sources of personal resilience among children who overcame significant disadvantages to succeed in school and life. This early research showed that resilience is an individual's capacity to thrive despite adversity. Now, it's recognized that employees who experience well-being also have strong resilience skills. What's more, the *Harvard Business Review* calls resilience the new leadership skill.[17] I would also call it a twenty-first-century organizational survival skill. For example, a growing number of cities around the world – some that have had to cope with floods, earthquakes, fires, and other catastrophes – recognize the importance of cultivating resilience within the community and its organizational ecosystem in order to prepare for future disasters.

Resilience involves psychological traits and personal behaviors that can be learned – a crucial insight for leadership development.

Resilient people don't bounce back; they bounce forward, finding new strength and equilibrium. They move to a new normal that enables them to keep progressing toward a better future. Resilient people don't just adapt to change, they find opportunities and renewed strength as they confront it. In the language of positive psychology, the goal is to help organizations and their members flourish and thrive. A meta-analysis of thirty-seven studies found that resilience-building programs can have a modest effect in workplaces as a form of primary prevention.[18] A major benefit of resilience training is developing individuals' capabilities and resources as protective factors for psychological well-being. Personal resilience is related to positive mental health and protection against stress, particularly post-traumatic stress disorder (PTSD). A leading example is Professor Martin Seligman's program with the US Army to foster "post-traumatic growth" among soldiers and prevent PTSD.[19] The program has resulted in a decline in PTSD symptoms and related healthcare costs.

My psychologist colleagues Dan Bilsker and Merv Gilbert call the resilience that training can build "psychological safety skills." But resilience training only goes so far. Workers need a supportive environment to be resilient. That's why it is so important for leaders to cultivate resilience, both personally and among their employees, in order to effectively manage the constant challenges, changes, and pressures of organizational life. To do this, leaders must develop their own resilience. Resilient leaders skillfully and proactively respond to stressors, learn from failure, develop renewed strengths, and show others how it is possible to thrive when the going gets tough. In this way, they foster a resilient workforce that is prepared to deal with the unexpected.

## Psychological Capital

However, some psychologists argue that today's leaders need more than just resilience. So they have developed the broader concept of psychological capital (PsyCap) to encompass a person's capacity to be not only resilient, but also hopeful, confident, and optimistic.[20] All these attributes can be learned, which has practical implications for organizational learning and development programs. PsyCap is related to a range of organizational outcomes essential for sustainable success. Leaders with well-developed PsyCap have better overall physical and mental health than their colleagues who lack PsyCap. They are also better able to manage the stresses of their job and are less likely to experience burnout.

A few years ago at a conference where I was speaking, someone in the audience asked an important question: "Does the engagement–resilience link mean that we just hire more resilient people?" The short answer is no. Organizational leaders must recognize that resilience is also an outcome of a psychologically healthy workplace. The Standard can help you to put in place the support system needed to cultivate resilience and other PsyCap attributes in your workforce (see box 3.1).

**Box 3.1 Features of a Psychologically Healthy and Safe Workplace That Contribute to Psychological Capital**

1 Supportive managers and coworkers
2 A culture that values individuals' well-being
3 Skilled people leadership
4 Respectful working relationships
5 Support for employees' personal growth and development
6 The resources needed to manage workloads and job demands
7 Employee involvement in decisions
8 Recognition for contributions
9 The flexibility needed to achieve work–life balance

## An Organizational Resilience Strategy

I encourage you to think about developing resilience as part of your healthy organization strategy. Any organization can apply the above insights about resilience and psychological capital to develop the workforce and organizational characteristics it will need to thrive in an uncertain future. The City of Christchurch, New Zealand, illustrates how this happens, as I learned while conducting a healthy organization workshop for local employers in 2014.[21] The massive February 2011 earthquake destroyed about half of the downtown area, killing 185 people and injuring several thousand.

As part of its recovery and rebuilding efforts, Christchurch became one of the first cities in the world to develop a resilience strategy designed to protect it against future shocks.[22] The city committed to spending 10 percent of its budget on developing resilience.[23] With floods, fires, and other natural catastrophes likely to increase as a result of climate change, cities such as Christchurch understand that preparedness is essential. The goal is to build a city "that will be stronger, smarter and more resilient to the physical, social, and economic challenges that are a growing part of the 21st century." City employees were on the front lines of helping others in the community to recover and rebuild in the wake of the earthquake. A three-year plan was developed to repair and rebuild council facilities, including a new city hall. It was immediately clear that staff needed tangible signs that the council cared about them. So council provided the support, flexibility, and other resources its employees needed to deal with post-disaster personal and family needs – basically, helping them so they could help others.

After the earthquake, Dr. Rob Gordon, a specialist in disaster psychology from Australia, presented his four stages of disaster recovery to various community groups in Christchurch.[24] These four stages are survival, endurance, identity crisis, and recovery from recovery. Council managers and HR staff realized that support for their employees, and the required budget, had to address changing needs as people went through these stages over time. In response, council took steps to develop what I would call a healthier and more resilient organization. Senior managers were briefed on the council's post-quake internal and external environment and encouraged to build flexibility into the organization, strengthen communication networks, and be innovative in their people practices. Improving staff well-being became a goal in the council's strategy. Resilience sessions were provided for all staff, developed jointly by the council's OHS and organizational development staff. These sessions addressed the emotional liquefaction (borrowing a term from earthquake science) people were experiencing after the earthquake. And team training provided tips for managing workload and staying resilient.

The council's Senior Leadership Group also acknowledged the efforts of staff by providing up to nine days annually, attached to a weekend, for rest and recovery. Employees felt valued and were appreciative of this leave. Employees were also offered heart health checks, including a follow-up with a nurse, and health risk screening. The council also held a half-day wellness expo with a popular (and fun) "smoothie bike" (I invite readers to imagine what this looks like!). And among employees, there was a 25 percent increase in mental health consultations by MDs, suggesting they were taking care of themselves. Council created a personal health resources website for employees, which included the Canterbury All Right? campaign's five pathways to well-being and resilience. And it collaborated with the New Zealand Mental Health Foundation in this program as a way of promoting mental well-being.

As recovery efforts progressed, employee fatigue set in. Training sessions for managers focused on the signs of "un-wellness" they were observing among their staff and how best to help. Later, as council building repairs were completed, employees were informed of them before they were expected to return, engineering reports were made available, and sessions with engineers were held so that staff could ask questions about their building's safety. There were also sessions with health and safety advisors to establish a return-to-the-building plan, including the emotional and social support staff would need. Council used its annual staff engagement survey to assess employees' post-quake well-being and workload, adding four new items:[25]

- The support initiatives the Council put in place post-earthquakes have had a positive impact on how I feel about working here.
- I am coping effectively with managing anxiety resulting from the earthquakes.
- Most of the time my workload is at a manageable level; I feel confident that my manager would help me prioritize workload.
- Most of the time I can get my work completed on time.

By 2015, workload had become the focus of council's workplace improvement efforts. The council was now into what Dr. Gordon labels the "recovery from recovery" phase, focusing on ways to ensure that its employees – who had been on the front lines of disaster relief and rebuilding – could achieve a decent quality of work-life.

## High-Quality Healthcare Organizations

My work with various healthcare organizations further illustrates how positive work experiences contribute to employees' quality of work-life as well as to high-quality patient care. As I've mentioned, a sense of engagement with one's work is one of the hallmarks of a psychologically healthy and safe workplace. A high level of engagement is also a strategic goal for a growing number of organizations in many industries, including healthcare. Increasingly, healthcare employers are taking steps to strengthen this people–performance link. However, a lack of good data on employee engagement in Canadian healthcare organizations has made it difficult to use the concept as a workplace improvement tool. To help fill this gap,

I examined results from the first wave of the Employee Experience Survey (EES), jointly developed by the Ontario Hospital Association (OHA) and NRC Health. Survey respondents were over 10,000 employees in sixteen Ontario hospitals.

High-performing organizations have healthy and engaged employees. In these outstanding organizations, work environments are designed to support the development and utilization of the people capabilities required for success. These basic ideas have taken root in healthcare. Experts and practitioners are calling for a comprehensive, strategically focused approach to measuring and reporting the quality of healthcare work environments. This is a big step beyond workplace health promotion programs, because it integrates employee well-being within a comprehensive framework for improving the quality of healthcare services. For example, research conducted on England's National Health Service confirms that hospitals with higher levels of staff engagement provide higher-quality care and have better financial performance.[26]

To support this approach to evidence-based human resource practices, I worked with the OHA to create the Quality Healthcare Workplace Model (figure 3.2).[27] The model outlines how health system performance depends on a capable workforce in a healthy and productive workplace. The OHA's model suggests that the quality of the work environment for staff and physicians is a key determinant of a high-performing healthcare organization. By integrating healthy workplace, human resources, quality, and patient safety goals within a performance-focused framework, the model offers a useful guide to research and practice.

The development of the EES was guided by the model in figure 3.2. The ninety-five-item questionnaire assesses the drivers, individual outcomes, and organizational outcomes specified in the model. A companion survey for physicians was also developed. NRC Health was a partner in the development of both surveys, and I was the project consultant.

**Figure 3.2** Quality Healthcare Workplace Model

Enabling context: strong values - compelling vision - clear mission - committed leadership

Source: Ontario Hospital Association.

Engagement influences other major human resources goals, such as retention, job performance, absenteeism, and (indirectly through the employer's reputation) recruitment.[28] Human resources experts recommend a multidimensional approach to measuring engagement, which combines a number of questionnaire items into a scale, yielding a single engagement score.[29] The resulting score can be useful to employers for tracking progress on actions taken to improve employee engagement. The engagement scale developed for the EES measures three core dimensions of engagement with six survey items (table 3.1).

Table 3.1  Engagement Dimensions and Measures Used in the Employee Experience Survey

| Dimension | Questionnaire Items |
| --- | --- |
| Emotional | • I am proud to tell others I am part of the organization.<br>• I find that my values and the organization's values are similar. |
| Rational | • I am satisfied with (my) job overall.<br>• Overall rating of the hospital as a place to work (from poor to excellent). |
| Behavioral | • I look forward to going to work.<br>• This organization really inspires the best in me in the way of job performance. |

To simplify data analysis and reporting, I grouped engagement scale scores into low, medium, and high categories, based on the distribution of scale scores. I was especially interested in identifying the job, work environment, management, and other organizational factors that most influenced engagement. Statistical modeling found that over 70 percent of the variation in engagement scale scores among all survey respondents could be accounted for by ten questionnaire items. Here are the top ten work environment drivers of engagement, rank-ordered by their net influence on individual employee's engagement scores:

1  I feel I can trust this organization.
2  I have an opportunity to make improvements in my work.
3  The organization values my work.
4  Senior management is committed to high-quality care.
5  I have clear job goals/objectives.
6  I feel I belong to a team.
7  My organization promotes staff health/wellness.
8  I have a good balance of family/personal life with work.
9  My supervisor can be counted on to help with difficult tasks.
10  I have adequate resources/equipment to do my work.

Trust is most closely associated with high levels of engagement. However, trust can also be considered an outcome of these other work experiences. As I will discuss in chapter 4, trust is a complex and dynamic feature of organizational life, being both a cause and effect of work experiences and performance. Still, after removing trust from the statistical model, the list of the top ten drivers of engagement remains largely the same.

The OHA Quality Healthcare Workplace Model suggests that highly engaged employees are better able than their less-engaged colleagues to achieve patient care and other organizational goals. That indeed turned out to be the case when we looked at four outcomes: retention, perceived quality of patient care or services provided by the respondent's team/unit, patient safety culture, and patient-centered care (or client-centered services for non-clinical hospital staff). To summarize these outcomes, nine in ten highly engaged employees planned to stay with the organization, at least for the near future, compared with about half of those who were disengaged. This would reduce turnover costs. In both clinical and non-clinical units, two thirds of highly engaged employees reported that their work units "always" provided top-quality service, compared with only about one in five of the low-engagement group. There is a strong positive relationship between being engaged and clinical employees' ratings of having a patient-centered work environment and a strong patient safety culture – both of which are priorities for healthcare systems in Canada and many other countries.

Furthermore, a work environment that's safe for patients is also safe for care providers, as measured by respondents' self-reported injuries or illness. And finally, highly engaged employees were far less likely to experience frequent job stress (24 percent), compared with their less-engaged coworkers. About 60 percent of this latter group experienced most workdays as quite or extremely stressful.

In summary, highly engaged employees experience pride, value congruence, and job and organizational satisfaction. They feel inspired, enthusiastic, and effective in their work. In the hospitals I studied, engagement levels were consistently related to a range of mission-critical organizational outcomes. An engaged workforce benefits patients and reduces turnover costs. This point is nicely put by researchers who conducted an in-depth study of engagement and healthcare performance in England's National Health Service: "cultures of engagement, positivity, caring, compassion and respect for all – staff, patients and the public – provide the ideal environment within which to care for the health of the nation. When we care for staff, they can fulfil their calling of providing outstanding professional care for patients."[30]

## Engagement Enablers

For healthcare leaders and policy-makers, along with employees and their unions and professional associations, creating the enabling conditions for high levels of employee engagement must be a priority. Everyone stands to benefit. Critical for unlocking higher levels of engagement is for managers at all levels to build trust with employees. Demonstrating basic respect, fairness, and integrity in all dealings with staff is the basis for trust. As we will see in the next chapter, culture becomes the vital link between positive staff experiences and organizational performance.

The Royal Victoria Regional Health Centre (RVH), located in Barrie, Ontario, exemplifies how healthcare organizations are linking employee and physician goals with patient care goals.[31] In 2009, the hospital's first staff survey (using the EES) documented room for improvement. Over the next several years, hospital leaders took an integrated approach to improving employee and physician engagement, knowing this would help to achieve patient care excellence. Employee and physician surveys were conducted annually. A corporate engagement strategy supported managers to guide effective survey action-planning with their teams and then to introduce needed changes.

A new strategic plan for the hospital, called My Care, brought a sharper focus on patient care improvements, with staff wellness and engagement being the prerequisites for these. Survey results were used to report psychological health and also to measure how deeply embedded the hospital's values had become. A number of activities were introduced to bring the hospital's values to life. One was "Mission Possible," a daily twenty-minute values-based activity used at team meetings and new staff orientation sessions. It focused on day-to-day challenges faced by team members and how these can be overcome by following the RVH's values. Another innovative initiative invited all teams to make their own short YouTube video showing how they lived the values. Winners were announced at a big awards ceremony. By watching these videos, staff across the hospital also gained an appreciation of what each other did in the interests of patients and the community. Subsequent surveys showed higher engagement levels – all during a time of senior leadership changes and a move to a new facility.

## Closing the Inspiration Gap

There are basic steps you can take to improve the work environment and provide more inspiring work experiences. Here I am speaking directly to managers, who have considerable power to ensure that vibrant workplace ingredients are in place. Actually, one of the most effective steps in this regard is relatively inexpensive in financial terms, but will require personal commitment.

To venture in this direction, a manager would have to make a determined effort to understand the filters employees use for assessing their jobs and work environment. These filters are people's work values, which define what is fundamentally important to them in a job, workplace, and career. The manager would also need to address major gaps between employees' work values and what they actually experience on a daily basis. I call this discrepancy between what employees want and what they have the inspiration gap. Most employee surveys provide only one of these pieces of information: assessments of various working conditions. So I would encourage HR professionals and others who manage employee surveys to find out what really matters to their workforce by also tapping into basic work values. Comparing these values findings with individuals' assessments of their working conditions will show the inspiration gaps you need to close. For readers who work in smaller organizations, these can become topics for discussions at team or all-employee meetings.

Earlier, I identified positive influences on employees' perceptions of whether or not their work environment is healthy. As for the negative influences – stressful and hectic jobs, heavy workloads, conflicting demands, bullying and harassment, uncaring supervisors, unhelpful coworkers – they obviously require remedial action. You can readily diagnose these problems in your workplace by using an appropriately designed employee survey, focus groups or employee forums, or other assessment tools or consultation techniques. Doing so will address some of the biggest concerns employees and employers have voiced about unhealthy psychosocial work environments. However, removing these toxic factors from a work environment does not make it healthy, never mind vibrant. But it is certainly a first step toward that goal. There must also be a range of positive factors put in place, such as those listed earlier as the top ten drivers of engagement in Ontario hospitals. Employee input on where to start is critical. Useful information in this regard can be gleaned from a basic gap analysis of employee survey results – assuming you have asked parallel questions about work values and work experiences.

Here is how to do this gap analysis and what you might expect to find. Using the list of positive influences on perceptions of a healthy work environment, such as those listed above and in the next chapter, imagine that you also have employee survey data on the importance, or value, your employees place on each factor. By comparing their assessments of these factors with how important each one is, you can calculate an inspiration gap score. Most employee surveys use rating scales on a negative-to-positive continuum. The most common would be a five-category rating scale that goes from "strongly disagree" to "strongly agree." The same statements used to assess job and work environment features can also be used to ask employees what they consider most important. A similar five-category rating scale is employed, but ranging from "not at all important" to "very important."

When you have the survey results, compare the answers with the assessment and importance questions for each job or workplace dimension. Put them side by side in an Excel spreadsheet, and simply subtract the percentage who answered "strongly agree" on the assessment from the percentage who answered "very important" on the values version of the same question. This procedure will give you the gap score. Look closely at the relative size of the gaps and then create a ranked list of priority issues you can address by discussing solutions directly with employees.

## The Dynamics of a Healthy Organization

Managers and professionals in OHS, wellness, and HR now have the evidence and practical insights they will need to plan and implement changes aimed at improving employees' work experiences and productivity. What energizes a healthy organization is having talented and motivated employees who know they are in a supportive, respectful, and well-resourced workplace. Simply put, this is a vibrant workplace. This is the context that enables your workforce to provide better results for customers, communities, and society that can be sustained over time.

To fully grasp the dynamics of a healthy organization, we need to further explore how the defining characteristics of quality jobs and healthy work environments are related. We also need to better understand other parts of the organization's systems, culture, policies, and practices. There is solid evidence, as we've seen, suggesting a logical sequence whereby quality jobs in healthy and safe work environments enhance an employee's quality of work-life and well-being and, as a result, contribute to the organization's success.

However, organizational life can be more complicated, because this neat chain of cause and effect can be influenced by many factors. Growing concerns over the past decade about mental health issues in the workplace, resilience, work–life balance, engagement, collaboration, innovation, leadership, and more have given new urgency to sorting out how job and workplace factors influence employees' work experiences and behaviors.

I encourage you to examine these issues in your workplace, using your own survey data and with the benefit of input from your employees or coworkers. Test out some of the ideas presented in this chapter. For example, are your most satisfied workers also highly motivated to innovate and collaborate – and if not, why? For your workforce, what changes in working conditions are most likely to improve employees' well-being? What would energize your employees or team members to feel more inspired about their work and how it contributes to making other people's lives better? The point is, you need to explore ways to put in place the workplace ingredients of a healthy organization that fit your unique context.

Now is the time to consider the role that the two other building blocks of a healthy organization play. The healthy organization model in chapter 2 depicted culture and leadership as foundational, because they also play a powerful enabling role. Change agents – be they senior managers, HR professionals, wellness or OHS committee members, or frontline employees – must step up to raise the issues, initiate conversations about potential improvements, and find opportunities to design and implement solutions. That means taking leadership. Perhaps even more critical as an enabler of workplace improvements is culture. The next chapter examines how a positive culture, based on strong people values, is the foundation for a healthy organization.

## CHAPTER 4

# Positive Cultures

Brian Scudamore is the founder and CEO of O2E (Ordinary to Exceptional) Brands, a Canadian business that owns 1-800-GOT-JUNK, Wow 1 Day Painting, You Move Me, and Shack Shine. He is a frequent voice in the business community on the importance of a positive culture for a successful business. As he explains: "Companies that have a vibrant culture didn't get it by accident. It all starts with a set of values and a vision that describes the kind of company you are and what you want to do. Having these hammered down is just as important as having a viable business plan. Then you have to take steps to bring them to life."[1] At O2E, a core value is transparency, which is reinforced by an open-concept office layout. Scudamore has a desk but no door, so that he can be accessible to employees.

The Mayo Clinic is one of the world's leading healthcare organizations. Excellence in patient care, research, and medical education – the clinic's three areas of activity – are grounded in a solid culture of respect for patients and for coworkers. As Len Berry and Kent Seltman explain in their book on management lessons from the Mayo Clinic, "Mayo's culture leverages the inherent power of respect. Feeling respected is a universal need in the workplace. To be respected on the job means to be trusted, to be listened to, to be included, to be treated as a contributor, to be treated fairly. Teamwork cannot be sustained without mutual respect, for teamwork depends on trust, listening, inclusion, teammate contribution, and fair treatment – the attributes of respect."[2] At Mayo, teamwork is essential for achieving its mission of putting the needs of the patient first.

Japanese reporter Miwa Sado was found dead in her bed, still holding her mobile phone, after putting in 159 hours of overtime.[3] Japan's notorious long-hours work culture is deeply rooted. Now the government is trying to change this culture, recognizing that while long hours have traditionally been a sign of hard work, reducing work hours would be a far better way to boost national productivity. The government now annually reports *karoshi* deaths, which result from overwork, and is considering legislation that would limit monthly overtime to 100 hours.[4] But as a manager at Panasonic observed of how this is trickling down into company culture, "change is slow." Such is the influence of pervasive national work values at both the individual and organizational levels.

These three examples highlight how culture is the critical link in an organization's employee well-being–business performance chain. A company's culture reflects the often unspoken values and assumptions that underlie decisions and behaviors. You can't see it or touch it, but culture exerts powerful influences on how managers and employees go about their day-to-day. As I will discuss in this chapter, successful policies, programs, and practices for achieving healthy organization goals are grounded in a positive culture. I offer ideas that will help you to strengthen your organization's culture so that it can become a solid foundation for improving employee well-being. To start, I would like to summarize the action implications of our discussion of culture in this chapter so that you can keep them in mind as you read on:

1 Positive cultures have widely shared people-centered values that guide managers and employees to act with stakeholders' best interests foremost in mind.

2 Negative cultures are unhealthy, unethical, toxic, and potentially disastrous for employees, customers, and society.
3 Successful organizations view their culture as a strategic advantage that gives them a competitive edge and provides a rallying point for a talented and motivated workforce.
4 The sense of community in healthy organizations reflects a culture of trust and ethical responsibility, strengthening an organization's relationships with its stakeholders.
5 Cultures can be changed by energizing or updating the best of the organization's existing values and including managers and employees in the process.

## What Is Culture?

I am frequently asked why some organizations are better places to work and provide better services or products than others. A big part of the answer is culture. Essentially, "culture" refers to the assumptions, values, and beliefs shared by the people in an organization about how organizational life ought to be conducted. An organization's culture expresses its unique personality, character, and philosophy. If the culture is negative, employees will be disgruntled – as in a Dilbert cartoon – and words such as "indifferent," "self-serving," and "uncaring" will be fitting descriptions of customers' and other external stakeholders' experiences. In contrast, a positive culture has strong and authentic people values. It instills pride and loyalty in employees, giving their work a greater sense of purpose and meaning. Top management sets the tone and direction for a positive culture, but they will not be its only keepers. Everyone in the organization owns the culture and must feel a responsibility for contributing to its ongoing vitality.

Edgar Schein, the MIT professor credited with coining the term "corporate culture," separates culture into three levels.[5] The first and most visible level is the organization's artifacts, including the physical workspace and its furnishings, corporate branding, employee dress, how employee contributions are recognized, and styles of personal interaction. The second level consists of the ways that the culture gets expressed in mission and vision statements, values, codes of conduct, corporate annual reports, and the like. The third and least visible level includes the unwritten assumptions about how organizational life should be conducted.

Schein's third level is most important for health, safety, and overall well-being. It reflects what is carried around in the heads of employees and managers. The genuine expression of these beliefs can bring everyone in the organization together around common goals and how best to achieve them. In this way, a healthy culture will be co-created by all members of the organization rather than imposed from the top.

## Negative Cultures

Sometimes, strong cultures can have negative consequences. Just think of the individualistic values – what critics called raw greed – that dominated investment banks and hedge funds leading up to the 2008 global financial crisis, blinding otherwise clever financial professionals to the inherent risks in mortgage-backed derivatives. More common are weak cultures, which leave employees feeling socially disconnected and unmoored. Employees in such an environment lack clear guidelines for how to do their jobs. Left to their own devices, workers in weak cultures fall back on their own informal work rules. This becomes the default culture. Sometimes, the default culture may be toxic, with dire consequences for employees and the organization as a whole.

Sexual harassment is an ugly indicator of a negative or toxic culture. The #MeToo movement has empowered more women to speak out about being sexually harassed at work. Getting to the root causes of workplace harassment and bullying requires fixing organizational cultures. Premier Brian Pallister of Manitoba, a Canadian province, publicly stated that the provincial government's culture has to change after a study showed that hundreds of civil servants had experienced sexual harassment at work, but most did not report it.[6] He said: "We really take seriously the need to change the culture because people should not be afraid to report instances of harassment, they should not fear reprisal." Pallister was responding to a report of consultations with more than 3,000 employees about a culture of sexual harassment in government. More than 500 of those consulted said they had experienced harassment. One in ten was currently experiencing sexual harassment. Most employees said they didn't report the harassment because they were afraid of reprisal or hurting their career prospects.

Civility and respect are core values that must be baked into an organization's culture for there to be zero tolerance of harassment or bullying. Civility and respect are prerequisites for a psychologically safe, healthy, and productive work environment. When these values are present, managers and employees consistently show esteem, care, consideration, and overall respect for the dignity of the other person. In the absence of these core values, abuse of power is likely. As Peter Cappelli, a professor of human resources at the Wharton School in Philadelphia, explains, a toxic workplace arises "when the boss acts like a dictator and actively punishes people who articulate different views or express disagreement."[7] The result for employees will surely be psychological injury and reduced contributions.

High-profile organizations are open to close public and media scrutiny, making it more likely that a toxic work environment will be exposed, either by whistle-blowers or the media. Amnesty International is a prime example.[8] The organization commissioned an independent review of its workplace culture after two staff members died by suicide in 2018. At stake was the health and well-being of its staff, and its credibility as a global human rights advocate. The review found that internally, the organization was a human rights night-mare. Based on a survey of staff at Amnesty's London office, plus many interviews, the review concluded that the office operated in a perpetual state of emergency and was rife with bullying and public humiliation by managers, adversarial relationships, discrimination, unfair treatment, lack of trust, and high levels of stress. Some of these problems could be traced back to a restructuring of the organization, which did not go well. Furthermore, because employees were per-sonally committed to Amnesty's mission, they put up with these con-ditions and took on inordinately heavy workloads. As one employee explained: "A 'martyrdom culture' is present, which encourages people to sacrifice their own well-being because of the critical impor-tance of the work."[9] As a result of the review, senior leaders accepted responsibility for this state of affairs, and five left the organization. The lesson emerging from the tragic events of 2018 is that Amnesty, especially its managers, must give utmost priority to staff well-being.

## Culture as a Change Barrier

The Japanese example of *karoshi* shows how an entire country's dominant work ethic trickles down into workplace cultures, which in turn shape individuals' work behavior. The strength of these work values stands in the way of making improvements, as the Panasonic manager I quoted knows all too well. Acknowledging how an organization's culture can be a change barrier is an impor-tant first step in designing a healthy workplace strategy able to get around this barrier, with the goal of gradually shifting the culture to be more positive and people-focused.

A good example of how strong cultures get in the way of healthy change comes from a major Canadian study of work–life conflict. Linda Duxbury and Chris Higgins's extensive surveys have docu-mented the challenges many employees face juggling the multiple demands of work and family. Given the high personal, family, and employer costs of this role overload, Duxbury and Higgins recommend that employers institute formal policies and practices providing paid time off for dependent care, leaves of absence for caregivers, compressed workweeks, compassionate care leave, and enhanced support through EAPs.[10] To be effective, these policies must be fair and transparent in their administration and their use tied to managers' performance pay to ensure access across an organization. While this is sound, practical advice, these two researchers warn that these changes on their own are "unlikely to make much of a difference to caregivers if the culture of the organization 'punishes' those who use them."[11] So even before leaders can get to the point of developing supportive policies, they must first recognize that employees' caregiving responsibilities are a legitimate workplace issue. Only with that recognition can meaningful cultural change begin to happen.

## Integrating Health into Corporate Culture

An emerging best practice for creating healthier workplaces is for employers to promote a culture of health. According to the US Centers for Disease Control, a culture of health "is the creation of a working environment where employee health and safety is valued, supported and promoted through workplace health programs, policies, benefits, and environmental supports. Building a culture of health involves all levels of the organization and establishes the workplace health program as a routine part of business operations aligned with overall business goals. The results of this culture change include engaged and empowered employees, an impact on healthcare costs, and improved worker productivity."[12] Or as a team of workplace health promotion experts emphasize, developing a culture of health requires an organization to integrate health into how it operates, thinks, and acts.[13]

The culture of health concept has been adopted by some of the world's largest corporations as a guide to their health promotion strategies.[14] A culture of health is also being advocated by the Wellness Council of America (WELCOA), the leading nonprofit organization advocating for workplace wellness in the US. With over 5,000 corporate members, it has studied the requirements for successful workplace health promotion. In a select group of what WELCOA calls America's healthiest companies, the focus has shifted from activity-based programs to a results-oriented approach that impacts corporate performance by embedding wellness into the companies' corporate culture.[15] This won't be achieved if the corporate culture prioritizes quarterly results.

Despite these signs of progress in the corporate world, more efforts are needed on the culture front. For example, the 2018 Sanofi Canada Health Care Survey highlighted for Canadian employers the importance of having a long-term philosophy that explains why they offer health benefits and that can guide decision-making regarding wellness. Companies with what the Sanofi survey report calls a wellness culture are far more likely to have such a philosophy. As one health benefits advisor suggests: "No matter the size of the employer, a good starting point to determine philosophy is for them to answer the question, 'Do you see your health benefit plan as a cost or an investment?'"[16] Most companies surveyed that year were focused on managing benefit plan costs. This is consistent with the 2017 Sanofi Canada Health Care Survey's finding that just over half (53 percent) of employees surveyed saw their organization's corporate culture as supportive of health and wellness.[17]

## A Culture of Health and Safety

Workplace wellness practitioners must think beyond health to incorporate safety, just as occupational health and safety professionals must give equal emphasis to health and safety. A strong commitment to promoting employees' health and safety in tandem pays off in business performance and sustainability.

Consider the superior stock market performance of US companies that achieved high scores for health and safety in the Corporate Health Achievement Award (CHAA), sponsored by the American College of Occupational and Environmental Medicine.[18] The CHAA recognizes companies that have achieved excellence in their occupational health, safety, and environmental management and outcomes. Applicants for the award are judged on four areas: leadership and management; healthy workers; healthy environments; and healthy organizations. Companies with the highest scores in employee health, wellness, and safety outperformed their lower-scoring peers in share price appreciation. As the study's authors conclude: "Companies that integrate their health and safety efforts, building a culture of health and wellness along with a culture of safety, are likely to have a competitive advantage in the marketplace."[19]

The CHAA assessment process demonstrates the advantages of an integrated health, safety, and wellness strategy. This comprehensive and integrated approach is considered best practice and advocated by the Total Worker Health framework reviewed in chapter 2. And you may recall from chapter 3 that, from a worker's perspective, a healthy work environment is also a safe place to work. There is untapped potential for cross-fertilization and coordination between wellness, occupational health and safety, and corporate social responsibility – three areas that typically have been separate areas of corporate policy and practice.

## Climate and Culture

One helpful insight that healthy workplace advocates can glean from workplace safety research is the distinction between climate and culture, a point we touched on briefly in chapter 3. "Safety climate" refers to employees' shared perceptions about the importance of working safely in their roles.[20] A strong safety climate reinforces for employees that safety takes priority over production goals, thereby resulting in safe work behavior. Because "climate" refers to employees' perceptions that are at the surface in a workplace, it is more directly measurable with employee surveys than deeper features of an organization's culture, such as unwritten and unspoken assumptions, beliefs, and values. When managers and OHS practitioners talk about a safety culture, they most likely are referring to climate – in other words, employees' perceptions about how much safety matters as they go about their jobs day to day.

The key enablers of a strong safety climate are management's investments in developing, implementing, and enforcing OHS policies; putting in place an OHS management system that proactively identifies and eliminates safety risks and hazards and promotes safe work practices; providing relevant training; and demonstrating leadership on all safety matters.

Safety culture exists at Schein's third level and, as such, is the foundation for a safety climate. "Safety culture" refers to the values, attitudes, beliefs, assumptions, and behaviors that guide an organization's commitment to safety.[21] For large firms, developing and maintaining a safety culture can be an explicit goal. However, among small- and medium-size enterprises (SMEs), the lack of an OHS management system, or even basic safety policies, puts greater importance on the role of the company's overall culture in promoting safe practices as everyone's job.[22] There is a close alignment between a safety culture and a culture of health. To see this, all you have to do is substitute "health" for "safety" in the previous three paragraphs.

## Assessing Your Culture

A team led by Dr. Ben Amick at the Institute for Work and Health collaborated with health and safety professionals in Ontario to create and test the Organizational Performance Metric (IWH-OPM), an eight-item questionnaire to help organizations assess and improve their health and safety performance (box 4.1).[23] The IWH-OPM is now recommended by provincial workers' compensation systems across Canada as an evidence-based tool for measuring leading indicators of health and safety performance and helping to develop a safety culture.[24]

---

**Box 4.1 Institute for Work and Health's Organizational Performance Metric**

1 Formal safety audits at regular intervals are a normal part of our business.
2 Everyone at this organization values ongoing safety improvement in this organization.
3 This organization considers safety at least as important as production and quality in the way work is done.
4 Workers and supervisors have the information they need to work safely.
5 Employees are always involved in decisions affecting their health and safety.
6 Those in charge of safety have the authority to make the changes they have identified as necessary.
7 Those who act safely receive positive recognition.
8 Everyone has the tools and/or equipment they need to complete their work safely.

---

This is because a company's IWH-OPM score is an accurate predictor of its past and future injury claims rate. In short, the IWH-OPM score is a leading indicator of safety performance. I'm reproducing the questionnaire so that you can see the key indicators of a strong safety culture, which closely parallels a strong culture of health. The IWH-OPM can be used by health and safety committees and by work teams, or to survey the entire workforce. Respondents indicate how frequently each practice takes place in their organization or workplace, ranging from 0 to 100 percent in 20-percentage-point increments. Pay particular attention to IWH-OPM items 2 and 3, which assess how embedded safety is in the way the company operates. The same questions could be usefully asked focusing on employee health and well-being. How would your organization rate?

## Strengthening the Trust–Well-Being Link

Some of my examples of healthy organizations are on the best workplaces lists produced by the Great Place to Work Institute in different countries. The assessment tool for these lists is the Institute's Trust Index employee survey, which is used annually by thousands of organizations in over ninety countries. The Trust Index measures three big drivers of trust: management credibility; respect; and fairness. This mirrors the Standard, which considers organizational culture an important influence on psychological health and safety. The Standard defines culture as "a mix of norms, values, beliefs, meanings, and expectations that group members hold in common and that they use as behavioural and problem-solving cues."[25] The Standard emphasizes that a culture based on trust, honesty, respect, civility, and fairness can make a workplace psychologically safer and healthier. In short, there is a general consensus that mutual trust is a cornerstone of a positive culture that promotes workers' health, safety, and well-being. But how exactly does trust contribute to these healthy organization goals?

To answer this question, I partnered with Great Place to Work Canada (GPTW) to find out. At the core of GPTW's methodology is its Trust Model. The model is the basis for its Trust Index survey. Survey results are used to produce the US list of 100 Best Companies to Work For, published in *Fortune* magazine,[26] and the Canadian list of Best Workplaces in Canada, published in the *Globe and Mail*.[27] Great workplaces aren't defined by eye-popping perks, pay, and benefits. Rather, all of these workplaces have a deeply rooted trust-based culture. And GPTW has set the standard for defining and measuring what it means to be a high-trust workplace. GPTW's research shows that a trust-based culture drives superior business performance precisely by promoting employee well-being.[28] This connection between trust and well-being deserves closer scrutiny, given that more employers are trying to move beyond traditional occupational health, safety, and wellness by embracing the broader concept of employee well-being.

Employers can improve employee well-being by taking a holistic approach to promoting physical, psychological, and emotional health and safety. For this to happen, leaders must make a demonstrated commitment to improve employee well-being and embed this goal into how the business operates. This is how the importance of well-being as an end in itself becomes woven into the cultural fabric of the organization.

## Measuring a High-Trust Culture

GPTW's research reveals how this happens. Employees trust managers who are concerned about their well-being. Trustworthy managers listen and respond to employee input, are open and honest about organizational changes, and do what they say they'll do. In a high-trust culture, strong core values – such as fairness, respect, and integrity – guide day-to-day interactions among coworkers, between managers and employees, and between employees and their customers or clients, suppliers, business partners, and the larger community. Employees take pride in their work and feel a true sense of camaraderie with coworkers. The synergy between trust, pride, and camaraderie inspires collaboration, creativity, and innovation. As a result, employees flourish and their overall work experiences are positive.

That's because a high-trust culture promotes psychological well-being, the main goal of the Standard.[29] I explored this connection between trust and psychological well-being by analyzing GPTW survey data using the Standard's framework of workplace psychological health and safety. Great Place to Work Canada provided me their data from 48,281 respondents in the 201 Canadian organizations it surveyed with the Trust Index in 2017 and 2018. In-depth analysis of these data led me to this conclusion: cultivating a trust-based workplace culture is a sure way to achieve high levels of psychological well-being for employees. Trust Index survey results shed new light on this organic connection between a high-trust culture and employee well-being.

## High-Trust Workplaces Are Healthy and Safe

GPTW's Trust Index survey asks respondents to rate how true the following statement is for them: "This is a psychologically and emotionally healthy place to work." This single question provides a global indicator of whether or not a workplace promotes employees' psychological well-being.

Workplaces with the highest trust levels are experienced by employees and managers as psychologically and emotionally healthy. This becomes clear when we compare the top twenty organizations (i.e., the top 10 percent), based on their overall Trust Index score, surveyed by GPTW Canada during 2017–18 with the other 181 organizations the institute surveyed. Four out of five employees in a high-trust workplace also consider it to be a psychologically and emotionally healthy workplace (figure 4.1). This compares with fewer than half in all the other organizations GPTW surveyed. Essentially, a psychologically and emotionally healthy workplace is a great place to work.

Also relevant is that four out of five employees in the top twenty high-trust organizations examined in figure 4.1 believe that their

**Figure 4.1** Key Well-Being Indicators Comparing 20 Best Workplaces in Canada with All Other Organizations Surveyed by GPTW Canada in 2017–18

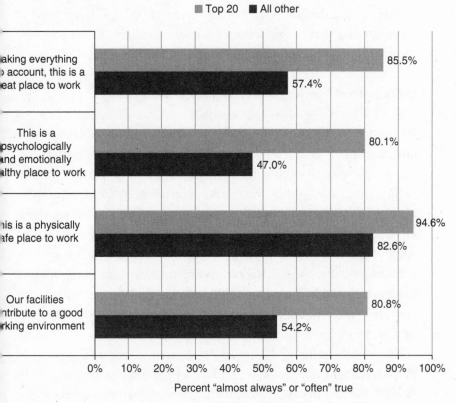

■ Top 20    ■ All other

aking everything
account, this is a
eat place to work — 85.5% / 57.4%

This is a
psychologically
nd emotionally
althy place to work — 80.1% / 47.0%

is is a physically
afe place to work — 94.6% / 82.6%

Our facilities
ntribute to a good
rking environment — 80.8% / 54.2%

Percent "almost always" or "often" true

© Great Place to Work Institute Canada. Based on 201 organizations with 48,281 employees and total average Trust Index scores (average of 58 items in the survey). All group differences statistically significant (p < .001).

employers' facilities contribute to a good working environment, far more than do employees in organizations with lower trust levels. And almost all (95 percent) of the employees in the top twenty high-trust organizations consider their workplaces safe, which is entirely consistent with the Rethinking Work survey evidence I presented in chapter 3.

Interestingly, physical safety is also positively rated (83 percent of respondents) in all the other organizations surveyed by GPTW. This likely reflects the successful efforts by many Canadian employers to reduce lost-time work injuries that are invariably physical in nature, as well as the decline of physically demanding jobs. Even so, it is worth noting that employees in lower-trust organizations consider their workplaces somewhat less safe.

## Workplace Influences on Psychological Well-Being

Recall from chapter 2 that the Standard identifies thirteen specific workplace characteristics that can either enhance or diminish the psychological well-being of workers. The Trust Index survey results shed new light on the relationship between these factors and employees' perceptions of the psychological health of their work environment. Using one Trust Index item as a direct measure of each of the Standard's thirteen workplace factors (see figure 4.2), I compared differences in the positive responses (combining "almost always true" and "often true" responses) to these items by employees' assessment of their workplace as psychologically and emotionally healthy (answered using the same response scale).

The results in figure 4.2 are an eye-opener. Around 90 percent of employees who rate their workplace as psychologically and emotionally healthy also very positively assess all thirteen factors in the Standard. In contrast, the same is true for only about half of survey respondents who give neutral or negative assessments of their workplace as psychologically and emotionally healthy. The one exception is physical safety. This should not be surprising; it corroborates my argument in chapter 3 that most Canadian workers perceive their workplace to be physically safe, reflecting employer progress in this regard over the past several decades. However, the new insight in figure 4.2 is that the most psychologically healthy workplaces are also highly rated for their physical safety.

I've already noted that workplace health and safety experts advocate creating a culture of health and a safety culture as building

**Figure 4.2** Characteristics of a Psychologically and Emotionally Healthy Workplace Based on the National Standard of Canada for Psychological Health and Safety in the Workplace

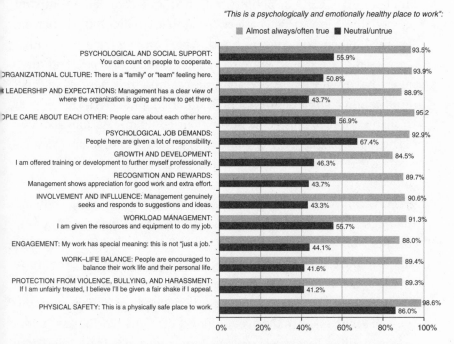

*"This is a psychologically and emotionally healthy place to work":*

■ Almost always/often true   ■ Neutral/untrue

PSYCHOLOGICAL AND SOCIAL SUPPORT: You can count on people to cooperate. — 55.9% / 93.5%

ORGANIZATIONAL CULTURE: There is a "family" or "team" feeling here. — 50.8% / 93.9%

LEADERSHIP AND EXPECTATIONS: Management has a clear view of where the organization is going and how to get there. — 43.7% / 88.9%

PLE CARE ABOUT EACH OTHER: People care about each other here. — 56.9% / 95.2

PSYCHOLOGICAL JOB DEMANDS: People here are given a lot of responsibility. — 67.4% / 92.9%

GROWTH AND DEVELOPMENT: I am offered training or development to further myself professionally. — 46.3% / 84.5%

RECOGNITION AND REWARDS: Management shows appreciation for good work and extra effort. — 43.7% / 89.7%

INVOLVEMENT AND INFLLUENCE: Management genuinely seeks and responds to suggestions and ideas. — 43.3% / 90.6%

WORKLOAD MANAGEMENT: I am given the resources and equipment to do my job. — 55.7% / 91.3%

ENGAGEMENT: My work has special meaning: this is not "just a job." — 44.1% / 88.0%

WORK–LIFE BALANCE: People are encouraged to balance their work life and their personal life. — 41.6% / 89.4%

PROTECTION FROM VIOLENCE, BULLYING, AND HARASSMENT: If I am unfairly treated, I believe I'll be given a fair shake if I appeal. — 41.2% / 89.3%

PHYSICAL SAFETY: This is a physically safe place to work. — 86.0% / 98.6%

0%   20%   40%   60%   80%   100%

© Great Place to Work Institute Canada. Based on all organizations surveyed by GPTW Canada in 2017–18. 201 organizations with 48,281 employees responding to the survey. This chart compares 2 groups of respondents: those answering "almost always true" and "often true" with those who answered "sometimes true/sometimes untrue," "often untrue," and "almost always untrue." All group differences statistically significant (p < .001).

blocks for a healthy organization. Now we know that achieving these goals can happen only in a climate of trust. Employees and managers must trust one another, and managers must take employees' best interests into account in what they say and do. In sum, all workplace relationships must rest on a foundation of mutual trust in order for the work environment to be truly healthy, safe, and productive. Let this be a guiding principle for any employer planning to implement the Standard.

## Building Trust

Tobias Lütke, CEO of Shopify, a Canadian e-commerce company, coined the term "trust battery." The trust battery is 50 percent charged when someone is hired. The battery's charge is either increased or decreased with every interaction coworkers and managers have with that individual. Basecamp (an American Internet application company) founders Jason Fried and David Heinemeier Hanson adopted this concept for their company. As they explain: "The reality is that the trust battery is a summary of all interactions to date.... A low trust battery is at the core of many personal disputes at work. It powers stressful encounters and anxious moments."[30]

How can you charge up the trust batteries of your employees and managers? A research team at the University of Florida compared results from 132 studies looking at the relationship between trust and two big outcomes: risk-taking and job performance.[31] The study made a useful distinction between trust and trustworthiness. Trust in a relationship between two people depends on the trustworthiness of each person in the eyes of the other. "Trustworthiness" refers to the qualities that must be present for someone to trust you. These qualities include loyalty, openness, caring, fairness, availability, receptivity, consistency, reliability, and discreetness – all of which can be learned. Consider incorporating trustworthiness into your leadership training and development as part of efforts to build a healthier organization.

Trustworthy leaders consciously use every encounter to charge up their employees' trust batteries. The more that managers are trustworthy, the more that employees feel committed to the organization, perform their jobs well, take risks in their work, and are good citizens by helping others and contributing to a positive work environment. From the employees' perspective, these examples of trustworthiness add up to a more vibrant workplace. When trustworthiness is widespread among managers, employees are less likely to exhibit harmful or counterproductive behaviors. These include disregarding safety procedures, making threats, tardiness, absenteeism, and other actions subject to discipline.

When you trust someone, you are able to take risks in your relationship with them. You will feel comfortable opening up and sharing ideas, revealing confidential information, asking for advice, offering help, willingly cooperating, and being vulnerable in other ways. Being vulnerable feels safe only if you perceive the other person to be trustworthy, knowing they will behave in expected and respectful ways and that their actions will take your interests into account. It is at this micro level of personal interaction that trust is built. As philosopher Robert Solomon and business consultant Fernando Flores comment in their book, *Building Trust in Business, Politics, Relationships and Life*: "Without trust, the corporate community is reduced to a group of resentful wage slaves and defensive, if not ambitious, managers."[32] This picture is poles apart from that of a healthy organization with a trust-based culture that promotes everyone's well-being.

## Culture Change

How do you change a culture to make it more positive and values based? One of the first things to consider is the level of trust in the organization, as we just discussed. To be successful, culture change must take deliberate steps to build or preserve trust. Also important is recognizing that trust is a by-product of the organizational change process itself. Generally speaking, there are two quite different approaches to organizational change. One approach advocates transformational change: reinventing the organization, shaking it up, ushering in a new era, and radically altering how people work together and how the business operates. A contrasting approach views organizational change, including culture change, as incremental. Based on my interpretation of the research on change and

my consulting experience, I'm in the latter camp. I consider successful change to be more evolutionary than revolutionary. Over time
and with persistent effort, it is possible to incrementally strengthen
a culture in ways that look and feel transformational.

The operative word here is "evolve." To quote McGill University
management expert Henry Mintzberg on this point: "You don't
change cultures – you revitalize existing cultures. You can't take
a company that has existed for years and just throw out its culture and drop a new one in place. What you do is bring back the
energy that is still there."[33] Change agents can take some comfort
from this view. Surely, constructing the kind of culture required in
a healthy organization becomes a less daunting task if approached
as step-by-step improvements rather than as having to orchestrate a
radical makeover. And if at each step, you are increasing the level of
trust in the culture, rest assured that you also will be contributing to
the goal of a psychologically healthier and safer workplace.

To make the culture change process real, I would like to provide
an example of how one organization carried it out successfully. The
HR vice president at a large hospital engaged me to conduct what
her leadership team called a "culture audit" of an outpatient unit.
Basically, they wanted me to help them to identify the root causes in
the work environment that were making the unit increasingly dysfunctional. After I interviewed all staff and physicians in the unit, it
became clear that the unit was not a toxic work environment. Rather,
a number of organizational factors had cumulatively undermined
the team's capacity to work together in the interests of patients.
From this organizational perspective, the unit's culture reflected
unit members' responses to mounting structural impediments to
providing outstanding patient care – a goal they all highly valued.

The unit faced significant leadership, workload, staffing, work
process, and teamwork problems. Solutions to these problems were
developed and implemented by the unit itself. However, success in
this renewal process required three things: the hospital's leadership

had to make a commitment to support the change process; the hospital's organizational development staff expertly facilitated the change processes; and a new unit manager was recruited with a clear mandate to guide this renewal process over several years.

Here's how the hospital's leaders and members of the unit itself defined a toxic culture. For many, working on the unit was stressful, frustrating, and exhausting. Tensions would increase as staff and physicians struggled just to get through their shift. But counterbalancing this, most unit staff and physicians emphasized their commitment to the unit's mission and its patients. Because of this commitment, most enjoyed their job and liked their coworkers. However, tension and conflicts among staff had escalated as a result of years of turbulent change: increasing patient loads; turnover in the unit's management that left the senior manager position vacant for months; moving to a new facility; an external peer review of the unit's performance with less-than-glowing results; budget cuts and restructuring; and lack of consistent leadership. The resilience that helped staff cope with these changes had been depleted. And the cumulative impact of all these changes had left staff and physicians feeling that they were not valued or supported by hospital leadership, a sure recipe for low trust.

At first glance, concerns about the replacement of registered nurses (RNs) with registered practical nurses (RPNs), who are less qualified and have a more limited scope of practice than RNs, looked like professional turf protection. But on closer examination, this issue had more to do with the nature of the change process and loss of nursing experience in the unit than jockeying for professional turf. The unit had oriented many new RPNs and RNs over several years, not all of whom had stayed. This created workload problems because the experienced nurses felt constant pressure to find time to orient and train new hires.

Unit staff and physicians all agreed on what was needed to get the unit back on track: fill the vacant unit manager position; provide full staff to meet the current patient load; more effectively utilize existing staff; and adopt more efficient patient care systems and processes. Staff and physicians offered a checklist of what characteristics they would like to see in a unit manager. Overall, strong management and people leadership skills were considered to be more important than clinical knowledge. Staff and physicians on the unit also wanted to participate in designing and implementing improvements to their immediate work environment and to patient care delivery. The unit team was able to look into the future and articulate a common vision of a work environment with less stress and tension. They envisioned a harmonious and welcoming workplace that is an attractive place to have a career – a place where everyone pulls together, things run smoothly, and morale is strong.

This improvement plan was launched during an unprecedented meeting between the hospital CEO (who previously had not met with the unit) and two executives. These three senior leaders endorsed the unit's recommendations and made a commitment to involve the team in a step-by-step improvement plan. This was a huge boost to the team's hope that the needed changes were coming. Above all, it translated three of the hospital's core values – compassion, collaboration, and patient-focused care – into tangible actions. That put the unit on track to re-energize its culture, rebuild trust in each other and in senior management, and achieve its potential for excellent patient care – the one value that everyone rallied around. Describing this project makes me wonder how many other work units or teams there are in healthcare or other industries facing similar problems, and with the untapped potential to make the same shift in their culture.

## Strengthening Your Culture

How can your organization's culture be strengthened? As you think about this important task, bear in mind the systemic nature of culture. You cannot isolate culture as a target for change. Just as in the above outpatient unit example, culture will shift in a positive direction as employees and managers work together to improve work relationships, processes, and practices. You therefore can't afford to ignore culture when trying to change other parts of your organization. However, culture can be elusive. Its features cannot be grasped concretely, the way, for instance, putting your hands on a marketing plan, an employee benefits handbook, or an organization chart can. The practical implication, then, is that it is not always easy to pinpoint what needs changing in a culture. Here are a few examples to help you identify ways to strengthen your culture.

As we just saw in my hospital example, positive cultures are modeled by the actions of senior management. This observation is based on a recurring theme in my conversations with many HR and organizational development (OD) practitioners: their diagnosis of a need to transform the organization's culture. Transformation is the solution, they explain, because the existing culture blocks the path to a healthier and higher-performing workplace. Yet further discussions with these professionals reveal that the changes sought have more to do with visibly aligning senior managers' actions with existing organizational values, such as respect, integrity, and learning and innovation. For example, senior managers at a public agency participated in a values assessment, which showed that they believed operational efficiency and cost control were paramount for the organization's success. In contrast, all the organization's espoused values were about people. To address this disconnect, HR facilitated discussions with the senior management team about how they could better achieve operational goals through the application of specific corporate values.

Culture cannot be taken for granted. Doing so creates a blind spot when management implements a new organizational system, structure, policy, or process. To illustrate, a large telecommunications company wanted to notch up its customer service levels. New service standards and incentives focused on customer service quality rather than on the volume of calls handled. In preparation, supervisors and managers were trained to coach call center customer service agents to be more responsive to customers' needs. But the existing culture placed more value on supervisors boosting call quantity (a key performance metric) than on customer service quality. A values shift, enabled by training and coaching, was required to support the new customer service objectives. Because this issue was not put on the table for discussion during training sessions, elements of the existing culture actually held back progress.

Organizational restructuring requires careful attention to culture. This is especially evident in mergers and acquisitions. For example, a large healthcare organization providing rehabilitation services was created through the merger of two successful and well-established institutions, one focusing on services to children and the other serving only adults. Each had a distinctive culture. Little time was invested in creating a blended culture, other than developing statements of the new entity's mission, vision, and values. Senior managers and HR and OD professionals who led a post-merger strategic planning initiative recognized that a unified culture would make it easier to successfully implement that plan. These change agents did not want to signal to staff that the existing culture was broken. Rather, they wanted to build on the best of the old culture while at the same time focusing everyone on the future of the unified organization. Timing was good, given a recent move from two separate facilities into a new, state-of-the-art building. So senior managers initiated an organization-wide conversation on the organization's future that included a revitalization of its values.

Progress on culture change may be uneven. A large regional health service organization had clearly committed to becoming a healthy organization. The organization combines several facilities, each with its own unique history and culture. The overall vision was healthy people in healthy communities, and a healthy workplace was a priority in the strategic plan. A healthy workplace council was established to coordinate actions on healthy workplace goals. Staff volunteered to be on the council, so membership was diverse, from frontline employees to senior executives and union officials. As a member of the council put it, their work injected more humanity into how employees and physicians were treated. As the council became a catalyst for regenerating the culture, it realized that progress would be uneven across departments and sites. This fit the council's community development approach to change. From this perspective, the council cultivated work-unit leadership and empowered teams to act on issues they considered important, at their own pace.

## Strong Values

I recently gave a talk on how vibrant workplaces inspire employees at a corporate educational forum. Forum organizers had chosen quality as the theme – quality improvement, quality client services, and quality workplaces. I asked the employees attending the forum how well they knew their organization's values. Someone in the front row admitted that while she could not recite the values, she "knew where to find them." This was a good opener for what turned out to be a frank discussion about how the values could support the organization's quality goals. What became clearer to these employees during a seventy-five-minute interactive session was that they personally needed to see their own values reflected in the organization's values. This point was driven home by a number of participants, who explained how they feel most inspired about their job when, at the end of the workday, their personal values are reaffirmed because they and their team have done something they truly believe makes a positive difference for customers and society.

## The Importance of Values

Values act as cultural glue, holding together the people and groups in an organization. The *Oxford English Dictionary* defines values as "the principles or standards of a person or social group; the generally accepted or personally held judgment of what is valuable and important in life."[34] Sociologists refer to values as the beliefs that guide the behavior of individuals and groups. In organizations, values often appear alongside the corporate mission (its purpose) and vision (its aspirations). The mission expresses "what we are in business to do" and the vision articulates "where we want to go," while the organization's values express "how we will run the business and go about achieving our goals and aspirations." More specifically, an organization's values should do six things:

1 Influence relationships with all stakeholders.
2 Guide decision-making and priority-setting.
3 Link employees to the mission and vision.
4 Inspire and empower employees in their jobs.
5 Provide the foundation for the organization's culture.
6 Stand the test of time.

Rosabeth Moss Kanter, a Harvard Business School professor, studied some of the world's largest corporations to understand how they were able to quickly develop creative solutions to major social and environmental challenges.[35] The agility of these huge multinational companies – IBM, Procter & Gamble, Omron, CEMEX, Cisco, and Banco Real – defied conventional thinking about lumbering bureaucracies. Kanter's conclusion: "A foundation of values and standards provides a well-understood, widely-communicated guidance system that ensures effective operations while enabling people to make decisions appropriate to local situations."

This echoes the conclusion that Jim Collins and James Porras reached in their best-selling book, *Built to Last: Successful Habits of Visionary Companies*.[36] Companies featured in this study had strong core values, which guided their adaptation to massive economic, political, and social changes in the twentieth century. Collins and Porras refer to core values as enduring principles that keep everyone focused on long-term viability as opposed to short-term financial expediency.

I will present three cases that illustrate the importance of values to an organization's success. The first, the Vancouver Organizing Committee for the 2010 Olympic and Paralympic Games (VANOC), was a new organization with a short life span. The second is IBM, which adapted its early twentieth-century founder's values to the twenty-first century. The third is mining company Teck Resources' smelter operations, where senior managers launched a values exercise that led to a set of guiding principles with clear behavioral expectations.

## New Values

Achieving a successful Olympic and Paralympic Games presents huge organizational challenges in full public view. People from very different backgrounds – administrators, lawyers and accountants, engineers, former elite athletes, media experts – have to be forged into a high- performing team, knowing that the team will disband soon after the last athletes leave the games venue. The Vancouver Organizing Committee for the 2010 Olympic and Paralympic Games rose to this challenge by crafting a clear vision, mission, and set of values.[37] The vision and mission were appropriately lofty for the games but also realistic, given the potential spin-offs:

• VANOC's vision is: A stronger Canada whose spirit is raised by its passion for sport, culture and sustainability.

- VANOC's mission is: To touch the soul of the nation and inspire the world by creating and delivering an extraordinary Olympic and Paralympic experience with lasting legacies.

However, it was the following explicit values that unified a diverse and expanding group of employees at VANOC:

- *Team* – We recognize that success and excellence can only be achieved and sustained by a deep commitment to working as a team and the practice of focusing on collective rather than individual effort and rewards.
- *Trust* – We act consciously to inspire the trust of everyone whose lives we touch by modeling the highest standards of honesty, integrity and ethical behavior at all times.
- *Excellence* – We model individual and collective performance by working as a team with our partners to promote social, cultural, health and sport excellence. Improve the sport performance of Team Canada and deliver on our vision.
- *Sustainability* – We proactively consider the long-term interests of all stakeholders in the Games, both here in Canada and throughout the World, to ensure that our impact is positive and our legacy sustainable for all.
- *Creativity* – We embrace new ideas, encourage input to foster breakthrough thinking and solutions that will allow us to amaze even ourselves in our ability to exceed expectations and deliver on our vision.

By following each single-word value with a description of how it plays out in practice, VANOC provided existing and prospective employees with a clear set of behavioral expectations. Because the organization had been in a steady recruitment mode, the values proved useful for screening applicants and orienting new recruits. Indicative of the importance VANOC placed on values fit, its website provided a values assessment that prospective applicants were encouraged to use to determine if they shared VANOC's values. The message: do not apply if you do not already believe in our values.

## Renewed Values

IBM is a good illustration of a well-established organization with a distinctive brand and culture. Thomas Watson, the company's founder, laid down what he called "basic beliefs" in 1914: respect for the individual, the best customer service, and the pursuit of excellence. However, when the digital information revolution took off in the late 1980s, the company faltered. It struggled to find a new footing in a global information technology market, where its dominant role as a manufacturer of mainframe and then desktop computers had been eclipsed by nimble, low-cost newcomers. IBM had to reinvent its business model, moving out of manufacturing and into information technology, business consulting, and outsourcing services.

In 2003, IBM's newly appointed CEO, Samuel J. Palmisano, sought to re-energize employees.[38] He launched an ambitious project to redefine the company's values using a high-tech, high-involvement process. IBM had developed an intranet-based tool that facilitated and summarized discussions on key business issues across all IBM's operations. Palmisano presented four concepts – respect, customer, excellence, innovation – to a meeting of 300 executives to test the idea of values renewal. "Respect" was jettisoned because of negative connotations; IBM had gone through a painful period of layoffs. The result was three draft values – commitment to the customer, excellence through innovation, and integrity that earns trust – that were proposed to employees in IBM's "values jam" online forum. There was lively debate and reflection on issues like internal silos, trust, integrity, and respect. After the values jam, Palmisano told an executive meeting: "You guys ought to read every one of these comments, because if you think we've got this place plumbed correctly, think again." An employee team sifted through the voluminous transcripts and results from pre- and post-jam surveys. The result was three new values:

1  Dedication to every client's success;
2  Innovation that matters, for our company and for the world; and
3  Trust and personal responsibility in all relationships.

In 2004, another jam was conducted in which more than 52,000 employees exchanged best practices for seventy-two hours. This event focused on finding actionable ideas to support implementation of the values identified previously. A new post-jam ratings event was developed to allow IBMers to select key ideas that supported the values. What's significant about this values renewal at IBM is its process. New values were not imposed from the top but were the creation of employees from across the sprawling global company. IBM has since adapted this grassroots consultation approach to its business development. For example, it launched an online "innovation jam" to consult with employees, their family members, and IBM customers about future products. IBM's use of executive blogs and its active encouragement of staff to discuss the company's future direction and products in open forums show how it lives its corporate values and stays ahead of its main competitors.

## Values-Based Behaviors

Canadian mining company Teck Resources' Trail Operations in British Columbia is one of the world's largest fully integrated zinc and lead smelting and refining complexes. The sprawling facility also produces other specialty metals, chemicals, and fertilizer products and generates its own hydro power. Mining and smelting have a long history in the mountainous Kootenay region of British Columbia. The Trail Operations has become a global leader in smelting and refining technology. Several years ago, senior management developed and implemented a comprehensive people strategy to ensure that the facility maintained its competitive positions in global commodity markets. The strategy responded to its human resource challenges, which included maintaining the highest standards of workplace safety and health, unprecedented retirements due to an aging workforce, and recruitment and retention pressures created by a competitive labor market for skilled trades.

Like IBM and other companies with long histories, the Trail Operations had a values statement, but it no longer resonated with managers or employees. So, as part of developing the people strategy, senior managers also revisited the old values and came up with a draft of new values, with the idea of consulting with line managers, supervisors, and employees to consolidate them. The people strategy's specific action items were implemented. These included improvements in new employee orientation; strengthening a safety culture; a wellness initiative; service recognition; enhanced leadership development; and profit sharing.

However, the discussion of values was put aside for more than a year after the implementation of the people strategy. The senior management team returned to the draft values that the people strategy had successfully launched. A candid discussion identified concerns that are often voiced when executives scrutinize the meaning of specific values: they are too vague; they do not get close enough to explicit behaviors; they need to reflect what managers will actually do; and they are not really values but operational goals. For example, references to excellent results were seen not as values, but rather as operational goals. This realization led the Trail Operations' top management to think in terms of guiding behavioral principles rather than values. They agreed that, first and foremost, any values statement had to be a meaningful guide to how they worked together and showed leadership. The guiding principles they developed were subsequently rolled out to managers, supervisors, and non-union professional and administrative staff (box 4.2).

**Box 4.2 Teck Resources' Trail Operations' Guiding Principles**

- These guiding principles define what we value, how we behave, and what we expect of others. Living by these guiding principles will ensure Trail Operations' future success.
  - We act with *integrity*, treating all with *dignity*, *fairness*, and *respect*.
  - We commit to everyone going home *safe* and *healthy* every day.
  - We take *personal responsibility* for our actions and results.
  - We *support* each other to achieve our fullest potential.
  - We *act responsibly* to support a sustainable future for the *communities* and *environment* in which we operate.

The senior management team agreed upon specific behaviors that reflected how the principles translated for them personally into effective leadership. They went one step further. In order to communicate the importance of the guiding principles, not as abstract concepts but as explicit guides to good management practices, they also illustrated each value with examples of how a member of the senior management team had followed one of the principles when making a decision or taking an action. These guiding principles became the basis for strengthening leadership skills across the Trail facility.

## Revitalizing Your Organization's Culture

To summarize, healthy organizations consistently treat employees as their core business asset and the key to long-term sustainable success. Managers are guided in their decisions and actions by strongly felt, people-oriented values. They actively cultivate trust with all members of the organization. Culture comes alive in the trust-based relationships that bind employees with each other, with managers, and with customers. Culture reinforces ethical imperatives, and it reaches deep into the foundations of performance excellence. Positive cultures help to address an organization's people challenges, especially by finding better ways to encourage employees to excel in their jobs and supporting them to meet their personal needs and professional goals. This is how an organization's cultural qualities are decisive in shaping its future.

A positive culture enables all the organization's relationships to be rewarding. It also contributes to a psychologically healthy and safe work environment. The attributes of a positive culture transcend values and beliefs about employee well-being. Positive cultures have values that run wide and deep – such as trust, which as we have seen is fundamental to business performance and responsible dealings with customers and communities. Even if you consider your culture to be healthy or positive, a closer analysis may reveal that it is necessary to minimize some things on the negative side of the cultural ledger and maximize other things on the positive side. In other words, your culture may need to evolve.

Senior managers must face the fact that their organization's culture is critical to attaining the high quality of work-life employees want, the excellent performance shareholders and customers want, and the ethical and responsible behavior other stakeholders in society expect to see. So it is important that culture be openly discussed and reflected upon, starting with top management. These conversations may not come easily, but you must look for opportunities to raise the issues we have just discussed. For some senior managers, talking about culture falls outside of their comfort zone. I have been inside organizations where the senior HR manager specifically asked that the word "culture" not be used in discussions with the executive team about developing a healthy workplace strategy. I also have been asked by managers to remove slides from presentations for leadership development workshops that list the organization's corporate values, because the values are dormant and showing them could provoke questions about why this is the case.

In this chapter, I have provided various examples of organizations at different stages of cultural evolution. My intent is to help you to plan next steps that can contribute to a more positive culture in your workplace. Some organizations have already advanced down this path. Indeed, on numerous occasions, I have heard employees and managers enthusiastically describe an organizational culture of mutual respect, pointing out how people trust one another and that everyone's contributions are valued and recognized. Conversations about culture in these workplaces have a different objective: how to keep the culture fresh, alive, and owned by everyone in the organization.

When you are considering how to revitalize or strengthen your culture, it helps to bear in mind key points about culture change. It is more useful to talk about revitalizing positive aspects of an existing culture that are critical for the organization's future direction than to talk about creating a different culture. As one newly appointed CEO of a financial services firm put it reassuringly at an all-staff conference: "I'm not here to change your culture but to help you to harness its strengths." Harnessing the strengths of your culture requires collective reflection on the values that are going to guide you into the future. A way to kick-start the process of revitalizing your organization's culture is to find ways to breathe new life into its values, which may still be relevant but dormant. This revitalization takes time and commitment from the top. View cultural change not as an end in itself, but as an evolving process that can be furthered through any type of change in the organization. This is how to recharge the collective trust battery. And strive to involve, consult, and empower employees to strengthen the culture so that it becomes theirs. The last point underscores why inclusive leadership also is a healthy organization building block – and it is the subject of chapter 5.

## CHAPTER 5

# Inclusive Leadership

Emile is a health and safety coordinator at a large manufacturer. Several years ago, he was asked by the company's HR manager to look into wellness programs. The human resource plan for the year included a wellness program feasibility study. Emile had fixed parameters in which to work. A thorough needs assessment of the company's thousands of employees was out of the question. And any plans would need the blessing of several unions. So his approach was to convene a series of focus groups representative of professional, administrative, and production staff and also invite key union reps. Focus groups identified current strengths in occupational health and safety that could be expanded to address wellness and agreed that a wellness initiative was needed. In the following year, a union-management wellness committee was launched. Emile was a member of the committee, but not the chair. Off to a slow start, the committee moved into action after making site visits to other unionized worksites that had comprehensive wellness programs. These visits showed what union and management cooperation could achieve. The committee's work opened the door to addressing a wide range of people issues vital to the future of the business.

Lin is the vice president of human resources in a large healthcare organization. The organization offered a long menu of programs in safety, health, and wellness, learning, and career development.

Some showed success, such as reduction in lost-time injury rates and improvement in the return-to-work process for injured workers. Yet employees faced a bewildering array of support services, often not clearly understood and therefore underutilized. Lin and her team saw the need to consolidate and streamline these people initiatives, so the team developed a healthy workplace framework that tied them together. The framework grew out of a vision of what a healthy workplace looks like, developed by the HR-OD team at a retreat. The executive did not accept the need for what it saw as yet another HR initiative. Undeterred, Lin and her team adopted the framework as their internal guide, never losing an opportunity to communicate to the executive the strategic value of taking a holistic and integrated approach to workplace and workforce issues. After several years and a new CEO, a revised corporate strategy recognized that fostering healthy employees in healthy work environments is key to healthcare excellence.

These real cases illustrate that the actions required to create healthier organizations can be led from many places and positions. In this chapter, I suggest that positive cultures and vibrant workplaces – two healthy organization building blocks – are products of combined efforts by many people. Healthy organizations do not result when a few lead and many follow. Certainly, it helps when senior managers make a commitment to improving the workplace and strengthening the culture by walking the talk. But top-down leadership is not sufficient. In quite different ways, Emile, Lin, and their coworkers show that even without executive-level commitment, progress is still possible with adequate time, determination, and patience. In fact, the greater the number of healthy organization champions there are in a workplace, the more likely it is that these changes will put down roots.

Regardless of your specific healthy organization goals, the change agenda has to be owned by everyone. In this way, progress will be the result of ongoing and coordinated actions of all members of the workplace community. Impetus for a healthy organization can come from the bottom, middle, and top of the organization. Even if the full support of senior management is lacking, others in the organization have considerable scope to make improvements, often more than they might think. Any employee should feel motivated and enabled to make the organization healthier. The key action implications for how to build a healthier organization flowing from my discussion of leadership in this chapter can be summarized as follows:

1 Achieving healthy organization goals requires an inclusive approach to leadership. Making improvements must be a shared responsibility.
2 Everyone in your organization has the potential to play a leadership role in achieving healthy organization goals. They need to be empowered to do so.
3 Each employee can show leadership in day-to-day relationships through values-based behaviors that contribute to a positive workplace community.
4 Training managers, supervisors, and employees in resilience or psychological capital will build collective capacity for healthy change.
5 When managers and supervisors adopt a transformational leadership style, they will encourage all employees to take initiative and make improvements in their work environment.

## Leading the Way to a Healthier Organization

There are three main reasons why an inclusive approach to leadership, inviting others to participate actively in shaping their work environments, makes sense in organizations today. First, from a health promotion perspective, inclusive leadership enshrines the proven principle that people thrive in an environment that they have intentionally created to be health promoting. Second, it is sound organizational development practice. The impetus and ideas for improving the organization's systems, structures, and culture spring organically from within. And third, it is consistent with the growing emphasis many knowledge-based organizations place on collaboration and innovation to also encourage employees to positively shape their work environment and jointly promote well-being.

## Who Are the Leaders?

Let's start by challenging the conventional view of leadership as a few people at the apex of an organization who lead and the many below then who dutifully follow. This outmoded view reflects a twentieth-century model of bureaucracy – a top-down chain of command and narrow job descriptions. Inclusive leadership breaks through bureaucratic rigidities and the tendency these structures impose for employees to passively follow or react to edicts sent down from the executive suite. In the spirit of shared responsibility, employees, too, must seek out new ways to contribute, leverage the knowledge of others, and improve how work gets done. They too can become successful change agents.

Successful twenty-first-century workplaces move beyond bureaucracy to become flexible, flatter, collaborative, and smarter. In short, there is a constant search for ways to develop and use employees' capabilities. This calls for an updated approach to leadership. There no longer needs to be a distinct line drawn between leaders and managers. I encourage you to reflect on your personal views in this regard. How would you answer these six questions?

1 Do you view leadership as exclusive or inclusive?
2 Do you assume that the CEO and other executive team members are the organization's leaders?

3 Or do you believe that all employees should be encouraged to take initiative and lead change?
4 In your organization, are the words "leader" and "leadership" used mainly to refer to the CEO and executive team, or do they extend to roles further down in the organization?
5 To what extent do frontline supervisors or managers show leadership?
6 Are people leadership skills required, and further developed, for individuals in those roles?

Warren Bennis, a pioneer in leadership studies, made important distinctions between managers and leaders. Not all managers are leaders by virtue of their formal authority. And leaders don't necessarily have formal responsibility to supervise other employees. Rather, leaders must be self-aware, and through this be tuned in to how others are thinking and feeling. Making personal connections with others is how leaders inspire and motivate fellow workers. And through the process of developing strong personal connections, work environments become psychologically healthy. Two of Bennis's favorite sayings capture the difference between managers and leaders: "The manager has his eye on the bottom line; the leader has his eye on the horizon," and "The manager does things right; the leader does the right thing."[1]

Other leadership experts argue that all managers can become good leaders. And so can employees throughout the organization. Henry Mintzberg challenges the exclusive view of leadership – the cult of the lone executive whose personal vision and determination guide the company to greatness. Mintzberg convincingly argues: "Let's stop the dysfunctional separation of leadership from management. We all know that managers who don't lead are boring, dispiriting. Well, leaders who don't manage are distant, disconnected. Instead of isolating leadership, we need to diffuse it throughout the organization, into the ranks of managers and beyond. Anyone with an idea and some initiative can be a leader."[2] In this chapter, I expand on Mintzberg's point to help anyone interested in shaping a healthier and more productive work environment.

An inclusive approach to leadership converges with the goal of employee engagement, which I discussed in chapter 3. Today more so than ever, functional management positions require soft people skills in order to inspire, develop, and retain staff. Increasingly, these activities are no longer something HR does through programs and policies, but rather are incorporated into the roles of managers and supervisors. One sign of this is the popular idea that managers should be coaches and mentors. I hear more managers today than ten years ago talking about wanting to inspire their staff, which is another way of saying they want to be great people leaders. What's more, inspired frontline employees will display innovation and initiative in their jobs and teams, which is another way of saying they are leading improvements. From this perspective, the answer to the question "Who are the leaders?" is that everyone in your organization is a potential leader.

## When Employees Thrive They Can Lead

Leadership means taking action to achieve a shared vision of a vibrant workplace, knowing that this will benefit you and your coworkers, customers, and the larger community. The features of a vibrant workplace depend on both personal and organizational leadership. Leadership is not something separate or special, reserved for specific times and places. We all can show leadership by how we go about our daily work and in all our interactions with coworkers, direct reports, customers or clients, and external stakeholders.

Inclusive leadership happens at the personal and organizational levels. As I have emphasized, there are many initiatives you personally can take, regardless of your position. These include a commitment to be guided by personal and organizational values, to develop relationships based on mutual trust and respect, and to be responsible for learning and for teaching others, offering suggestions and ideas for now to do things better, being open and honest in all communication, supporting your coworkers or direct reports, and recognizing others' contributions. At the organizational level, managers and professionals can ensure that the right support systems are in place. Professionals in HR, OHS, organization development, learning, wellness, CSR, and related areas become change agents by crafting the policies, programs, resources, and systems that support employees to succeed in their jobs.

The good news is that leadership skills can be learned. Leaders are made, not born. The qualities of leadership are not innate characteristics that individuals bring into the workplace as part of their personality or character. Leadership skills are "soft" people and interpersonal skills, not "hard" technical skills. Leadership experts James Kouzes and Barry Posner observe that leaders motivate others to act on values and make visions a reality.[3] The action verbs Kouzes and Posner use to describe the practices of exemplary leaders in all walks of life are "model," "inspire," "challenge," "enable," and "encourage." They also argue that leadership is everyone's business, because all members of an organization must take personal responsibility for showing leadership within their own sphere. Leading by example is showing others the way forward.

## Setting Examples at the Top

There are many examples, backed up by research, illustrating how senior executives, line managers, and supervisors can have a huge positive impact on employees' well-being and job performance. This underscores the critical role that manager–employee relationships play in healthy organizations.

At the tops of organizations, some CEOs are championing healthy work practices. For example, CEOs are speaking out about the importance of a "regular" workweek of forty hours or less.[4] Jason Fried, CEO of Basecamp (a project management platform), advocates eight hours a day and no more than forty hours a week, arguing it is a "useful constraint" that focuses your attention on only what really matters. Annie Tevelin, CEO of Skin Owl (a beauty products brand), encourages her team to work a four-day week, from 8:30 a.m. to 2:30 p.m. Monday through Thursday. She knows that people work hard when at their job. As Tevelin observes: "I'd rather have people come in, work their hardest, feel present, and enjoy their lives after work rather than be a slave to the workplace. My team leaves when the sun is still out, which contributes to their quality of life and their work ethic."

There's no doubt that senior leaders set the tone for the entire organization, as demonstrated by Blake Mycoskie, the founder of TOMS, a shoe company. Mycoskie led the growth of a successful global company that became well known for its "one-for-one" social enterprise commitment to donate a pair of shoes for every pair it sold. As a result of this commitment, millions of pairs of shoes have been donated to children in need.[5] Searching for new ways for him and his employees to make an even greater social contribution, Mycoskie spent time reflecting on how social enterprises can help with international development.[6] As he learned about the coffee trade in Rwanda, he saw an opening and decided to create TOMS Roasting, which also followed a one-for-one model, providing a week's worth of clean water to a person in need for every bag of coffee it sold. This not only left Mycoskie feeling more energized and committed; it was also a source of inspiration for the company's employees. However, Mycoskie openly admitted that all this work took a personal toll on him. As he told the 2019 Society for Human Resource Management conference, he had sacrificed his personal well-being and was recently diagnosed with mild depression – a rare admission by a successful corporate leader.[7] He used this personal experience as an opportunity to help others make the lifestyle changes that would reduce work pressures. To do this, he partnered with researchers to identify ten habits that can improve well-being, and will be launching this self-help mental health program in 2020.

We can gain a more detailed understanding of effective leadership behaviors from the 2018 Employee Recommended Workplace Awards, created in Canada by the *Globe and Mail* newspaper and employee benefits provider Morneau Shepell. The awards recognize excellence in achieving a healthy, engaged, and productive workforce.[8] Based exclusively on employee feedback, they show that the highest-rated employers practice effective people leadership. In these organizations, leaders lead by example, there is open communication, managers listen closely to staff and new hires, and there is spontaneous recognition of employee efforts. Under these conditions, employees believe that senior management cares about them as individuals – one of the hallmarks of a healthy organization.

Researchers have also documented effective management practices. Organizational psychologist Michael West and his colleagues examined results from England's annual National Health Service Staff Survey and other health system performance data. They were able to identify management behaviors that simultaneously improved workers' engagement and well-being, enabling them to deliver higher-quality patient care.[9] According to these researchers, "good management" consists of the following practices: well-structured staff appraisals that set clear objectives, help improve job performance, and leave the employee feeling valued; encouraging a team environment based on cooperation, collaboration, and continuous improvement; ensuring that employees receive relevant training; and designing jobs so that they provide meaningful tasks and involvement in decision-making.[10] As West and his colleagues conclude: "When we care for staff, they can fulfill their calling of providing outstanding professional care for patients."[11]

More generally, this list of good management practices should be basic activities for managers in any organization. As we can see, managers' actions directly impact, for better or worse, their employees' well-being. Gallup's research involving hundreds of organizations and surveys of more than 15 million workers has identified a single survey question – whether their supervisor cares about them as a person – that can accurately predict employees' well-being.[12] When a manager truly cares about a worker as a whole person and views their well-being as an important end in itself, the results include better job performance, higher-quality work, fewer sickness absences, loyalty, and fewer injuries on the job. And frontline workers will feel safe stepping forward to raise the alarm when things are going wrong. Without this basic safety to speak up and know they'll be listened to, we can't expect rank-and-file workers to exercise anything close to leadership.

To drive home this point, consider what can happen when employees feel they have no voice. A current example of this is the Canadian government's failed introduction of the Phoenix pay system, which is a payroll processing system for all federal government employees. The system has failed to properly pay over 150,000 public servants. This debacle is going to cost Canadian taxpayers $2.2 billion to fix. Canada's auditor general, Michael Ferguson, concluded that the Phoenix problems are a result of a culture within the public service in which employees are fearful of communicating failures upward to superiors.[13] In stark contrast, organizations that support everyone to be a leader encourage open and constructive discussion about how to learn from and correct mistakes.

Setting the stage for inclusive leadership also requires management practices that empower workers to deal effectively with the stresses of their job. It's not enough for workers to have a supportive supervisor and coworkers when faced with excessive job demands. Equally essential is having autonomy to make decisions and access to appropriate job resources. This combination of autonomy, resources, and social supports contributes to workers' well-being because workers are able to proactively control the demands of their job. The same conditions drive higher performance. A meta-analysis of fifty-seven studies in this area confirmed that the quality of an employee's relationship with their supervisor, a sense of psychological empowerment, and a supportive culture and leadership contribute to job performance.[14] This approach would have saved Canadian civil servants the anxiety of inaccurate paychecks and taxpayers a lot of money.

Here's another way of looking at what it takes for employees to show leadership, drawing on our discussion in chapter 3 of what inspires employees. Gretchen Spreitzer and Christine Porath, writing in the *Harvard Business Review*, neatly summarize what it means to thrive – or feel inspired – at work: "Think of a thriving workforce as one in which employees are not just satisfied and productive but also engaged in creating the future – the company's and their own."[15] Thriving employees have an edge because they feel energized – but they know how to avoid stress and burnout. Thriving employees seek out opportunities to innovate and learn. They also build relationships with colleagues at work that will energize them and transfer that work energy to their personal lives.

It is also helpful to think of the workplace as a community in which everyone is a good citizen, contributing to its overall betterment. The community metaphor is used by Jeffrey Pfeffer in his discussion of a culture of caring.[16] When the workplace is truly a community, employees know that they can rely on each other when things get tough at work. Expanding a wellness program doesn't do much to cultivate a caring community. Rather, companies that are committed to supporting their workforce not only motivate employees to engage in mutual caring; they also ensure that management decisions don't add to workloads, job insecurity, or stress. In a caring culture, everyone feels accountable for being a good organizational citizen. It is an expected part of how you go about your job. This describes a psychologically healthy and safe workplace, as discussed in chapter 2.

## Inclusive Leadership Qualities

Now let's apply these ideas to describe the leadership qualities needed in a healthy organization. Six qualities define the kind of leadership that anyone can bring to their roles and relationships: inspire yourself and others; be caring and connected; be trustworthy and trusting; be action oriented; empower others; and be self-aware. By cultivating these qualities, you will become a healthy organization change agent.

1 *Be inspirational.* Inspire yourself. Encourage and support others to set and achieve higher goals for quality of work-life and performance. Employees who do not have management responsibilities should focus on what they can bring to their own role and to their team, work unit, and internal network. Simple things can contribute to the long-term goals of a healthy organization. These include bringing a positive attitude toward one's job and clients or customers, seeking out opportunities to improve teamwork, helping and being supportive of coworkers, and strengthening the ties between the workplace and its larger community by volunteering. Managers have more scope in this regard. As I will discuss below, when managers inspire and energize their employees, these individuals are able to initiate significant change.

2 *Be caring and connected.* Whether as a manager or a coworker, you need to care about and be connected to those with whom you work. This attitude extends to appreciating others' contributions and viewpoints, providing honest and constructive feedback, and valuing and acknowledging the capabilities they bring to the organization. Creating a sense of connection among employees fosters a workplace community. Leaders keep the big picture in view and understand how their actions contribute to the workplace community and the organization's mission. They

connect people to a bigger purpose and encourage learning and reflection as part of the process of achieving the mission.

3 *Be trustworthy and trusting.* Effective leadership requires a high level of mutual trust, as discussed in chapter 4. When employees feel respected, they will feel safe offering new ideas and pointing out mistakes and errors as opportunities to learn and improve. Everyone is more willing to take risks that can lead to better internal processes, services, or products. This high-trust work environment is diametrically opposite to a command-and-control bureaucracy, where everyone is risk averse, won't speak up, and slavishly follows the rules. We know that these traditional workplaces can stifle initiative and suck the meaning out of work. Leadership is about inspiring others to collaborate to achieve outstanding results, knowing that they can trust you and everyone else in the organization.

4 *Be action-oriented.* Developing a common language for talking about a shared vision, values, and healthy organization goals is the prelude to action. As leadership expert Michael Fullan puts it: "The litmus test of all leadership is whether it mobilizes people's commitment to putting their energy into actions designed to improve things. It is individual commitment, but it is above all collective mobilization."[17] The leadership mind-set required in an environment of constant change, according to Fullan, results in ongoing organizational development and performance enhancement. Leading involves understanding the change process, fostering in others a higher purpose, making sense of the whole, creating and sharing knowledge, and, above all, building relationships. It is not the goal that matters as much as the process for taking action to reach that goal together.

5 *Be empowering.* Employee empowerment and autonomy have been promoted by management experts for decades, but have come to take on a hollow ring. Yet people do want a say in their jobs and workplaces – regardless of the label manage experts

place on it. So a key ingredient of effective leadership is enabling others, especially your direct reports if you are a manager, to be actively involved in making and implementing decisions. Margaret Wheatley, a respected authority on leadership, offers a view of leadership that taps into our deep-seated personal need to shape our own life.[18] For managers, this way of thinking opens up opportunities to harness people's capacity to figure out how to do things better. The guiding principle here is that if people create something, they will support it and use it. That neatly expresses what a healthy organization is all about.

6 *Be self-aware.* At a personal level, leadership also requires you to use the principles of a healthy organization as a mirror for reflecting on your own actions. It is important to take time to reflect on how your intended actions will affect others and contribute to larger goals, beyond getting the task at hand done. Strong leaders are self-aware. This is a major step toward being tuned in to others' needs, interests, and emotional experiences in the workplace – what Daniel Goleman calls emotional intelligence. To quote Goleman: "Imagine the benefits for work of being skilled in the basic emotional competences – being attuned to the feelings of those we deal with."[19] If managers are expected to model healthy behaviors, they must have an adequate level of self-awareness about those behaviors in the first place.

## Developing Inclusive Leadership

Let these six qualities guide your roles and relationships in the workplace. Learning to lead the way to a healthier organization involves cultivating behaviors consistent with these six leadership qualities. It also means practicing the values of the organization and showing others how its vision for its customers, employees, and society is being achieved – even if by small steps. Guidelines need to be fleshed out with specific behaviors relevant to your organization's situation.

Once you have identified behaviors, update your training and development programs so they equip managers, supervisors, and employees with the skills needed to put the behaviors into practice.

Teck Resources' Trail Operations in southern British Columbia provides a useful example of how leaders can use their organization's values or guiding principles to develop leadership behaviors, then use these behaviors as the basis for skill development, a process that also reinforces the values as collective guideposts of behavior. Senior managers at the Trail Operations translated their guiding principles, described in chapter 4, into behaviors they could expect of each other and of other managers and employees. This showcases how any organization can involve managers and employees in discussions about how to lead by example.

## Living the Guiding Principles

In chapter 4, I described how the senior management team at Teck Resources' Trail Operations created a set of guiding principles. The goal was to develop clear behavioral guidelines that the management team would commit to following and that would lead the rest of the organization to foster a more positive, healthy, safe, and productive work environment. This initiative was not a defensive reaction to problems. In fact, the Trail smelter had achieved record productivity, profits, and safety levels. But the leadership team, under the guidance of a new general manager and including several new members from outside the organization, felt it could achieve even higher levels of performance and at the same time improve working conditions – as long as everyone was part of the process.

Through a facilitated discussion of revised values, the senior managers crafted five guiding principles that expressed what they individually and collectively believed could help to guide the organization into the future. Each manager then had the opportunity to reflect on the principles. They provided descriptions of the behaviors they felt were essential to actually "live" by the principle every day in the workplace (box 5.1). Here's an example of how the first guiding principle was communicated with a list of simple but effective actions:

### Box 5.1 How Leaders at Tech Resources' Trail Operations Live One of Their Guiding Principles

*Guiding principle: We act with* integrity, *treating all with* dignity, fairness, *and* respect. *Behaviors that show how they "live" this principle:*

- Always respect others' opinions and viewpoints.
- Avoid negative, behind-the-back comments or gossip about others.
- Speak to a person directly if you have concerns about their behavior.
- Have courageous conversations about performance (others' and your own).
- No hidden agendas.
- Listen first, and then speak.
- Don't jump to conclusions.
- Be courteous. Use language you would use at home with your family.
- Be forthright and honest with everyone, regardless of their position.
- Show respect for others by showing up for meetings on time and prepared.
- Try to make tough decisions so they are "win-win."
- Be honest about mistakes, learn from them, and improve.
- Expect honest feedback from others.
- Act ethically and honestly with business partners, even if you don't think they are doing the same.

To bring these behaviors to life, the senior managers also offered one or two personal stories about how they had recently used each of the guiding principles. These stories were a powerful communication tool in discussions of the guiding principles with managers, supervisors, and staff. By telling these stories, senior managers modeled how other managers could positively reinforce the guiding principles by telling their own stories and encouraging their team members to do the same. And by telling personal stories, they also showed vulnerability, which is so important for building trust.

Just as in the Teck example, senior management teams in any organization must find their own way to connect with their workforce. What the Teck leadership team quickly realized was that they had to consistently do what they said they would do. Many workplaces suffer negative consequences when managers regularly say one thing and do another – or do nothing at all to follow up on a commitment. The wider the gap between what managers say and do, the more dysfunctional a workplace can become. Employees retreat into the narrowest confines of their jobs and grow cynical when senior managers fail to meet the behavioral standards set for all employees through corporate values, codes of ethical conduct, and vision statements. The workplace will lack a sense of common purpose if managers do not put words into action, and employees' sense of personal meaning in work will be diminished, along with their energy to do an excellent job.

Most managers know these facts, at least intuitively. In my discussions with middle managers, they often point out that employees interact not with organizations, but with their immediate supervisor and unit or department managers. As one manager put it: "We are the face of the organization for the employee." How individual managers and supervisors behave in their day-to-day dealings with employees is the most concrete expression of an organization's character. For this reason, people skills are the critical ingredients of effective leadership in a healthy organization.

## Managers Need People Skills

Managers' people skills are essential for making progress toward healthy organization goals. Most workers highly value the intangible rewards of their job, notably challenging and meaningful work, feeling part of a team, developing and applying their capabilities, and knowing their contributions are valued. In a vibrant workplace, these intangibles describe employees' experiences. The manager or supervisor to whom they report can help them to see their job in the bigger picture of team, department, and corporate goals. This will enable the pursuit of career development, foster team spirit, provide constructive feedback, support them to manage workload and work–life balance, and recognize work well done. I often hear employees and executives complain that if only supervisors and middle managers had these people skills, the organization would be a much better place to work.

Part of the problem is that supervisors and managers are often recruited on the basis of technical proficiencies. To rectify this, recruitment and training efforts for people in these positions must focus on people skills. According to Gallup research, managers account for 70 percent of the variance in how employees experience their workplace. In fact, the main cause of burnout is how employees are managed. This includes unfair treatment, low trust, lack of role clarity, an overwhelming workload, unreasonable time pressures, and lack of communication and support from one's manager.[20] A Gallup study of nearly 7,500 full-time employees found that 23 percent of them felt burned out at work very often or always, mostly for these reasons. Although burnout has come to be accepted as part of the job for some workers, its organizational costs are substantial: absenteeism; reduced performance; and turnover. As Gallup researchers conclude, employee burnout can trigger "a downward spiral in individual and organizational performance."

Other studies reinforce these Gallup findings. A Mental Health America study of over 17,000 employees in nineteen industries in the

US showed that 44 percent of respondents felt that skilled employees were not given recognition in their workplace. Furthermore, just over one in three respondents felt that they could rely on their supervisor and colleagues for support. Lack of support and recognition in the workplace contributed to higher levels of workplace stress and isolation, as well as job dissatisfaction. The report concludes: "Unsupportive and unstable workplaces fostered psychological distress and contributed to a decline in employee engagement."[21] In Canada, a survey of about 800 HR managers by the Human Resources Professionals Association and *Canadian HR Reporter*, a practitioner publication, found that 73 percent spent considerable time dealing with problems caused by bad managers.[22] Over one-third said their employer tolerated bad behavior from problem managers who get results. Among the most common problems were treating employees disrespectfully (cited by 62 percent) and bullying or intimidation (cited by 57 percent). Bad managers may lack training in people skills, but training won't be useful for those whose values and attitudes are inconsistent with those of the organization.

The incidence of workplace bullying and harassment would steeply decline if managers and supervisors had better people skills and made effective use of these. Bullies use their power and position to psychologically harass and threaten others in their workplace. The 2018 Public Service Employee Survey, which includes all employees in Canadian federal government departments and agencies, found that 15 percent of about 163,000 survey respondents had experienced harassment in the previous 12 months.[23] Harassment is defined in the survey as "objectionable act(s), comment(s) or display(s) that demean, belittle, or cause personal humiliation or embarrassment, and any act of intimidation or threat." It also includes the meaning of harassment within the Canadian Human Rights Act (i.e., based on race, national or ethnic origin, colour, religion, age, sex, sexual orientation, gender identity or expression, marital status, family status, genetic characteristics, or disability).

The #MeToo movement has sparked constructive discussions about how to eliminate the underlying causes of sexual harassment from workplaces. As two Harvard business school professors observed: "Sexual harassment is not a women's issue but a leadership one. Women do not need to be 'protected' from the misbehavior of men in their workplaces. They need their managers to foster cultures in which sexual bullying is treated as the threat to the organization it is."[24] This is yet another strong inducement to nurture a positive, respectful, and inclusive culture in your organization. Start by ensuring that everyone in a management or supervisory position knows how to cultivate a civil work environment and models positive behaviors that others can follow in this regard – and is held accountable for doing so on a daily basis.

Yes, there are big gaps in supervisors' and managers' people skills. Based on my experience, and various Canadian workforce surveys I have conducted with EKOS Research Associates, senior organizational leaders increasingly recognize the importance of developing this critical skill set. However, supervisors and managers often face too many demands and a shortage of time. And they can be impeded by an organizational culture, reinforced by the senior managers above them, that only pays lip service to good people leadership. The sure way to remove these barriers to cultivating people skills is if those in the executive suite make supportive people practices a mission-critical priority.

## Developing People Skills

Training for managers and supervisors is a vital component of a comprehensive strategy to make workplaces healthier and safer. As I outlined in chapter 2, the US Centers for Disease Control recommends the Total Worker Health (TWH) approach, which can reduce work-related stress through three actions that have leadership

implications: implementing organizational and management policies that give workers more flexibility and control over their schedules; training supervisors on what they can do to reduce stressful
working conditions for direct reports; and enhancing workers'
stress reduction skills.[25]

Indeed, training supervisors and managers in TWH can pay off.
A fourteen-week TWH intervention tailored for construction crews
simultaneously improved safety, health, and well-being. Team supervisors were provided computer-based training and self-monitoring
activities on team building, work–life balance, and reinforcing targeted behaviors.[26] Supervisors and workers also completed safety
and health training in small groups. As a result, workers' health,
safety, and well-being improved. Specifically, family-supportive
supervisory behaviors improved, as did the frequency of daily
exercise, healthy diet support, team cohesion, sleep duration, and
blood pressure. Casting a wider net, a systematic search for studies published by peer-reviewed journals of workplace interventions
that provided managers with training on workplace mental health
found ten controlled trials that evaluated the impact of this training
on managers and their direct-report employees. A meta-analysis of
the pooled results from these ten studies found improvements in
managers' mental health knowledge, in non-stigmatizing attitudes
toward mental health, and in support provided to employees experiencing mental health problems.[27] More topics would have to be
covered in order for managers and supervisors to acquire all the
people skills I have mentioned. Still, what these studies show is that
focused people skills training can work.

Furthermore, we know from successful practices in the OHS area
that mandatory safety training increases the awareness of safety
issues throughout a company's workforce. The same no doubt
would apply to basic workplace health and well-being training –
although this remains an empirical question for future research to
answer. For example, a study of French apprentices at the end of

their schooling and start of their careers found that those receiving 'first aid at work' training in school had a much lower incidence of workplace injuries two years into their careers, compared with their peers who received no OHS training.[28] The researchers recommend providing broadly based OHS education rather than focusing narrowly on risks associated with specific jobs. Following the TWH approach, this also would include the promotion and protection of psychological health. However, there is no comparable research on the benefits of early-career healthy workplace training – for example, on workplace stress, respect, discrimination, harassment, bullying – but surely we could expect there to be benefits for students and their future employers.

## Cultivating Resilience

Resilience is a basic psychological safety skill that can be developed by individuals and teams, resulting in a more resilient workforce. The field of positive psychology emphasizes that positively oriented psychological strengths and capacities – including resilience – can be developed and measured in a workforce. The goal is to help organizations and their members thrive. There is evidence that resilience training contributes to these goals, although there is no consistent evidence of which training format or content is most effective.[29] The biggest benefits of resilience training seem to be developing individuals' capabilities and resources as protective factors for mental well-being.[30]

Let's expand our focus to team resilience, which is more than the combined personal resilience of individual team members.[31] A resilient team performs well when faced with adversity, perhaps undergoing a small decline in performance, and then becomes stronger in the process. Even though teams can be temporary, lasting for the life of a project, for example, a team's resilience can still be developed and strengthened. A resilient team takes stock of workplace pressures, assesses the risks of stress and burnout, and identifies actions to proactively address these. In resilient teams, members are mutually supportive, have a clear sense of purpose, and collectively adapt to changing circumstances. And taking a cue from positive psychology, teams also need to identify sources of positive energy and do what they can to strengthen and cultivate these.

Research has identified unique team-based features of resilience that contribute to higher team performance.[32] Practically, this emphasizes the need to focus on group as well as individual resilience. Psychologist Monique Crane offers advice for managers and team leaders on how they can support individual employees and teams to be more resilient.[33] This boils down to four actions managers and team leaders can take:

1  Reducing unnecessary drains on individual and team resilience;
2  Promoting adaptive workplace thinking and behaviors when faced with difficulties;
3  Supporting the development of personal and social resources; and
4  Enabling employees to access these resources.

While this advice will help to develop individuals' and teams' psychological resilience, it is clear that drains on resilience include many organizational features – such as unnecessary bureaucracy, unrealistic deadlines, understaffing, or administrative requirements – that in themselves are a source of stress for employees.

## Linking Resilience and Leadership

With this background on resilience, I would now like to share relevant insights from an action research project that examined how resilience, leadership, and well-being are interconnected. I was the research consultant on the Resilience in Leadership Project, which the Alberta School Employee Benefit Plan (ASEBP) conducted in collaboration with educational system leaders across the province. ASEBP administers a province-wide group insurance program offering a wide variety of health benefits, employee and family assistance, and loss of life and disability insurance to employees and their dependents in the educational sector.[34] The project's starting point was the recognition that educational leaders face heightened risks to their well-being given the demands of their role in an educational system defined by rapid change, rising expectations, and resource constraints. Leaders are expected to support school system improvements, most notably those aimed at making education more inclusive and promoting healthy school communities.

The project's survey of educational leaders confirmed that resilience and leadership are closely linked and in turn influence educational leaders' well-being and school system performance. Resilience, as I've noted, is a person's capacity to bounce back from adversity and to find a new and healthy normal. Yet, as noted in chapter 3, today's leaders need more than resilience; they also need the capacity to be hopeful, confident, and optimistic.[35] When combined, these positive psychological traits – called psychological capital (PsyCap) – are better predictors of well-being and performance than each attribute on its own. Studies link PsyCap to a range of individual well-being and workplace performance outcomes, such as absenteeism, intentions to quit, job satisfaction, commitment, and organizational citizenship behaviors.[36]

The latter attribute is central to inclusive leadership, because it refers to employees going beyond their job descriptions to help coworkers or in other ways benefit the organization. An effective way to develop resilience in a workforce is through leadership styles that promote the psychological capacities captured by PsyCap. This requires managers to connect on a personal level with the employees who report to them. When leaders are positive and authentic, thoughtful and transparent, and build confidence and commitment among their staff, they will be actively cultivating PsyCap for themselves and their team. PsyCap is positively contagious; as described by experts, it "trickles down and ripples out," leading to positive behaviors by others in the organization.[37]

Among the educational leaders we studied, PsyCap had a significant and positive relationship with their health, well-being, and stress levels. Respondents with greater PsyCap – in other words, those who feel optimistic, confident, resilient, and hopeful – were far more likely than their colleagues with low PsyCap to report very good or excellent general health and mental health and high life satisfaction. They also experienced less stress and reported fewer symptoms of burnout. One of the project's objectives was to illuminate the relationship between educational leadership, well-being, and resilience. So the survey also measured transformational leadership behaviors from a widely used and validated leadership assessment tool, the Multifactor Leadership Questionnaire.[38]

Transformational leaders contribute to the future success of their organizations by encouraging their colleagues to see opportunities and challenges in new ways. They also motivate others to strive for higher levels of performance, are admired and trusted, stimulate creative thinking, and are attuned to individuals' growth needs by acting as a coach or mentor.[39] In short, transformational leaders go far beyond a "transactional" or goal-oriented management style by enabling individuals to achieve their potential, find innovative solutions to challenges, and embrace change. The practical implication is that psychological capital – which includes resilience – contributes to school system performance by supporting a transformational style of leadership and higher engagement among senior administrators.

## Assessing Psychological Capital and Leadership

The study and follow-up consultations were a catalyst for reflection and action. The results helped to raise awareness about the importance of connecting psychological skills, leadership style, and well-being. The professional association representing educational leaders in Alberta used the findings in its leadership development program, succession planning, and supporting its members' health and wellness. Leaders themselves were better informed, having evidence-based insights to guide how they could involve other staff in promoting organizational health.

If you and your organization are interested in developing the psychological capital and leadership skills just described, I am providing short assessment tools for the key behaviors that define psychological capital (box 5.2) and transformational leadership (box 5.3).

### Box 5.2 Psychological Capital Assessment
*Here's a checklist you or your coworkers or team members can use to assess PsyCap. Do you or your team do any of the following?*

1  Always look on the bright side of things at work.
2  Feel optimistic about your/their future career.
3  Manage difficulties one way or another at work.
4  Take stressful things at work in stride.
5  See yourself/themselves as being successful at work.
6  Think of many ways to get out of a jam at work.
7  Feel confident contributing to discussions about organizational strategy.
8  Feel confident presenting information to a group of colleagues.
9  Avoid taking work stress home.

**Box 5.3 Transformational Leadership Assessment**

*Listed below are the behaviors associated with a transformational leadership style. You can assess your own leadership style by asking how frequently you do the following:*

1  Articulate a compelling vision of the future for your team and for the organization as a whole.
2  Express confidence that organizational goals will be achieved.
3  Seek differing perspectives when solving problems.
4  Get others to look at problems from many different angles.
5  Go beyond self-interest for the good of customers or clients, employees, and communities.
6  Act in ways that build others' respect for you.
7  Consider the moral and ethical consequences of your decisions.
8  Communicate the importance of having a strong sense of purpose.
9  Help others develop their strengths.
10  Teach and coach your staff.

We've now seen how strong psychological capital and a transformational leadership style set the stage for inclusive leadership by inviting employees to take responsibility for making their workplace better. It certainly helps in this regard if senior managers signal to others in the organization that through dedicated collective effort, specific improvement goals can be achieved. Senior managers must regularly and consistently communicate the importance of the organization's people to its success, using language that resonates right down to the front lines.

## Encouraging Bottom-Up Change

When senior managers are fully committed to the goal of employee well-being, they can mobilize others in the organization to also pursue that goal. This is what happens on effective wellness committees, which have a clear mandate and the necessary resources to make improvements. So if senior management endorses a specific healthy workplace initiative, they can empower frontline employees to become leaders. For example, a large Canadian municipality launched a one-month campaign on sleep for its employees. A wellness needs survey identified sleep as a major health concern for its workforce, especially those working in protective services (i.e., fire, police, and ambulance). Some 60 percent of survey respondents wanted more sleep and to feel more rested. So the city established an ambassador network, involving interested employees from each worksite and program area early in the development of the program. The city's employee assistance program provider was a partner in the project, providing a sleep specialist and helping to develop resources that were promoted by the ambassadors, such as a list of "top ten sleep tips" and a sleep self-assessment.

That's a good example of a top-down initiative that taps into frontline employees' potential to be leaders. An equally powerful catalyst for change can result when those same frontline employees take initiative without direction from senior managers. This bottom-up approach to change inverts the authority pyramid found in many organizations. It is a powerful way for employees who aren't in management roles to lead change. The Institute for Work and Health (IWH) provides relevant examples of this bottom-up approach to leading change. An IWH research team led by Dr. Lynda Robson identified the factors leading to what it calls "breakthrough change" in a firm's safety performance.[40] The team conducted case studies of Ontario firms that went from poor OHS performance (based on workers' compensation claims) to strong performance over a ten-year period. Four in-depth case studies (two manufacturers, a grocery, and a social agency) identified the importance of organizational learning and "positive deviance" – or the intentional departure from past practices.

Critical in this regard was the role of what the researchers call a "knowledge transformation leader" (KTL). This individual translated new OHS knowledge into useable internal knowledge, spurring coworkers and managers to take action based on this knowledge. The KTLs were in various organizational positions, not necessarily in formal OHS roles. They were able to generate positive social dynamics in joint health and safety committees to make improvements, and gained senior leadership support for these change initiatives. As described by the researchers, "the KTLs had productive interactions with external OHS management consultants, learned new OHS concepts, and then disseminated and embedded that new OHS knowledge internally, by interacting as required with individuals from across the organization. The KTLs were notably adept at working collaboratively and communicating with others in the organization."[41] This combination of frontline initiative, learning, and diffusion is consistent with my observations of how many organizations have developed effective health and wellness initiatives.

Here's an example from the nonprofit social services sector showing how leadership skills can be developed among frontline staff. Ronald McDonald House (RMH) provides houses in fourteen locations in Canada where families of sick children can stay while their child is being treated at a local hospital. The goal is to keep families together and help kids' recovery. At two RMHs in Alberta, a unique project was led by a University of Alberta graduate student, Jonathan Lai, in partnership with the Healthy Workplaces for Helping Professions project (a collaborative effort involving the university and social service organizations across Alberta) and staff at RMHs in the cities of Red Deer and Calgary. The goal was to increase employees' stress management capabilities and develop more collaborative relationships between departments in the two houses. The intervention included changes to weekly team meetings, providing staff thirteen minutes without a manager or supervisors present when they could discuss wellness issues, and five two-hour workshops on how to be a "wellness leader."[42] As a result, participating frontline staff felt more empowered and became more capable of taking initiatives that made their work environment healthier and more supportive.

## Shared Leadership Responsibility in Healthcare

Additional ideas about how organizations cultivate shared leadership responsibility can be found in healthcare. As I outlined in chapter 4, team medicine is the hallmark of the Mayo Clinic's excellent patient care and outstanding reputation. Everyone's talents are combined in teams so that patients' needs can be best served. The diverse expertise of all medical and support staff is always available for patients. As Berry and Seltman put it in their book on management lessons from the Mayo Clinic, "collaboration, cooperation, and coordination are the three dynamics supporting the practice of team medicine at Mayo Clinic."[43] This is how personalized care for patients is delivered collectively. This spirit of collaboration also provides fertile ground for each individual staff member to take initiative – that is, to show leadership – in the interests of patients.

Other examples of shared leadership come from the Ontario Hospital Association's Quality Healthcare Workplace Awards, a recognition program that ran from 2011 to 2015. The award-winning hospitals actively involved frontline staff in improving patient care, and through this process boosted employee engagement and well-being. Below are five examples of inclusive leadership in action, all of which empowered frontline staff to make improvements that benefited patients and, at the same time, contributed to their own well-being.

A regional hospital actively involved frontline staff and managers in quality improvement through its Lean Forward program. Its quality and safety board redevelopment by the inpatient surgery staff is a good example of staff-led improvements that had positive results for patients and also increased staff pride. The hospital introduced extensive consultation opportunities, from daily rounding (check-ins with patients by clinical staff) to leadership safety walkabouts, which encourage two-way communication between staff and hospital leaders and invite staff input.

A small community hospital had achieved high levels of staff engagement by pursuing quality improvements through initiatives that directly involved staff. Staff members were able to self-schedule, resulting in low absenteeism. Staff also had the ability to reallocate employees between departments as needed, helping them to directly manage their own workloads. As a result, the use of overtime and banked hours was substantially reduced at the hospital.

A large teaching hospital implemented numerous initiatives to involve staff and physicians in improving patient care quality and safety. The CEO conducted weekly walk-arounds, providing opportunities for two-way communication. Staff had the autonomy to make improvements in patient care through numerous continuous quality improvement councils and initiatives, with documented positive patient outcomes. The hospital adopted Toyota's Lean methodology, another way that frontline staff can be directly involved in continuous improvement processes.

At a large regional hospital, staff and physicians regularly participated in workplace and patient care improvements. The hospital's strategy, mission, actions, and performance metrics supported these improvement initiatives by giving priority to staff health and safety. Staff autonomy and improvement initiatives were encouraged through workshops on Lean methodology. The collaborative "transformation of care" initiative was an innovative approach to redesigning workloads and improving care. Staff input also included peer interviewing of prospective new hires to assess how they would fit into the team, which reduced first-year turnover. Another good example of staff-led improvements was the pharmacy team's reduction of medication selection errors.

At a community hospital in a northern Ontario city, a values-based culture supported staff involvement in continuous improvement initiatives. This approach to Lean generated $2.3 million return on investment over two years. Employee focus groups and task teams found ways to improve staff decision input and teamwork, resulting in measurable improvements in communication and consultation. Lean methodology is now part of the hospital's strategy, achieved by promoting frontline staff autonomy and initiative. In daily huddles, teams discuss the means for achieving these goals. Fifty completed Lean projects were all guided by a simple principle of inclusive leadership: "those who do the work change the work."

## A Healthy Organization Is a Shared Responsibility

To recap, leadership in a healthy organization is a shared responsibility. Everyone has a role to play. Everyone feels a responsibility to contribute to a healthy, safe, and productive work environment. While senior managers' support and actions are big enablers of progress, healthy organization goals are easier to achieve when there are opportunities for all employees to become involved in that process. We have seen how healthy organizations approach leadership in inclusive ways, empowering employees down to the front lines to take ownership of work environment improvements. In this chapter, I have provided many examples of how you can develop the leadership capabilities your organization will need for sustained improvements. As we've seen, there are different avenues for this, ranging from training supervisors in people skills, to developing resilience or psychological capital skills at all levels of the organization, to equipping managers to act as transformational leaders.

Now it's up to you to find opportunities in your organization for managers to encourage others to lead. Leadership is all about bringing people together to achieve purposeful change that will benefit the entire organization and its stakeholders. But here's the catch: someone has to take the initiative. That is why leadership is one of the basic building blocks of a healthy organization. Otherwise, an organization will be paralyzed by inertia, suspended in a state of limbo where any talk of creating a more vibrant workplace and improving employee experiences remains just that – talk. To avoid this inertia trap, change agents at all levels of an organization must understand the change process itself. This will equip them to play the most constructive role possible, working with others to implement improvements. Chapter 6 explores the dynamics of change involved in creating healthier organizations.

# CHAPTER 6

# Healthy Change

My work as a consultant over the past two decades has given me a front-row seat for observing how organizations in different industries have gone about creating a healthier workplace. Whether the organization called what they were trying to do a plan, program, or strategy, each was committed to forging stronger people–performance links. Despite detailed preparations, however, results sometimes were disappointing. Carefully planned change initiatives never fully took root. These experiences have led me to ask a fundamental question, one that I now will pose to readers: How do you think about and then design a process that will successfully result in sustainable healthy change?

That's the question I will answer in this chapter. I offer practical lessons from a wide range of organizations that have charted their own path to a healthier, safer, and more productive work environment. What I do not offer is a step-by-step guide. As I suggested in chapter 4, organizational change is too contextualized and complex to follow a straightforward, project-management, one-size-fits-all approach. More realistically, successful change has three defining characteristics. First, it takes into account the entire organizational system. Second, it is an organic and emergent process that evolves as people reflect upon and learn from each step they take, altering course as they go. And third, as I suggested in chapter 5, a successful change process should bring together many people from different places in the organization and combine their energy, expertise, and ideas, sometimes with external partners.

There is no easy recipe for creating a healthy organization. Rather, your creative challenge is to collaborate with others in your workplace, and community partners, to find the most suitable way to connect the goals of improved employee well-being, better working conditions, and sustainable organizational success. This customized approach to change will have to be tailored to the unique circumstances, culture, and needs of your organization. This requires you to creatively design an appropriate healthy change process that outlines in broad brushstrokes your direction, all the while recognizing that the details of the change will emerge at each step along the way.

Some organizations have achieved remarkable overall health and sustainability. Indeed, these companies' successes have been recognized on lists of best workplaces, best employers, best-run and most admired businesses, and most environmentally and socially responsible corporations. While much can be learned from this top tier, their so-called best practices are not readily copied. So this chapter is mainly directed at the large middle group of organizations that are neither dangerously unhealthy nor exceptionally healthy in terms of the vibrancy of their workplaces, the resonance of their culture, or the level of well-being and inspiration experienced by their employees. Mostly, my examples are good organizations striving to become better. Their journeys provide tips that you can use to seize opportunities, navigate twists and turns, avoid pitfalls, and make progress toward your own healthy organization goals.

## Moving from an Individual to an Organizational Focus

Many workplace wellness programs target the health behaviors and attitudes of individual employees and stop there. What can you do to reach beyond this individual focus and take into account how organizational systems influence, and are influenced by, employee well-being?

A narrow focus on individuals' health attitudes and behaviors misses important opportunities to improve the physical and psycho-social work environments, which exert powerful influences not only on employee well-being but also on their job performance. A Stanford University study points out that workplace stressors increase a worker's probability of poor health outcomes by 50 percent, the same extent as exposure to secondhand smoke – a known carcinogen that is strictly regulated. The study's authors argue that "if initiatives to improve employee health are to be effective, they cannot simply address health behaviors, such as reducing smoking and promoting exercise, but should also include efforts to redesign jobs and reduce or eliminate workplace practices that contribute to workplace-induced stress."[1] That's one way to think about what an organizational focus entails, in contrast to a more limited focus on individuals.

A systematic review of studies assessing the economic and health benefits of workplace wellness strategies identified common success factors, based on documented positive outcomes.[2] The researchers summarize six critical success factors as follows:

1 The corporate culture encourages wellness to improve employ-ees' lives, not only to reduce costs.
2 Employees and leaders provide strong support and input for the wellness programs.
3 Employees are motivated by corporate policies and a physical environment that encourages participation.
4 Programs are adapted over time to the changing needs of the workforce.
5 Community health organizations are partners, providing support, education and treatment.
6 Technology is used to facilitate health risk assessments and wellness education.

If you already have a wellness program, you can use this list of success factors to take stock of your current approach to workplace wellness. Before even considering how to use your existing program as a springboard for taking an expanded organizational focus, you first may find it useful to address the challenge of encouraging employees to use these existing wellness resources. A review of workplace health promotion programs found a median participation among eligible employees of only 33 percent.[3] That's why successful worksite health promotion strategies actively involve employees during all program phases, right from the start – an essential requirement for making deeper changes in organizational systems, structures, and culture. When employees participate in designing, implementing, and monitoring worksite wellness initiatives, they take greater ownership for their overall health, safety, and well-being. And they will be benefiting the organization by practicing inclusive leadership, as I described in chapter 5.

Also important as you consider how to expand the focus of your workplace wellness initiatives is to assess to what extent they meet two criteria for maximum program effectiveness. As I've already emphasized, successful wellness or employee health promotion programs are both integrated and comprehensive. Being integrated means being able to overcome the traditional silos that have separated occupational health and safety, human resources, workplace health promotion, HR, and CSR. And being comprehensive entails addressing a range of mental and physical health determinants and risk factors at the individual and organizational levels, as well as building the capacity needed for managers and employees to achieve their well-being and job goals.

How do you reach that turning point where lots of employees and managers want to be involved in co-creating a healthier organization? I'm reminded of a recent corporate wellness conference where one of the presenters got the audience thinking about the change process by asking a simple diagnostic question about how any organization is positioned for change: "Are you mobilized or paralyzed?" In the ensuing discussion, it became clear to all present that when an organization is mobilized to initiate healthy change, it has a critical mass of change-ready thinkers prepared to imagine a new and better future. An organization that fully embraces healthy system-wide change needs to be more than change-ready. It will have a culture that encourages innovation and continuous improvement. It will also tap into the capabilities of the workforce to design and implement needed changes. The upshot: you and your colleagues must think carefully about how your organization can become mobilized and, as a flip side to this, what factors are likely to contribute to change paralysis so that you can anticipate and then overcome these barriers.

## Generating Change Capacity

There are many theories of organizational change. The one that I find helpful for designing a healthy change process is proposed by Richard Beckhard, a pioneer in the field of organization development.[4] OD practitioners plan and implement system-wide changes in an organization's processes, structures, and culture. They often target how people work together and with customers and community stakeholders. Beckhard suggests that it is possible to design change to improve organizational health, as long as the focus is on the change process as well as the change goals. The usefulness of an OD approach to healthy change has been reinforced through my work with managers and employees. As we will see in the examples below, many types of change can be designed to strengthen the organization's ability to collaborate, learn, and innovate in its pursuit of healthy organization goals. This capacity-building is an outcome of the journey, not an end goal.

The key word here is "capacity." Anthony Buono and Kenneth Kerber offer advice on how to develop an organization's capacity for sustainable change.[5] Critical for developing change capacity is having an organizational context that supports change, a culture that facilitates learning, and a focus on successful implementation. Buono and Kerber distinguish their approach, called "guided change" because it involves all members of the organization in exploring new and novel ways to improve, from top-down directed change or planned change sponsored from the executive suite. Their change model is best described as emergent, grassroots change that can start anywhere in the organization. This is consistent with the incremental approach to culture change I discussed in chapter 4. But as Buono and Kerber explain, "managers must be willing to give up control based on rules, procedures, and tight supervision and substitute an approach based on overall direction, principles, values, and commitment."[6] By following three basic principles, your organization will be able to cultivate the capacity for sustainable change: involve employees directly in designing change so they feel a sense of ownership; encourage everyone to be open to a wide range of possible solutions; and evaluate and learn as you go in the spirit of continuous improvement.

Another reason to devise a grassroots, capacity-building, and continuous improvement approach to organizational change comes from Richard Axelrod, also an organizational development expert. Axelrod argues that when top managers are the change cheerleaders, negative consequences for the organization's structure and culture can result.[7] The main drawbacks include greater cynicism, resistance, bureaucracy, and reinforcement of top-down control. Axelrod calls such organizations "Dilbert organizations," named after the hapless character in Scott Adams's comic strip that depicts a seriously dysfunctional office. The failure of many change initiatives can be traced to the rigid change management process used, because it "disengages the very people whose support is essential to success." As a solution, Axelrod recommends widening the circle of involvement by using democratic principles of participation that create the trust and confidence needed for change to succeed.

Axelrod's observations are backed up by academic experts on organizational change, who state: "The more people are involved, the more the change effort is their change effort. The more individuals can see that they can succeed in the future state, the more empowered they feel."[8] My assessment of truly healthy workplaces identifies strong commitment from top management, reinforced by their individual behavior, as a key success factor. Equally essential, however, is the meaningful involvement of all groups – frontline workers, all levels of management, unions, and professional associations – in the organization. This key ingredient of successful organizational change resonates with a core idea of health promotion. The WHO's definition of health promotion, which I provided in chapter 1, suggests that workers' involvement in the process of creating and maintaining healthier working conditions is a prerequisite for achieving a healthy workplace and workforce.[9] Real progress is possible when the impetus for change comes from the bottom and middle of the organization, not just from the top.

That said, there are cases where decisive action by top management marks a crucial first step in moving an organization to a healthier place. Robert Sutton's refreshingly frank book, *The No Asshole Rule*, illustrates the kind of change that senior managers can initiate to foster a civilized workplace.[10] Sutton describes the "culture of fear" that engulfs workplaces when managers and employees get away with bad behavior, demeaning others, and generally acting like jerks. Fear leads to change paralysis. People retreat or quit, usually in that order, often at considerable personal and organizational costs. Sutton describes how a new CEO at a *Fortune* 500 company fixed an unhealthy culture by purging about two dozen toxic senior managers and rigorously applying the existing performance management system to prevent bullying and harassment. The CEO's moves restored a large measure of humanity to the organization and set the tone for civility in all workplace relationships, as well as for future healthy change.

Perhaps the CEO in Sutton's example followed his own moral compass or was encouraged by the board to clean house. Regardless, this is an example of positive change coming right from the top. In sharp contrast, grassroots or organic change happens when employees find common cause and pressure senior management to act. The #MeToo movement has sparked such actions recently, including the firing of high-profile CEOs and media personalities for sexual misconduct, signaling that a fundamental culture shift has begun.

Google provides a good example of how frontline employees can initiate change. More than 20,000 Google employees staged a walkout – called the Walkout for Real Change – in 2018 protesting the company's handling of sexual misconduct cases. Anger arose among employees after the *New York Times* reported that Google had generously paid off male executives accused of sexual harassment, all under a veil of silence. As one female product manager observed, "Google is famous for its culture. But in reality we're not even meeting the basics of respect, justice and fairness for every single person."[11] Just 31 percent of Google's global workforce and one in four of its executives are women. In response, Google agreed to end its practice of private arbitration of sexual harassment or assault complaints (which had required people to waive their right to sue and to sign confidentiality agreements). Alice Lemieux, a Google software engineer, encouraged employees to keep organizing and providing internal feedback. "Laws and policies change because of people like us," she said.[12] Employee pressure is still on Google to provide a fairer and more respectful work environment. It has since come to light that some of the female leaders of the walkout have experienced retaliation, which only further undermines a culture of fairness and respect.[13]

## Constant Communication

People cannot become enthusiastic participants in a change process if they do not know about it. Open and constant communication is a key success factor in any organizational change initiative. Creating healthier workplaces is no different. One of the complaints I often hear from workplace health promotion or wellness practitioners is the low level of participation in available programs. This usually reflects two weaknesses. Often missing is a lack of continual communication using language that is meaningful to the diverse demographic groups in the workforce. Also missing from program design is a process that meaningfully involves employees in ways that give them a sense of ownership. This can be accomplished through committees, councils, or ongoing consultation mechanisms.

Equally important, everyone in the organization must be kept fully informed about the goals, strategies, and progress milestones for change. Traditional change initiatives driven from the top often suffer from communicating too little, too late. As change expert John Kotter warns, most corporate change initiatives under-communicate by a factor of ten.[14] If change is flowing from the front lines of an organization, change agents must keep senior management informed about the impact of the initiative and use multiple channels to communicate progress to coworkers. Ideally, the change effort will have the active support and involvement of one or more executive "champions." Also important is helping all managers to adjust their thinking about what drives performance, especially corporate values and other cultural factors.

Shifting people's thinking is an important step in changing how they act. Effective communication is the means to this end. New thinking can come about only if a common language can be found for talking about health and performance within your organization. After a workshop I facilitated on how to improve job quality, one of the participants, who was a workplace wellness coordinator, raised the importance of language. She noted that different labels – "healthy organization," "healthy workplace," "quality jobs," "engaged employees," "health and productivity" – all point to similar determinants and outcomes. Depending on the type of organization, one label will work better than the others, so you will need to settle on language that makes sense in the context of your workplace. Using locally meaningful language, you will be able to expand the possibilities for how decision-makers think – and take action – about the impact of the work environment on health, safety, and performance.

## Getting on Your Own Healthy Change Path

Becoming a healthy organization is more of a journey than a destination. Yes, the "what" is important, but so too is the "how." Indeed, you need to set specific goals for the short, medium, and long terms. Yet as we have seen, the attributes of a vibrant workplace and positive culture take root over time. Thus, each organization will be at a different point along a healthy organization path, looking for opportunities to take the next step. What healthy organizations have in common is a commitment by employees and managers to achieve optimal results for all stakeholders. Everyone participates in the change process. As workplace culture expert Deborah Connors advises, people must feel empowered to ask a potentially transformative question: "What new practices can lead to a better future in this workplace?" By asking questions like this, you are inviting others to collaborate with you to generate a shared vision that can guide change.[15]

Consider the following examples of organizations in which change agents are making concerted efforts to move down a healthy path. These examples come from three of my consulting clients that took different paths toward similar well-being and performance goals.

A telecommunications company launched a new customer service strategy in its six call centers. The call center that went furthest in implementing supportive coaching and team-based learning achieved the highest customer service performance ratings, lowest turnover, and highest employee satisfaction. Employees at this center experienced less stress in their jobs because they had more autonomy to meet customer needs and more support from coworkers to get the information required to resolve customer problems. This approach to teamwork was encouraged by the regional vice president, whose motto was "Do whatever you can to meet customers' needs; just don't give away the store!"

Anticipating a wave of retirements, a city administration developed a detailed HR plan. But this was not enough to renew management ranks. Rising workloads, overly bureaucratic reporting structures, and difficulty in setting priorities had taken the fun out of work and ratcheted up workloads. Promising employees and supervisors turned down promotions to avoid the high levels of stress and burnout that they knew came with those roles. After wide discussion, there was a collective realization that the solution lay in more flexible career paths, giving employees and frontline supervisors authority and accountability for decisions, and a more supportive culture.

A logistics company measured its performance by how long it took to pick up, ship, sort, and deliver a package. Work was fast paced. Consultations with employees identified stress and work–life balance as major concerns. Based on this input, leadership training was revised to help managers address these issues. The director of occupational health and safety saw an opportunity for healthy change. He championed a pilot project that added to the corporate report card organizational OHS and HR measures, such as lost-time injury, short-term disability, turnover, and overtime utilization. These metrics quickly caught the attention of operations managers because they saw how healthy work environments affected the number of workers available on any given shift. This led to more realistic expectations for frontline workers' daily job goals.

Employees and managers in each of these organizations took decisive steps toward healthy organization goals. Keeping up momentum requires putting firmly in place two of the healthy organization building blocks we discussed earlier: a positive culture that supports employee well-being, and inclusive leadership that enables workers at all levels to participate in workplace improvements.

## The Role of Culture and Leadership

The culture building block of a healthy organization supports ethically responsible behaviors, including how people should be treated. Look to your corporate values to guide any type of organizational change. Or if these values do not address workplace relationships and employee health, safety, and well-being, you can craft a set of guiding principles to help you move forward with healthy change. Examples of healthy change reveal that what is needed is not better "change management," a popular concept among managers. Rather, change leadership must be demonstrated by many groups and individuals throughout the organization. Healthy change requires effort by numerous and diverse champions. Change agents need to till the ground, cultivating fertile conditions for new ways of thinking and acting to take root and eventually flourish. Improvements become a shared responsibility, which I described in the last chapter as inclusive leadership.

If you have a personal commitment to a healthier workplace, then you are an agent or champion of healthy change. As such, you should always be on the lookout for the language, opportunities, and allies to help make this happen. You will likely have a personal vision of a healthy organization or workplace. You probably do not accept the status quo, but, at the same time, you understand that positioning change depends a great deal on timing and organizational politics. You may even describe your approach as "change by stealth." This is a term one champion used in one of my healthy workplace strategy workshops, because he took one opportunistic step at a time, without the benefit of an official healthy workplace strategy. To be candid, I certainly have seen change agents quit their job in frustration. But in my experience, most people who truly believe in the importance of a healthy organization remain tireless advocates, nudging along the change process whenever and however they can.

Groups also can be powerful engines of change, diagnosing workplace needs and proposing action plans. Groups can trouble-shoot and solve problems that fall outside the scope, mandate, or resources of existing organizational arrangements. For example, a task force, committee, or project team can break through red tape, bridge functional areas, and do an end run around resistant managers. Organizational change experts recommend that groups leading change need a clear purpose, a design that fits this purpose, links to other parts of the organization, and a group culture that supports risk-taking and learning.[16] Change team leaders should coach team members to focus simultaneously on performance and culture. The goal of a change team is not to manage a new project, but to stimulate organizational development, learning, and innovation through the actions of others.

Consider the case of a newly formed wellness committee in a large police service. Members spent several day-long sessions fleshing out goals and timelines for a comprehensive wellness initiative. What really energized committee members was a discussion of the benefits each of them wanted to see result from the committee's efforts. It also helped that senior management had empowered the committee to come up with its own definition of wellness. The committee put its own stamp on wellness by identifying five organizational benefits (reduced costs, team effectiveness, productivity, retention, and morale) and five individual benefits (satisfaction, engagement, individual effectiveness, personal health, and work–life balance) that its wellness-related actions should achieve. By clearly communicating these wellness benefits to coworkers, the committee encouraged others to think more about organizational health goals rather than just individual wellness.

## Guidelines for Healthy Change

My approach to healthy change can be summarized in five general principles, which are based on my practical experience and reinforced by relevant research evidence. The five principles highlight the issues that change agents will need to consider as they move from thinking to action:

1 Understand your organization's change readiness and capabilities.
2 Develop the organization's capacity for sustainable change.
3 Link people initiatives to the business strategy.
4 Widen the circle of involvement.
5 View the change process as defined by learning, innovation, and continuous improvement.

A useful insight from the field of health promotion is the importance of a person's readiness to make changes in their health-related attitudes and behaviors. A person's readiness to change determines what will be realistic goals and timelines for them – and whether they stand a chance of making any progress at all. Readiness is assessed by past actions, knowledge, and awareness about change benefits, and the motivation to adopt new lifestyle practices.

Organizations also can be assessed for their readiness to change in a healthy direction. You can use the model of a healthy organization presented in chapter 1 to develop a vision that you and your coworkers would like to see your organization achieve. Use language in the vision that suits the character of your organization, which could range from "healthy organization," "healthy workplace," or "employer of choice" to "inspired employees" or "resilient workforce."

For example, work I did with the Ontario Hospital Association, which has over 150 hospitals in the province as members, altered its language from "healthy workplaces" to "high-quality healthcare workplaces." The reasoning behind the change was to encourage hospitals to move beyond a traditional health, safety, and wellness focus to make connections between the quality of the work environment, the quality improvement process, and the quality of patient care (see figure 3.2). As a result, many hospitals increased their capacity to simultaneously improve quality for both patients and staff. This was because the shift in language especially resonated with front-line clinical staff who were involved in ongoing patient safety and quality care initiatives. It provided them with a framework that tied these operational patient-focused projects with the health, safety, and engagement of themselves and their team members.

Once you have a healthy organization vision that sets out your shared aspirations for how the organization can improve, use that vision to assess to what extent the important components of your organization are "ready" to support or enable changes in the direction of the vision. As a start, some of the key organizational features to review are presented as a change readiness checklist in table 6.1.

As you consider the above organizational features, using checkmarks, rate each based on the following four criteria:

1 A current or potential source of **resistance** to introducing changes to realize your healthy organization vision.
2 A source of **inertia** created by the weight of tradition and/or indifference that will have to be overcome.
3 Ready to be tapped as an actual or potential **capacity** for healthy change.
4 Already generating **momentum** for healthy improvements in the work environment, the culture, or organizational systems.

For instance, if your EAP provider has recently included a range of workplace mental health resources on its website and provided on-site educational sessions for managers and employees on mental health, that would indicate increased capacity or momentum. So

Table 6.1 Change Readiness Checklist

| Organizational Feature | Check ✓ to indicate if the feature is a source of ... | | | |
|---|---|---|---|---|
| | Resistance | Inertia | Capacity | Momentum |
| Culture | | | | |
| Senior leadership | | | | |
| Line managers and supervisors | | | | |
| Mission and strategic plan | | | | |
| Your team or coworkers | | | | |
| Existing wellness and OHS programs | | | | |
| Employee assistance program (EAP) | | | | |
| CSR strategy | | | | |
| Support for ongoing learning and development | | | | |
| Quality improvement initiatives | | | | |
| HR, OHS, OD, CSR, and wellness professionals | | | | |
| Systems for communicating with employees and managers | | | | |
| Union leadership (if applicable) | | | | |
| Relationships with external health promotion, OHS, and other community partners | | | | |
| Anything else about the organization's current state you deem relevant | | | | |

check that box. In contrast, if the organization's executive team is fixated on quarterly results and has not supported health and wellness programs, that would be a checkmark for inertia.

Whatever your organization's readiness profile, the objective is to leverage the sources of capacity and momentum, find ways to reduce resistance, and break free of the inertia. And for those factors you assessed as either sources of resistance or inertia, think about what you and other change agents can do to move the factor to a state of readiness or momentum. Conducting this change readiness assessment should be an early step in planning a healthy workplace strategy. Tailor the change strategy to fit the picture that emerges.

## Removing Barriers to Change

Successfully implementing change requires putting in place enabling conditions to help make the organization change-ready, which include the capacity needed to undertake sustainable change. This requires you to identify and remove (or figure out how to work around) barriers. This is an important step toward closing "the knowing–doing gap."[17] A common barrier to change – doing what you know should be done to improve the organization – is inertia, marked by the deadweight of traditional practices and ways of thinking that have gone unchallenged. Lack of information about alternatives contributes to inertia. Remarkably, when larger organizations decide that employee development, engagement, recruitment, and retention are strategic priorities, and use employee survey results and HR data to measure progress, they often discover pockets of internal excellence. Sharing lessons from these areas of excellence – basically, high-performing and healthy parts of the organization – can help other units to overcome inertia and start making their own improvements. Thus, shared learning is a vital part of healthy change.

Heavy workloads and time scarcity also are major change barriers. In numerous discussions I have had with managers and employees, these barriers are invariably identified as holding them back from doing more to promote a healthy organization. As I told one organization struggling with a serious workload problem, you need to find the time to figure out how to escape the catch-22 imposed by overwork. Overworked employees won't embrace a new change initiative, even one aimed at improving their wellness or work environment. It will be dismissed as "just one more thing on my plate." For managers and supervisors, lack of time is reinforced by incentives that give priority to operational and business goals, not to using effective people practices that promote well-being. Managers can make more time for change in two ways. One is to tie healthy workplace goals (which could include employee engagement, learning and development, or community volunteer work) to existing operational plans for quality, service, or product improvement. Some industries call this "operational excellence," or, as I've illustrated, in healthcare it takes the form of Lean quality improvement. Another is to involve more employees in the process, which is an easy way to spread the change work around and mobilize more people.

This latter point reinforces our earlier discussion about how effective wellness strategies empower employees to improve their own working conditions. A broadly representative worksite wellness committee (WWC) can do this. WCCs play a critical role in the successful implementation of health promotion programs.[18] WWCs are able to respond to worksite needs at the local level, directly shaping how corporate wellness goals are achieved. And effective WCCs build the organization's change capabilities. Successful WWCs do five things:

1 Assess employee health risks and use these data to set priorities and targets.
2 Have the capacity to facilitate change in terms of an adequate budget, resources, skills, and authority.
3 Undertake systematic program planning.
4 Set the stage for implementation by providing required training, coaching, consultation, and communication.
5 Conduct ongoing monitoring and evaluation of the programs.

Resistance among frontline supervisors and middle managers can be the Achilles heel of organizational change. Historically, the greatest opposition to redesigned work systems came not from workers, but from supervisors who perceived a threat to their limited power base. Similar scenarios play out today if supervisors expect the change to impose on them greater responsibility, more accountability, and increased workload. Supervisors may also lack the skills needed to enable change, so managers at all levels need to be equipped to make constructive contributions. The best way for supervisors and managers to become enablers of healthy change is to directly involve them in improving drivers of health and performance for themselves and their team.

Another potential impediment to change is divergent perspectives within your organization's workforce on what's needed to make the workplace healthier and more productive. For example, a team of Australian researchers interviewed employees and senior managers in several workplaces in the state of Victoria with established workplace health promotion programs. The researchers asked about what organizational features contributed most to improving employee health and well-being.[19] Managers were more likely to see traditional occupational health and safety initiatives as the biggest contributors, whereas employees considered culture and the psychosocial work environment the key features of a health-promoting workplace. Such differences could be reconciled through frank and open discussions between frontline employees and managers. The result would be a common starting point for future healthy workplace initiatives.

## Participatory Work Redesign

I've emphasized the importance of having employees who will be directly affected by the change actively involved in its design and implementation. An interesting case of this participative approach to change is BMW's redesigned factory for workers age fifty and older.[20] A decade ago, BMW recognized that the average age of its production workers would increase to forty-seven by 2017. This demographic trend threatened the company's competitiveness. Its older workers were absent more and had to work harder just to keep up, yet their experience and skills were essential for quality and productivity. Project 2017, as it was called, recruited a team of age-fifty-plus production workers (supported by engineers and health professionals) to redesign all aspects of assembly line work with the goal of reducing physical strains and the chance of errors. In all, seventy worker-suggested changes were made. Most were simple and inexpensive, such as wood flooring, orthopedic footwear, magnifying lenses, adjustable work tables, large-handled tools, larger fonts on computer screens, rest breaks, and ergonomically optimal job rotation.

Follow-up projects have been launched in other BMW plants. An entire new BMW factory has been built based on Project 2017 ideas and employs only workers over age fifty. Beyond ergonomic design, the company's goal of retaining older workers has been achieved through its approach to training, employee health, knowledge sharing, and personalized retirement transitions. More generally, the BMW example represents an effective job redesign intervention in which workers modified their own job characteristics and work environment in order to improve their well-being and job performance. As a result, the company has the healthy and productive workforce it needs to achieve its future production and quality goals – a great example of human sustainability. The intervention has also strengthened a corporate culture that values employees' contributions and well-being, sending a message that workers of all ages surely appreciate.

By tapping into the research on job redesign, we can learn more about what's needed for change initiatives targeting the organizational level to succeed. My reason for shining a spotlight on job redesign is that it has the potential to get at some of the root causes of today's major physical and psychological health risks. In short, it is a method for engaging frontline workers in crafting viable solutions to what they perceive to be the biggest problems they face in their jobs and work environments, such as job stress and work–life imbalance. By definition, this is a healthy change process that follows the World Health Organization (WHO) definition of health promotion: directly involving those most affected in creating a healthier environment.

Let's consider a successful job redesign intervention at a call center.[21] This study deserves our attention because the changes to workers' jobs addressed two requirements of a psychologically healthy and safe workplace: giving workers more job control (more discretion over when and how to carry out tasks), and providing them with constructive feedback from supervisors on their job performance. Research shows that these two job characteristics impact employees' psychological well-being and their job performance as rated by their direct supervisor. And when these job characteristics are present, employees are more likely to believe that their employer has met what researchers call "psychological contract fulfillment," living up to its obligations to provide decent working conditions. The call center job redesign led to improvements in all three of these employee outcomes.

Here's how. The researchers used what's called quasi-experimental participative job redesign. They guided four of twelve call center teams (the other eight teams served as control groups) through a process of identifying problems, designing solutions, and implementing required changes in their daily work. The project began with call center agents and supervisors in the four experimental teams participating in a two-day assessment workshop, facilitated by the research team, where they worked in small groups to identify specific job tasks and the obstacles that prevented effective execution of these tasks. Teams rated different job redesign scenarios in terms of their impact on well-being and performance. In addition to assessing the current job design, teams developed three new redesign scenarios: one aimed at maximizing well-being; one that would maximize performance; and a third that optimized well-being and performance. Just as at BMW, and in my earlier examples of Lean improvements in hospitals, the teams were actively involved in crafting a better workplace.

After group discussions, the changes that would have a positive impact on both well-being and performance were adopted as potential job redesign initiatives. Discussions of specific changes helped employees to understand that not all aspects of their jobs would change. The workshop concluded with the teams agreeing to develop workable proposals for each initiative, which the researchers compiled into a report and presented at a joint meeting with employees and managers. As a result, the improvements introduced provided employees with more job control and feedback on their performance. When the four experimental teams were compared with the control teams, it was obvious that the participatory job redesign process benefited both employees and the company.

The practical takeaway from this job redesign study is that making successful changes to people's jobs and work environments requires a plan for meaningfully involving affected employees and supervisors throughout the process, as well as taking before and after measures of expected outcomes. While the BMW Project 2017 partnered production workers with the company's own engineers and health and safety experts, the call center change initiative was a partnership with a university. Depending on your goals and the local partners available, you also may be able to partner with university researchers who are able to design, implement, and measure the impact of changes at deeper organizational levels than a wellness program gets at. But this sort of partnership is not a prerequisite for success. Nor do you need a "quasi-experimental" methodology, although in the call center study it provided strong evidence that the redesign had the intended outcomes. Still, there

are numerous nonprofit health promotion agencies and professional bodies in the areas of OHS, HR, and workplace wellness and
health promotion that also can become helpful partners, depending on your focus.

## Improving Well-Being through Work Redesign

According to extensive research by Gallup, many workers in the
US desire more flexibility in their work schedules, including the
option to work from home. Gallup's survey results suggest that
access to flexible work arrangements is an important consideration
when employees quit a job or take a new one. As Gallup observes
in its 2017 *State of the American Workplace* report: "Employees are
pushing companies to break down the long-established structures
and policies that traditionally have influenced their workdays."[22]
American workers aren't alone in wanting flexibility. When the
2016 Sanofi Canada Healthcare Survey asked respondents to rank
in order of preference thirteen common workplace health promotion programs, the top-rated (41 percent would use it) was flexible
work arrangements.[23] This is an interesting finding, because it highlights how some HR policies are viewed by employees as health
promoting and contributing to improved work–life balance. How,
then, can you do as Gallup recommends, and break down deeply
rooted organizational structures and policies? Here are a couple of
examples that show how some companies have gone about redesigning work to be more flexible and family friendly, all the while
encouraging workers to "work smarter."

When an employer introduces more flexible work arrangements,
this opens the door for employees to become more innovative.
A good example of this is a New Zealand firm's six-week trial in
2018 of a workweek consisting of four eight-hour days. Perpetual
Guardian is a financial services company with 240 employs. The

company's founder and CEO, Andrew Barnes, came up with the idea of paying employees for five days a week but having them work only four – essentially a day off a week to focus on family and personal needs. As he said: "We want people to be the best they can be while they're in the office, but also at home. It's the natural solution."[24] The company partnered with a New Zealand university to measure the results of the four-day-week trial. While this was change initiated from the top of the company, its success required the active collaboration of all employees and a research partner.

Jarrod Haar, a human resource management professor at the Auckland University of Technology, used a wide range of before and after measures to assess the impact of the Perpetual Guardian trial.[25] And the benefits were striking. There was a big increase – 24 percentage points – in those saying they could successfully manage work–life balance. There also were significant increases in teams' psychological capital, which measured a team's strength based on resilience, optimism, hope, and confidence (as I outlined previously). Furthermore, teams felt empowered to find ways to work "smarter" – that is, more efficiently and effectively. As a result, productivity actually increased. Job satisfaction, engagement, and retention also improved. So did five key measures of well-being: life satisfaction, health satisfaction, leisure satisfaction, community involvement satisfaction, and job stress.

Supervisors confirmed that workers and teams had found ways to do their jobs just as well, or even better, in a four-day-week as they previously had done in five days. Simply put, workers were motivated to find ways to work smarter. Overall employee responses were positive. As Professor Haar concluded, "staff felt more energized and happy." And there was good news for Perpetual Guardian: "Everyone was more willing to help each other and everyone was very committed to being more productive."[26] Other benefits included reduced power bills for the company and, for the community, reduced traffic and pollution from commuting.

This comment from one of the employees in the study sums up the positive experience: "I can't stress how good the pilot program has made me personally feel about things. Yes, during the four other working days you're busier and more concentrated on your work but by taking a midweek day off I feel I come back in on the Thursday re-energized and refreshed for the last two days in the office, ready to get stuff done!"[27] After the trial, the company made the four-day week permanent for all full-time employees, taking a big step down its path to being a healthy organization.

Other organizations in New Zealand, Australia, and elsewhere are following suit. As the New Zealand Minister of Employment Relations commented, "I applaud this instance of working smarter and encourage more businesses to take it up," noting that too many workers in the country were putting in overly long workweeks.[28] The Perpetual Guardian trial echoes similar positive findings from the Swedish city of Gothenburg, where the municipality reduced the length of the workday to six hours, finding that employees got just as much work done. And a company in British Columbia, Canada, tested a new flexible work hours policy for a month before rolling it out. Digital marketing agency RingPartner Inc. moved from fixed work hours in a day to requiring employees to be in the office from 10 a.m. to 3 p.m., leaving it up to them to decide where and when they work for the rest of the day to put in a forty-hour week.[29] The main motivation for introducing the policy was talent attraction and retention.

A team of US sociologists, led by Professor Phyllis Moen, used a social determents of health perspective similar to the WHO's definition of health promotion, mentioned earlier, to help understand how a well-designed organization-level change initiative can improve workers' well-being.[30] The researchers examined the impact on information technology workers at a *Fortune* 500 company of organizational changes that provided these workers with more control over their work time and provided supervisors with the skills required to support employees' personal and family lives. The change initiative was called STAR (Support, Transform, Achieve, Results), developed by a US consortium of researchers and organizational development experts in the Work, Family and Health Network. The network's goal is to create an evidence-based organizational intervention that organizations can use to improve work–family balance and employees' health.

The study was guided by insights from stress process and job strain theories. In the former, stress is seen as a process resulting from a mismatch between a person and the demands their work environment places on them. The latter focuses on a worker's level of job control and their access to resources and support to meet the demands, or strains, of their job. Both theories emphasize the importance of increasing workers' resources and capacity on the job to improve their well-being.

The study design was a randomized field trial in which employees were randomly assigned to either an intervention (STAR) group or a control group. This powerful research methodology, rarely used to study the impact of workplace interventions, provided definitive results on the impact of the change. Measures of the intervention and key outcomes – job satisfaction, burnout, perceived stress, and psychological distress – were taken at baseline, six months, and twelve months. Control group teams had no changes made to their work. The STAR intervention had two goals: to increase employees' control over their work hours and schedules; and to increase employees' perceptions that their supervisor supported their personal or family life.

The study results confirm that designing work to give employees more control over their schedules and encouraging supervisors to support work–life balance can enhance workers' well-being on all four outcome measures. An unanticipated wrinkle during the course of the study was the company's announcement of its merger with another business. Fortunately, the researchers were able to account for the impact of the merger on study participants. Some of the study groups were not exposed to the shocks of the merger announcement, and these were the ones with the positive results. In contrast, other study groups who were exposed to the merger announcement experienced no benefits from the STAR intervention. In short, the potential benefits of work redesign can be canceled out if an organization is undergoing a merger, acquisition, downsizing, or other major structural changes.

This study highlights how organizational-level interventions can improve employee well-being and meet company goals. Workers in the experimental group were able to work wherever, and whenever, they chose as long as long as they delivered results by meeting goals on time. This not only provided them the kind of flexibility that Gallup surveys show many workers desire; it also encouraged them to find better ways of doing their jobs, just as in the Perpetual Guardian example. At the same time, managers received training on how to be more supportive of employees' personal issues. To help them become more supportive, managers were also encouraged to discuss their life outside of work with employees – a sure way to build trust. Compared with the control group that underwent no changes, employees in the intervention group not only were happier and healthier; they also slept better, experienced less work stress, and planned to remain with the company.

The research team summarizes the study's practical implications, sharply contrasting the difference between programs that focus only on individuals and deeper interventions, like STAR, that target organizational systems: "We provide clear evidence that specific conditions matter for well-being and can be changed. This necessitates more than 'helping' workers muddle through their stressful lives by teaching them individual coping strategies. Instead, this study demonstrates the value of an organizational initiative promoting greater flexibility and control for workers as well as greater supervisor support."[31] Because the organizational changes reduce workers' burnout, job stress, and psychological distress, employers can expect to benefit from a healthier workforce through higher productivity, lower rates of absenteeism and presenteeism, and better retention.

## Learning to Change

To make the organizational changes happen, the researchers and employees involved in the STAR project had to challenge and then shift strong cultural norms in the corporation. These norms assumed there was a clear dividing line between an individual's work time and the rest of their life, and also assumed that for workers to be productive they had to be present and visible at the office on a full-time basis. For norms like these to change, managers and employees had to learn about new possibilities. So they first had to become aware that there were potentially better ways to address their needs and the company's needs. This awareness is what sparks a new vision for the future.

While large employers have more resources than smaller ones to offer perks, health benefits, and wellness programs, I want to emphasize that the organizational changes aimed at making work more flexible, giving workers more control, and supporting work–life balance are not big-budget items. When it comes to healthy changes, small may be good. As Gallup's 2017 *State of the American Workplace* report observes about small US companies: "They are offering employees the flexibility, autonomy and development they want and establishing work environments that feel less like traditional, inflexible corporate cultures."[32] This is consistent with our discussion in chapter 3 of how the self-employed and employees in smaller organizations have more positive perceptions of workplace health and safety. That's because smaller organizations operate less formally, making it easier to cultivate supportive relationships and to meet employees' personal and professional needs.

In chapter 5, I mentioned research on breakthrough occupational health and safety change by Dr. Lynda Robson and her colleagues at the Institute for Work and Health. Her study also is relevant to the present discussion. Dr. Robson's team identified the enabling conditions that propel companies, small and large, to move from having a poor health and safety record to making significant, firm-level improvements in injury and illness prevention.[33] The initial motivation to change may have come externally, in the form of a Ministry of Labour order to fix unsafe practices or conditions, or an audit by the provincial workers' compensation board that identified deficiencies. But for the process of breakthrough change to be launched internally, someone in the firm has to act as a "knowledge transformation leader." This person could be in any position, as long as they are a trusted source of information on good health and safety performance and how to improve this. Other actors in the organization then use this new information – new for them, that is – to initiate improvements. The practical insight is that breakthrough change involves the dissemination of knowledge that helps workers to envision a better alternative. This in turn develops change capacity and mobilizes others into action.

Experts on learning organizations agree that people learn in workplaces through a process that extends over time, is collaborative, and is based on continual knowledge acquisition and dissemination. That's what the above examples illustrate. Learning also helps workers to avoid repeating mistakes and to reproduce successes. Management expert Michael Beer, using a health-related metaphor, argues that "the capacity to learn and change" is organizational fitness.[34] Especially important in this regard is learning from the results of ongoing and rigorous evaluations of change initiatives – a topic I return to in chapter 8. By reflecting on the experiences of implementing change, then refining and readjusting the action plan, it is possible to make change a process of continual organizational learning and improvement.

## Healthy Change as Organizational Renewal

This chapter has explored the expansive landscape of change through a healthy organization lens. My intent has been to provide practical ideas about how to embark on change in your workplace. I have emphasized that the change process itself must contribute to healthy workplace goals. In a word, it must be healthy. How people experience the journey is what moves you toward your vision of a more vibrant and inspiring workplace. That's why the change process itself must be a positive experience for all those involved, engaging them on a personal level and clearly heading toward a better tomorrow. If people experience change as stressful, imposed from the top, or inconsistent with the organization's people goals and values, then both the process and end results will be unhealthy.

Healthy organizations are built through gradual and cumulative changes over time. As a next move, consider how to use few resources to boost morale, well-being, and performance in your workplace. There can be big payoffs from small improvements. As management experts Felix Barber and Rainer Strack, writing in *Harvard Business Review*, observe: "Because employees represent both the major cost and the major driver of value creation, people-management moves that lead to even small changes in operational performance can have a major impact on returns."[35] The trick, of course, is to identify those small steps along your healthy organization journey. The suggestions in this chapter are intended to help you design an optimal way of doing just that.

Be aware, though, of a common trap. You will need to avoid getting stuck just thinking and talking about a vision of the ideal healthy workplace. Almost every organization has strengths to build on and opportunities to take bold steps forward. Building incrementally on these strengths and seizing present opportunities, however small to begin with, will start making the vision a reality. It will also develop change capacity in your workforce. As I will discuss in chapter 7, the pressures for workforce and workplace renewal, for strengthening community relationships, and for making wider social and economic contributions also offer promising opportunities to progress down your own healthy organization path.

## CHAPTER 7

# Sustainable Success

Advances in corporate social responsibility (CSR) over the past decade cast a bright light on what it means to be a healthy, sustainable organization. The Corporate Knights' annual Global 100 list of the most sustainable corporations in the world is based on how companies create value for society. As a Corporate Knights representative states: "On a hot, flat, hungry and crowded planet, there is a big market (estimated by the UN at $12 trillion by 2030) for businesses that create more value for society than they take away through negative externalities. This is fertile ground for a rising movement of corporate knights to roam in the quest for a sustainable world."[1] Since the first edition of this book, there are more "corporate knights" pursuing sustainable business practices. Organizations now have sustainability managers, CSR task forces, and human rights and environmental stewardship policies. Leading business schools now have courses or degree programs on corporate sustainability. As business scholars argue, there is now a "market for virtue" whereby corporate leaders, and their employees, I would add, are guided by values and ethics to self-regulate for the good of society and the environment.[2]

More large corporations are blending sustainability into their business strategy. For ten years until early 2019, Paul Polman was CEO of Unilever, the huge Anglo-Dutch multinational, which makes a wide variety of consumer products and has a market value of over $200 billion. Polman redefined the company's vision: its purpose was now to "make sustainable living commonplace." Polman dealt a blow to short-term capitalism by canceling quarterly earnings guidance for investors. He also banned the use of the term "corporate social responsibility," given how extensively Unilever had integrated a holistic, long-term approach to sustainability into its strategy and business operations.[3] Simply put, sustainability defined how the entire company operated.

Unilever is not alone in promoting social value instead of short-term gains for shareholders. Larry Fink, CEO of BlackRock, the world's biggest asset manager with more than $6 trillion invested, advocated for shareholders to support "purpose-driven companies" in his 2018 annual letter to them. Fink was reading the shifting public mood correctly: polls showed that two-thirds of Americans believe that companies have a responsibility to speak out on political and social issues.[4] The new bottom line is how companies can demonstrate their positive contribution to society, which enhances the financial bottom line. In the view of Fink and other big financial players, it actually enhances the long-term profitability of a company. Fink and other institutional investors are using their financial clout to nudge companies in this direction. Other big investment funds are doing the same – for example, by putting pressure on Apple to take into account the detrimental effects its products may have on children. And in the toxic cauldron of Trump-era US politics, other corporations have taken action to support LGBTQ rights, immigration reform, environmental protection, and other social issues.

"Corporate social responsibility" initially referred to companies taking responsibility for their impact on society and looking beyond just creating profits for the benefit of shareholders. More companies recognize that CSR, or what's increasingly called "sustainability," is good for business. It strengthens their unique brand, translates into higher revenues, and leads to customer satisfaction and positive relationships with stakeholders. While there is no consensus definition of CSR, it generally refers to voluntary actions taken by a company to include social and environmental concerns in how it operates and in its relationships with stakeholders.[5] CSR also reflects how a company ensures the sustainability of natural, social, and human resources. In the academic literature, the terms "CSR" and "corporate sustainability" are used interchangeably. A recent review of CSR reporting by *Fortune* 500 companies confirmed that "sustainability" is now the most commonly used term.[6]

My focus in this chapter is on the human sustainability of organizations, which emphasizes ethically responsible relationships with all internal and external stakeholders. A decade ago, CSR emphasized a company's relationships with external stakeholders. That left a large gap in our understanding of how CSR benefited, and in turn was influenced by, the firm's employees.[7] We have since learned more about what an employer's sustainability commitments mean for their employees. And it has become increasingly clear that for global corporations with extensive supply chains, sustainability commitments can improve the human rights, labor rights, and working conditions in this much larger workforce. As we will see, "doing good" for society can result in doing good for a company's employees and supply-chain workforce.

To summarize, here are the chapter's key sights for achieving sustainable success:

- Organizations become more sustainable by taking a holistic and long-term approach to success, balancing the needs and interests of all stakeholders.
- Healthy organizations have strong core values that guide the treatment of employees, communities, and the environment in enduring ways.
- Employees' perceptions of their employer's sustainability practices, and more fundamentally, the values and ethics that guide these practices influence their work engagement and performance.

- Social responsibility commitments open opportunities to embed social and environmental goals into business strategy, inspiring employees in the process.
- Healthy organizations integrate human resource strategies that promote employee health, safety, and overall well-being with their sustainability initiatives.

## Human Sustainability

Organizations that claim to be committed to sustainability goals must take better care of their employees. As Jeffrey Pfeffer argues, for this to happen the language of business must change: "Well-being and physical and mental health need to become much more focal in conversations and policies."[8] Sustainable companies will actively promote human sustainability by creating healthier and safer work environments.

Promoting a healthy and safety workplace reflects an organization's commitment to CSR by contributing to the well-being of employees, families, and communities. Workplace health experts define CSR as encompassing company-sponsored programs that improve the environment, the community, and workers' safety and health.[9] Earlier I described how US companies receiving the annual C. Everett Koop National Health Award achieved impressive cost-effective improvements in workers' health. These corporations view workplace health promotion as part of their broader social responsibility commitment. This comprehensive approach helps to explain why these award-winners financially outperformed their peers.

In short, human sustainability depends in large part on an organization's people practices. Basically, it comes down to how a company values and treats its employees, workers in its supply chains, and individuals living in the communities where it operates. Health promotion also can be viewed as a core dimension of CSR, both for the communities in which a firm operates and for its own employees.[10] This should be a natural connection for those firms that are strategically committed to worker health and safety. However, few studies examine how a firm's CSR activities contribute to health promotion, or more specifically the achievement of public policy goals in this area. A recent academic review of research on the links between human resource management (HRM) and CSR arrived at this conclusion: "Reducing harmful work conditions and 'toxic' work environments for workers in all the organizations forming a supply chain or ecosystem, as well as improving the living conditions of members of the local communities, in which these organizations operate, should constitute part of overall sustainable HRM."[11]

Effective CSR requires the active participation of middle managers and employees.[12] Managers, for their part, must be attuned to what employees have to say about the company's CSR practices, both positive and negative. Only engaged employees provide this sort of feedback. And for managers at any level, examples of unethical behavior will erode the employee trust that is so essential to sustain CSR initiatives. And there is untapped potential in the whole area of human resource management to encourage employees to adopt pro-environmental and other forms of sustainability behaviors – a topic that so far has not received much attention from academic researchers.[13] In the future, HR practices in a healthy organization will take into account external stakeholders, CSR will expand its focus internally to include the company's employees, and there will be greater collaboration between HR and CSR roles and professionals, each area benefiting from the expertise of the other.

Employees want to be involved in their employer's CSR initiatives. This opens up opportunities for expanding meaningful work to include social, environmental, and community benefits, and the pride and sense of fulfillment that can come when employees are part of those achievements. CSR also shifts the focus of employee engagement from the individual employee to the "we," or what the company's employees' can accomplish collectively for the benefit of external stakeholders.

As I've already noted in chapter 4, healthy cultures foster a community spirit in the workplace. CSR has the potential to expand that community to include supply-chain workers and contractors, customers, communities, NGOs, and other external stakeholders. This assumes, of course, that caring companies are motivated by positive values and ethics. Otherwise, as critics have pointed out, an emphasis on engagement can have a dark side, where companies impose cult-like values and behavioral expectations. This can happen through "corporate manipulation, invasions into employees' private lives, and the potential to create a 'total community' wherein loyalty to and actions supported by the corporation supersede other employee commitments and opportunities."[14] When companies look at the engagement scores obtained from their employee surveys, surely they will see potential for increasing engagement through genuine efforts to meaningfully involve employees in all aspects of their sustainability strategy and to reinforce positive corporate values.

Let's look at several more examples of how corporate CSR initiatives contribute to a positive employee value proposition, helping to foster strong values-based relationships with employees, customers, and other stakeholders.[15] IBM engaged its employees and retirees in its On Demand Community, which matched IBMers around the world to volunteer opportunities that would use their expertise for the good of the community. Salesforce.com, an IT company, developed a "1-1-1" model in which it donated 1 percent of its founding stock to help meet community needs, encouraged employees to donate 1 percent of their paid time to volunteer activities that fit the company's parameters for philanthropy, and gave 1 percent of revenues from customer subscriptions to nonprofits to improve their operating effectiveness. Consumer product giant Unilever involved employees in redesigning products to reduce trans fat, saturated fats, sugar, and salt. Its Sustainable Living plan committed the company to improving the health of one billion people by purchasing all of its agricultural raw materials from sustainable sources and reducing the environmental impact of all its products, all the while doubling the company's revenues. And Levi Strauss & Co. responded to a market downturn in the late 1990s by consulting widely with employees, managers, and stakeholders to identify the big challenges facing the apparel industry and its workers. The result was a corporate citizenship value proposition that committed the company to reflect the diversity of its communities, respect all workers in its supply chain, actively contribute to positive social change, and launch an HIV/AIDS initiative to help protect employees, workers, and customers. There are many similar examples showing how companies can tap into the creative ideas of their stakeholders to have positive social impacts.

## Accountability for Sustainability

Influential NGOs now track corporate performance on sustainability, environmental, and human rights goals. Catalysts for action on environmental goals came from the 2016 Paris Climate Accord, and on human rights and labor rights from the United Nations' 17 Sustainable Development Goals, adopted in 2015 and setting targets to be achieved by 2030.[16] Five of the goals can be met by ethical, fair, and sustainable corporate practices. These are poverty reduction, good health and well-being, gender equality, decent work and economic growth, and reduced inequality.

The *Academy of Management Journal*, a leading scholarly publication, devoted a special thematic issue in 2016 to CSR. The issue's editors noted that more than 8,000 companies from over 150 countries had signed on to the UN's Global Compact, which covers issues of human rights, labor standards, the environment, and anti-corruption. They went on to observe that discussions of CSR in the corporate world "have shifted from existential questions regarding organizational mission and shareholder value to the mechanisms and processes by which corporations conceptualize and enact their social obligations."[17] In sum, corporate sustainability has taken on both a strategic and a practical focus.

Now used by most of the world's largest corporations, the Sustainability Reporting Standards of the Global Reporting Initiative (GRI) are the gold standard for sustainability reporting.[18] The GRI standards have raised the transparency and accountability bar for corporate reporting on economic, environmental, and social sustainability practices, including the treatment of workers.[19] Reporting casts a wide net, covering all workers, including employees, contractors, other freelancers, agency workers, and volunteers. As the GRI standard for OHS states: "Workers, of any type, are to be included if the organization controls their work and/or workplace, because these forms of control position the organization to take action to eliminate *hazards* and minimize *risks*, to protect workers from harm."[20]

The GRI standards include relevant indicators for healthy organizations: employment practices and labor–management relations, occupational health and safety, training and education, diversity and equity, non-discrimination, child labor, indigenous peoples' rights, and customer health and safety. Full disclosure requires companies to describe management's approach to OHS. This includes the following information: details and metrics related to their OHS management system; the processes for identifying hazards, assessing risks, and investigating incidents; occupational health protection services provided; worker participation, consultation and communication on OHS issues (e.g., through joint OHS committees and other means); worker OHS training; voluntary health promotion programs and services; prevention and mitigation of OHS impacts that are linked to business relationships; workers covered by the OHS management system; work-related injuries and fatalities; and work-related physical and mental ill health.

Sustainability reporting continues to expand and evolve in positive ways.[21] Shareholders are pushing publicly traded companies to adopt sustainability practices, which can lead to improved financial performance.[22] Indeed, a corporation's economic, environmental, and social performance – as assessed and ranked by, for example, the Dow Jones Sustainability Indices (DJSI) – now play a significant role in investment decisions, with assets managed using these criteria rising to over $30 trillion US in Europe, Canada, the US, Japan, Australia, and New Zealand by 2018.[23] More executives and boards understand that long-term corporate success requires them to consider the social, environmental, and economic impacts of all management decisions.

Along with the DJSI, the Corporate Knights' annual Global 100 list is another high-profile independent ranking based on corporate sustainability performance.[24] The Global 100 list is based on research that pulls together key performance indicators in eighteen areas, ranging from clean technology, climate and carbon, leadership, and waste to health and lifestyle, and workplaces. This is the sort of information contained in annual corporate or sustainability reports, often using the GRI reporting standards. The indicators used to assess a company's people practices include lost-time injuries, fatalities, employee turnover, women's representation in the executive management team, women's representation on the board of directors, links the company makes between executive pay and sustainability targets, and pension fund status.

Considering the above sustainability reporting trends and resources, the pertinent question facing organizational leaders is not whether to adopt sustainability, but how to do it. Answering that question has led a growing number of organizations to forge closer connections between sustainability, HR, wellness, and health and safety. Still, we have much more to learn about how sustainability commitments and reporting influence a firm's internal people management practices and employees' attitudes and behaviors. The big issue for aspiring healthy organizations is understanding how their sustainability goals and practices impact and in turn are impacted by employees, who in CSR parlance are core stakeholders.

## Sustainability Trends

It took ninety seconds on April 24, 2013, for the Rana Plaza building in Dhaka, Bangladesh, to collapse. Five clothing factories located there were destroyed, killing over 111 workers and injuring more than 2,500 others. The horrific working conditions endured by workers in the fashion industry's global supply chain became a top news story for Western consumers. Because of actions taken by major clothing brands and retailers in response to the Rana Plaza disaster, fewer factories in Bangladesh are death traps today. Several global buyers voluntarily paid compensation to victims and their families after this catastrophe. The International Labour Organization coordinated a broader and more effective response, notably the provision of employment injury insurance for Bangladesh workers. About 250 companies signed the Accord on Fire and Building Safety in Bangladesh and the Alliance for Bangladesh Worker Safety. Yet dangerous working conditions still persist in Bangladesh garment factories. Since the Rana Plaza disaster, the country has experienced over 100 incidents caused by fire or building collapse, with more workers being injured or killed.[25]

### Corporate Responsibility for Human and Labor Rights

The Rana Plaza collapse is a glaring example of the complex challenges multinational companies face pursuing lofty social responsibility and human rights commitments within their global supply chains. Outstanding issues include forced labor, child labor, gender inequality, collective bargaining rights, and the protection of

whistle-blowers who report basic human and labor rights violations. Companies face competing pressures that often are difficult
to balance. According to one report, garment factory owners in
Bangladesh "complain that the brands want it both ways, pressuring factory owners to invest in safety upgrades, but still relentlessly
pushing for lower prices."[26] Most large corporations operating in
apparel, footwear, and other sectors at risk of labor abuses still fail
to meet basic UN human rights standards.[27]

Corporate Human Rights Benchmark, a UK-based NGO, annually assesses how large publicly traded companies perform on
human rights issues. While there are year-over-year improvements
in the overall benchmarks, progress is slow.[28] Few companies have
taken the steps necessary to ensure that workers in their global
operations are paid living wages – required to meet the UN's sustainable development goal of ending poverty. Fewer than one in ten
have made a public commitment to protect human rights defenders
in countries where they operate. And over half of companies in the
apparel sector included in the rankings fail to prevent child labor in
their supply chains.[29] There are, however, some leading lights from
which others can learn: Adidas is the top-scoring company on the
2018 list; Nike scored above average.

Chances are, either you or someone in your family wears Adidas
or Nike sports shoes and clothes. Both companies have come under
intense scrutiny for their human rights and sustainability practices.[30] And both companies are making progress supporting and
promoting human and labor rights throughout their extensive
supply chains. Adidas was the first sports company to adopt a policy of defending human rights. It also provided a mobile app for
hundreds of thousands of factory workers in Asia to report labor
rights violations. Among top fashion brands, Adidas ranked first
in the KnowTheChain partnership, indicating that it monitors and
addresses forced labor risks in its supply chain. Another UN sustainable development goal is to end modern slavery, which as shocking

as it may seem still persists in many developing countries where products consumed in North America and Europe are made.[31]

## Nike: Just Fix It

A close look at Nike shows how it adopted a sustainable business model. Nike is the world's biggest maker of athletic footwear and apparel, with over $34 billion annually in revenues. It is now widely recognized as a global leader in sustainability.[32] Nike uses the GRI Sustainability Reporting Standards, described above, in its annual Sustainable Business Report.[33] This report signals that Nike has come a long way since it faced allegations of poor working conditions in its supply-chain factories in the 1990s. The company well known for its "Just Do It" ads has taken a "just fix it" approach to meeting its social responsibility obligations.

CEO Mark Parker (who has been with the company over forty years) states that Nike is determined to "create a company culture where everyone has an opportunity to play an important role and be successful."[34] Nike measures progress in three areas: diversity and inclusiveness; equitable pay and benefits; and employee development and well-being. A priority for the company is to address supply-chain problems such as excessive work hours, use of child labor, the right to freedom of association and collective bargaining, and worker health and safety. It developed an Engagement and Wellbeing Survey for its supply-chain factories in Asia to address stress, compensation, safety, and management communication. For its employees, Nike's goals include retention, a positive workplace culture, healthy lifestyles, diversity, and engagement. Based on reviews from current and former employees, the career website Glassdoor ranked Nike as one of the best workplaces in America in 2018.[35] And *Forbes* magazine ranked Nike second on its 2018 list of the happiest companies to work for in the US.[36]

Nike's culture, leadership, and organizational design have contributed to its advances in sustainability. Its matrix structure and decentralized authority make it easy for sustainability staff to work directly with business units. For example, the sustainability office is on the same floor as the CEO in the Nike headquarters. About a decade ago, it changed the name of its CSR department to the Sustainable Business and Innovation Department to highlight the future-oriented, opportunity-seeking nature of its approach to sustainability – basically, how it wants to do business. Hannah Jones, until recently Nike's chief sustainability officer and vice president of its Innovation Accelerator, told *Fast Company* that it has had to rethink sustainability: "Sustainability was always framed as something that was counter to business success.... The reframe that happened is that we stopped seeing sustainability and labor rights as a risk and burden [and instead] as a source of innovation."[37]

Nike also publishes diversity statistics, holding itself accountable for the gender, racial, and ethnic composition of its workforce. In 2017, it reported that a majority of its US workforce was made up of ethnic and racial minorities and that its global workforce was 48 percent female. Diversity, inclusion, and equity go hand in hand, so Nike recently took action to rectify evidence of workplace misconduct and discrimination against women. In 2018, the company's female employees complained that Nike tolerated bad behavior by some managers and excluded women from its top jobs. In response to a company investigation of these allegations, about a dozen senior managers left. And after an internal pay review, about 10 percent of its 74,000 employees worldwide received a pay raise to achieve its goal of equal pay for men and women. Mark Parker issued an apology to employees for not seeing these problems and pledged to improve the company's management training and compensation systems to achieve pay equity and diversity.[38]

## Linking HR and Sustainability

Nike's sustainability story illustrates the need for a close alignment between an employer's HR policies and practices and its sustainability or CSR commitments. Helpful in this regard, human resource and organizational behavior researchers have been exploring the micro foundations of sustainability.[39] This means looking at a firm's sustainability strategy through the eyes of its employees. After all, a firm's commitments to its local communities and, more widely, to society depend in large part on the actions of its employees.

Employees' perceptions of their firm's sustainability practices, policies, and brand influence their volunteerism, which improves local communities. Multiple stakeholders – the NGO, the employees who volunteer, their employer, and groups within the community – benefit when employees are supported to volunteer on meaningful projects and when both employees and community organizations are able to develop their capabilities. Furthermore, employees' positive perceptions of their employer's sustainability record can encourage good organizational citizenship – voluntary, altruistic behaviors that help coworkers and improve the work environment.

A company's reputation as ethically, socially, and environmentally responsible also improves its ability to attract good talent.[40] And once hired, employees who consider their employer socially responsible are less likely to quit. They are also motivated to engage in organizational citizenship behavior, voluntarily making positive contributions to their workplace community.[41] Sustainability is important to employees, so employers should follow suit and market these activities to their own employees as much as they do to external stakeholders. Companies can even go a step further, involving employees in designing, implementing, and monitoring sustainability goals and initiatives. Doing so will strengthen trust between employees and the organization.

I concur with Jeffrey Pfeffer, who writes in his book *Dying for a Paycheck*, that a different kind of corporate leadership is needed if companies are to take employee well-being seriously.[42] Instead of adding wellness programs, companies need to make concerted efforts to consider the health and well-being impacts of business decisions that could result in layoffs, job insecurity, toxic cultures, or stress. And socially responsible companies will realize that by considering the human impact of their business decisions, they will benefit their bottom line and society by contributing to a better quality of life for workers, families, and communities.

As yet, little is known about how a company's social and environmental responsibility policies and practices influence voluntary pro-environmental behavior among employees. One of the few studies to shed light on this link emphasized the importance of how employees perceive their employer's CSR approach. Employees who perceive their employer as socially and environmentally responsible have stronger commitment to the organization. Interestingly, the study found that those employees who expressed personal empathy for the well-being of other individuals, including people outside the organization, were most likely to be positively influenced to engage in pro-environmental behaviors if they had a favorable view of their employer's sustainability approach. So employees' attitudes and personal attributes do influence sustainable behaviors in a company's workforce.

This is a new area of research with many important questions yet to be fully answered.[43] For example: How can employees' recruitment, appraisal, rewards, and training be aligned with a company's sustainability strategy? And how does an employer's approach to sustainability affect important HR outcomes such as employee absenteeism, turnover, innovation, creativity, and productivity? And an important question that's at the core of this book: How does a company's approach to sustainability impact its employees' well-being? The next section begins to explore this.

## Environmental Action and Employee Well-Being

The drive to reduce global warming by cutting greenhouse gas emissions has moved to the top of the public policy agenda in many countries. While some national governments are foot-dragging on Paris Climate Accord goals, other stakeholders are moving forward. In reaction to President Trump's withdrawal from the Paris Climate Accord, a number of leading US corporations formed a coalition with educational institutions and local governments, called We Are Still In, to achieve US commitments under the agreement. And as my examples of green buildings in chapter 1 revealed, commitment to environmental sustainability is a growing trend in the US and other countries, with good potential to mutually benefit employees and the environment.

In various countries, municipalities have been actively promoting what's called "active transportation," which basically encourages people to walk or bike to get to work and go about their daily business. These initiatives are being encouraged by employers. For example, a large hospital in Sydney, Australia, launched a successful plan developed by its sustainability task force. The goal was to promote active travel to and from work and reduce by 10 percent the proportion of staff driving to work.[44] Smart urban planning, the pursuit of environmental goals, and employee health promotion all converge in these active transportation initiatives. Desjardins, a Quebec-based financial services corporation with hundreds of branches and 45,000 employees, has included in its sustainability strategy numerous initiatives that make it easier for its employees to get to work using reduced-emission modes of transportation. These range from biking or walking, encouraged by the installation of lockers, showers, and bike lock-up facilities at its offices, to the use of car-sharing, carpooling, and public transit.[45]

And as evident from discussions I increasingly hear at health and safety conferences, many employers are finding ways to cut back on business travel by using Internet communication technology and other practices that minimize air and car travel. INGRAM Micro, a California-based information technology company operating in more than fifty-five countries, launched its global CSR initiative in

2016.[46] It is focusing on developing internal capabilities to take climate change action as well as contribute to the UN's 17 Sustainable Development Goals.[47] These goals set targets to be achieved by 2030 for eliminating poverty and hunger, reducing inequality, ensuring good health and well-being, promoting decent work and economic growth, achieving gender equality, ensuring access to affordable and clean energy, and taking climate action, to list just some. Achieving these goals will require more private sector partners, such as INGRAM. Part of the company's environmental stewardship policy is the reduction of business travel and encouraging alternate work schedules and the use of green and active forms of commuting, including telecommuting. Again, these environmental sustainability initiatives have the potential to enhance employee health and well-being.

## Community Connections

There are many potential links between workplaces and their immediate community, from the involvement of community partners in workplace health initiatives, to workplaces ensuring that workers are able to balance work with their family and community responsibilities, to organizations participating in community fitness or health promotion events. Prominent healthy workplace frameworks call for a much closer connection between healthy workplace and CSR goals, especially those targeting communities. As noted in chapter 2, the Total Worker Health framework for enhancing worker well-being encompasses work and non-work experiences that influence workers' health and quality of life.[48] One of the framework's five dimensions addresses factors external to the workplace in a worker's home, community, and society that can influence their well-being. Included here are a worker's life satisfaction (or happiness), financial health, social relationships, and community engagement. Implementing policies, programs, and other initiatives to promote worker well-being is best achieved through collaboration between employers, workers, and community partners.

Furthermore, the WHO's definition of a healthy workplace also links workplace health initiatives with community contributions. One of the hallmarks of a healthy and sustainable workplace, according to WHO, is workers and managers collaborating to find "ways of participating in the community to improve the health of workers, their families and other members of the community."[49] In Canada, this sort of partnership is illustrated by the joint efforts in the area of workplace mental health that I described in chapter 2. To recap, diverse organizations in the public, private, and NGO sectors continue to contribute to progress in this important area.

Corporations, too, are taking decisive action to encourage employees' community participation. Encouraging employee volunteering is a common form of community outreach. For example, Silicon Valley–based tech multinational Cisco Systems introduced in 2015 a volunteering policy, Time2Give, providing all employees five days of paid leave annually to volunteer at a charity or nonprofit organization of their choice.[50] The result was 424,000 employee volunteer hours in 2018. This reflects the company's commitment, developed with input from stakeholders, to have a positive impact on its employees, society, and the planet.[51] Fundamental to Cisco's "People Deal" (what its HR strategy is called) are attracting, retaining, and sharing great talent; fostering a culture of innovation, inclusion, and diversity; and supporting employees to have a positive impact on their communities. It is relevant to note that Cisco Systems was ranked fourteenth on the 2019 Corporate Knights Global 100 list, which I will return to shortly, based on an assessment of sustainability that includes workplace practices.

In the fall of 2018, Starbucks launched a six-month program to promote a culture of philanthropy among its US employees. In partnership with a nonprofit, Points of Light, it selected thirty-six employees in thirteen US cities to spend twenty hours of paid time doing work for a local charity for six months. According to Starbucks' vice president of global social impact and executive director of the Starbucks Foundation, the initiative is intended to inspire greater community involvement among employees and promote a positive work experience at Starbucks.[52]

One way to support both employees and their communities can be found in how some organizations address health promotion. Returning to an example I used in chapter 1, the World Bank Group (WBG) illustrates how a large multinational organization can take care of a diverse and global workforce. With offices in more than 130 locations around the world, the WBG takes an evidence-based approach to workplace health and safety. A survey of its staff revealed that one in three did not have a local primary healthcare provider, and 60 percent said they would participate in health promotion programs if they were available. In response, the WBG made healthcare services available to staff and their families through its global network of offices. It also took a more preventative approach, making it easier for staff to access on-site healthcare services, disease management programs, telemedicine, and wellness resources.

Often overlooked in discussions of corporate community involvement are people outside the organization who volunteer their time to public sector and nonprofit organizations. This important stakeholder group should be included in a comprehensive corporate sustainability strategy, as required by the GRI standard. In Canada, volunteers contribute more than 2 billion hours of work annually, making them one of the country's largest workforces. Volunteers face similar workplace hazards as paid workers, but do not benefit from the same health, safety, and well-being standards and policies and programs. Many nonprofit organizations rely heavily on volunteers to provide services.[53] More can be done to understand and reduce the health and safety risks to which these volunteers are exposed. This provides an opportunity for companies with strong health, safety, and wellness programs to help the nonprofit sector.

## Sustainability Is All about Values and Culture

Meaningful sustainability commitments reflect an organization's core values, which reflect its purpose. An outstanding example of this is the widely admired Mayo Clinic, a nonprofit organization. Len Berry and Kent Seltman describe the "social profit" created by the clinic because its patient care, education, and research create net benefits for society. As they explain, "Social profit involves investing financial and nonfinancial resources (such as knowledge) toward a better quality of life.... Social profit depends on a spirit of generosity."[54] Guided by the founding Mayo brothers' core philosophy that "the needs of the patient come first," in one year alone the clinic generated $7 billion in revenue, which benefited the larger community when the clinic invested more than $500 million in unpaid medical care to patients in need, medical research, and medical education.[55]

And as we saw in chapter 4, strong values define a healthy organization that inspires employees, so it is not a stretch to expect a company's environmental and social sustainability practices to filter down to employees. And looking at values from the bottom up, employees' social and environmental values also will influence and reinforce their employers' sustainability practices.[56] Employees in large corporations are increasingly holding these firms to account when their business practices contradict their environmental and social commitments. Amazon has taken steps to reduce its carbon footprint, such as relying on renewable energy at its data centers and cutting carbon emissions from its shipments. But employees reacted to lack of action and disclosure, plus the fact that Amazon was going to provide data services to major oil companies. The

Amazon Employees for Climate Justice is emblematic of a trend in large tech companies of employees calling their employees to account for practices deemed unfair, unethical, or destructive to the environment.[57] It is pressuring the company to transition more quickly and transparently to renewable energy. Digital technologies and social media are making it much easier for workers in a global workforce to network and take collective action on issues they care about, and to bring their concerns to the attention of employers.[58] Amazon and Microsoft employees have demanded their companies stop providing services to software company Palantir, which provides technology to the US Army and Immigration and Customs Enforcement (ICE). After last year's walkouts over Google's handling of sexual misconduct cases, employees signed a letter protesting Project Dragonfly, a new search engine that would comply with Chinese censorship. And employees at Salesforce, Microsoft, and Google have protested their companies' ties to US Customs and Border Protection, ICE, and the military.[59]

## When Sustainability Principles Guide Business Decisions

Adidas is a leader in corporate sustainability, having been on the Dow Jones Sustainability Indices for nineteen years in 2018 and ranked by the DJSI as the top company in the textiles, apparel, and luxury goods industry for its corporate economic, environmental, and social performance.[60] The UN has also recognized the company for its human rights practices and fair treatment of employees, and Toronto-based Corporate Knights ranked it as an industry leader on its 2018 Global 100 Most Sustainable Corporations in the World list.[61]

The company and its employees are on a relentless quest for sustainable athletic wear products. To this end, Adidas partnered with the nonprofit Parley for the Oceans to convert marine plastic waste into running shoes. It produced a limited edition sneaker, each with uppers made from the equivalent of eleven bottles of plastic ocean waste. Then it partnered with Parley to sponsor races in big cities around the world to raise money for Parley's oceans project, donating $1 for every kilometer run. Adidas now plans to make five million pairs of ocean plastic shoes. As Adidas executive Eric Liedtke explains: "Adidas teamed up with Parley to help spread awareness and transform ocean plastic pollution into high-performance sportswear, spinning the problem into a solution. The threat, into a thread."[62] And in 2019 it pledged to use only recycled plastic in all its products where feasible by 2024 and announced a 100 percent recyclable sneaker, called the Loop, with the aim of eventually eliminating all shoemaking waste. Developed by Futurecraft, an in-house Adidas think tank, this shoe is "made to be remade" and will be released in 2021.[63]

What better way to instill a sense of purpose and pride into a workforce than taking on challenges like ocean plastics or producing a totally recyclable running shoe? Even more powerful than these examples of weaving sustainability goals into its products is Adidas' overall sustainability strategy. In 2018, the company started combining detailed financial, environmental, and social reporting in its annual report (the information that the DJSI and the Corporate Knights use to compile their lists).[64] The 2018 annual report is the first to include the company's sustainability actions and metrics. The report describes how the company's unique culture drives its "Creating the New" strategy. The report clearly states that employees are the key to the company's success: "Their performance, well-being and knowledge have a significant impact on brand desire, consumer satisfaction and, ultimately, our financial performance."[65] The culture "cherishes creativity, collaboration and confidence," the three behaviors essential for achieving corporate goals.

## Detoxifying Work Environments

As the Adidas example shows, it's the actions guided by these values that count, starting at the top with the organization's executive team and board. However, corporate value statements can't be taken at face value. So when Rupert Murdoch explained to Fox News employees that he fired high-profile TV host Bill O'Reilly – accused of sexually harassing women over many years – because "we want to underscore our consistent commitment to fostering a work environment built on the values of trust and respect," this surely rang hollow.[66] Lacking at Fox, at the Weinstein Company and Miramax Films (companies operated by accused serial harasser Harvey Weinstein), and at Amnesty International and other organizations where abuse and harassment became a toxic norm were basic human values of civility and respect. When widely shared and acted upon, such values ensure that a workplace is psychologically safe and healthy – in other words, a sustainable environment.

Unfortunately, workplace violence and harassment are part of work-life for many women.[67] Analysis of results from Canada's General Social Survey on Victimization (a representative sample of 27,643 respondents) concluded that women were more than twice as likely as men to experience workplace violence. But according to a survey of Canadian CEOs conducted in 2017, only 5 percent see sexual harassment as a problem in their organization, believing that they had sexual harassment policies and a culture in place that prevented this – even though a third of these CEOs admitted they knew of specific cases of sexual harassment.[68] There are systemic barriers to preventing the mistreatment of women in the workplace, with women often being reluctant to complain of harassment to HR due to a lack of trust and fear of repercussions. In fact, some critics claim that HR departments are part of the reason for the perpetuation of sexual harassment, with HR more focused on protecting their employers from anti-harassment lawsuits.[69] This is despite the fact that surveys in Canada, Britain, and Japan document that around one in three women report having been sexually harassed at work.[70] Even companies, such as Google, that have worked to develop a reputation as a great workplace have not eradicated sexual harassment and discrimination against women.

Prevention of workplace violence, bullying, and sexual harassment has in the past decade also become a public policy goal in a growing number of jurisdictions. For example, in 2016 the province of Ontario expanded existing protections under the province's Human Rights Code by amending the Occupational Health and Safety Act to require employers to ensure a safe workplace free from sexual harassment by developing policies, complaints investigation procedures, and training aimed at prevention.[71] Governments and employers have complementary roles to play in addressing what is surely one of the most glaring examples today of corporate irresponsibility and unsustainable human resource practices.

## Shorter Work Hours

Work hours are another area where organizations can improve employee well-being and contribute to human sustainability. According to the Organisation for Economic Co-operation and Development (OECD), long work hours may impair personal health, create safety risks, and increase stress. One in eight employees in the OECD's thirty-four member countries works fifty hours or more per week.[72] The incidence of long weekly work hours ranges from a low of 0.5 percent of the workforce in the Netherlands and 1.1 percent in Sweden to 3.7 percent in Canada, 11.4 percent in the US, 12.7 percent in the UK, 21.8 percent in Japan, and 33.8 percent in Turkey. Vacation days also are important to consider. In 2017, Americans took 17.2 vacation days, less than in the period from 1978 to 2000. Project Time Off shows a slight improvement in the number of American workers taking their vacation entitlements since 2014. However, changing a long-hours work culture is progressing slowly, with just over half of workers still having unused vacation days in 2017.[73] In contrast, European Union legislation guarantees workers a minimum of twenty paid vacation days annually.

Analyzing the human costs of the trend over the past two decades of an "overwork premium" (the more you work, the more you earn and get ahead) in managerial and professional careers, notably business services such as law, finance, and consulting, the *New York Times* reported that America's obsession with long work hours has contributed to widening the gender pay gap, especially for university-educated professional women.[74] Many of these professional women step off the corporate treadmill when they have children, leaving their husbands to work punishing hours in order to maintain the family's comfortable living standard. Few American workplaces have family-friendly benefits, with only 38 percent offering paid parental leave to new parents.[75] Here, then, is another example of how organizations can merge employee well-being and sustainability goals.

## How Ethics Matter for Employees

We can find solid evidence of the organic link between corporate ethics and employees' experiences in Great Place to Work Canada's survey results. Recall that I used GPTW data from Trust Index surveys it conducted in 2017 and 2018 in my discussion of trust in chapter 4. Using the same GPTW surveys, I examined the data from two survey items that are relevant to the sustainability theme: "Management is honest and ethical in its business practices" and "I feel good about the ways we contribute to the community." GPTW uses the first of these as a measure of management credibility, and the second is a measure of employee pride in the company.

Generally speaking, honest and ethical business practices and community contributions are good indicators of an organization's sustainable relationships with external stakeholders. What we learn from the GPTW data is that high-scoring companies on the Trust Index receive exceptionally high ratings from employees on these two sustainability measures, clearly demonstrating what is achievable. Looking at the top 10 percent of companies surveyed by GPTW in 2017 and 2018 in Canada, between 99.4 percent and 100 percent of their employees – basically everyone – said they almost always or often feel this way about their employer. Among all other companies participating in the same GPTW surveys, between 84 percent and 89 percent of employees felt this way. Remember that this is a self-selected group of companies who have chosen to be evaluated for a ranking on the list of GPTW's Best Workplaces in Canada, so we can expect all of them to be well advanced toward a positive culture. To preserve confidentiality, I can't provide a list of the top ten companies, but I can report that they cover a range of industries, regions, and sizes – including some small- and medium-sized businesses.

The Rethinking Work surveys, which I have conducted in partnership with EKOS Research Associates, complement these insights from GPTW's Trust Index surveys. The 2012 and 2015 Rethinking Work surveys provide a representative view of the Canadian workforce. The typical worker feels that whoever makes decisions in their organization does not care about their interests. Corporate ethics, ideally, should ensure that an organization and its employees can be trusted by external stakeholders to consistently "do the right things." That is, these relationships will be honest, transparent, accountable, fair, and respectful of others' rights and interests – in a word, sustainable.

The 2015 Rethinking Work survey asked respondents: "To what extent do you trust the senior managers in your organization to take employees' interests into account when planning changes?" This survey item is a litmus test for ethical business practices, because it shows that senior managers and boards consider one of their core stakeholder groups – employees – an important consideration in decision-making. Just 25 percent of those answering the survey believed employers take employees' interests into account to a great extent. Far more (44 percent) said employers don't do this at all in their organization. There is little doubt that this perception negatively affects employees' feeling of work engagement and their overall well-being. Consider, for example, that three-quarters of employees who trust senior managers to take employees' interests into account are satisfied with their job, compared with one in seven (14 percent) who report that employers never do this.

The 2012 Rethinking Work survey further illuminates how employees view ethical practices by senior managers in their organization. This survey asked: "To what extent do you trust the senior managers in your organization to ... make ethical decisions?" Just under half reported that ethical decision-making happens to a great extent. Yet one in four see no signs at all of ethical decision-making, while just over a quarter see it happening to some extent. Clearly, in the eyes of Canadian employees there's room for improvement in ethical decision-making. I think we can accurately assume that employees' frame of reference for answering this question was any decision affecting internal or external stakeholders. And here's the big disconnect for employees, which likely generates cognitive dissonance: in the same survey, 88 percent said it was important for them to be able to trust senior management in the organization where they worked.

We should not be surprised that when employees fail to see ethical and considerate decisions being made by senior leaders, they revert to a self-preservation mode. That undermines their potential for organizational citizenship. This goes beyond employees being motivated to be team players and to proactively think of ways to help coworkers succeed in their jobs and personal lives. For example, organizational citizenship could be displayed by helping a colleague deal with a family medical emergency, sending a coworker relevant articles or websites for a new project, offering to pitch in and help others who are overloaded, or volunteering to organize work group social or recreational events. These are the small ways that individuals rise above their own immediate interests, putting others' needs first. For this to happen, it certainly helps for senior managers to demonstrate the same spirit of collective caring. When all of this happens, the organization surely will become more humanly sustainable.

## Closing the Well-Being Gaps

In a socially responsible organization, keeping stress in check is viewed as essential for workers' well-being, developing their capabilities, and generating sustainable success. But doing so requires closing existing gaps between what employees need and value in their work with what they actually have. Drawing again on results from the 2015 Rethinking Work survey, we can document just how far some employers will have to go to provide a healthy and safe psychosocial work environment.

The survey asked respondents what job characteristic they would consider to be most important if they were looking for a new job. The nine job characteristics respondents rated can be seen in figure 7.1. All of these characteristics contribute to a psychologically healthy and safe workplace, according to the Standard. After identifying the most important characteristic for a new job, respondents were asked to what extent they had that in their current job. Figure 7.1 reveals some wide gaps between what workers want and what they currently have in their jobs.

The biggest wants were for (1) a flexible schedule that allows good work–life balance, and (2) freedom to decide how to do your job as well as having a say in workplace decisions. Only 53 percent and 58 percent, respectively, reported having these characteristics to a great extent. Flexibility, autonomy, and input are critical job features than can reduce stress and improve work–life balance. Yet many workers who highly value – and therefore need – these features in their job lack them. Also relevant to our discussion is the fact that

**Figure 7.1** Most Important Job Characteristics, Ranked, Showing % of Those Who Have This Characteristic in Their Present Job

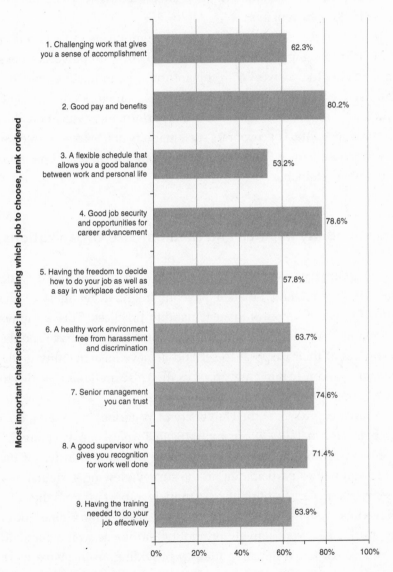

Percent who have the "Most Important" characteristic "To a Great Extent"

Most important characteristic in deciding which job to choose, rank ordered

1. Challenging work that gives you a sense of accomplishment — 62.3%
2. Good pay and benefits — 80.2%
3. A flexible schedule that allows you a good balance between work and personal life — 53.2%
4. Good job security and opportunities for career advancement — 78.6%
5. Having the freedom to decide how to do your job as well as a say in workplace decisions — 57.8%
6. A healthy work environment free from harassment and discrimination — 63.7%
7. Senior management you can trust — 74.6%
8. A good supervisor who gives you recognition for work well done — 71.4%
9. Having the training needed to do your job effectively — 63.9%

Source: *Rethinking Work*, EKOS Research Associates & Graham Lowe Group, Canadian workforce survey, December 2015. Base n=6,813

just over 60 percent of workers who place a high priority on having challenging work, a healthy work environment free from harassment and discrimination, and job-related training reported having these in their current job.

In sum, findings like these should give employers cause to reflect on what these gaps look like in their workforce. Employee surveys can provide the answer. With this information in hand, employers can make changes to improve the psychosocial work environment, and with it employees' well-being and performance. Viewed within the broader context of corporate sustainability or CSR commitments, closing these gaps will contribute to making the organization more humanly sustainable.

## Sustainability in Small and Medium-Size Organizations

Large companies such as Unilever, Nike, Adidas, the World Bank, Teck Resources, and others I have highlighted get most of the attention when it comes to sustainability practices. This is understandable, given the wide impact these companies can have and the resources at their disposal to set and achieve sustainability goals. Yet small and medium enterprises (SMEs) also are taking strides to make communities more sustainable.

A research project at the University of Waterloo, in Canada, documents sustainability efforts by SMEs in Toronto and Vancouver.[76] The study's findings are very promising, with eight in ten of the 1,695 companies participating in the survey viewing sustainability as important, very important, or extremely important. And they displayed clear signs of becoming healthy organizations: nine out of ten businesses were actively promoting employee well-being, and seven out of ten were committed to providing an inclusive work environment and doing community outreach. Just over four in ten had designated an employee or team to address sustainability issues.

The most common motivation for these actions was not cost savings, but an improved reputation in their community. And for many SME leaders, pursuing sustainability is consistent with their personal values – a point that must not be overlooked, as I've illustrated with earlier examples in this regard. While this is not a representative survey of SMEs, the results are nonetheless encouraging.

In some communities, SMEs are banding together to support each other's sustainability goals. The Better Way Alliance (BWA) is an initiative by small- and medium-sized employers in Toronto and other communities in Ontario to promote ethical, humanly sustainable business practices. The BWA's website has this tagline: "Investing in employee well-being for our bottom line and the health of Canada's economy."[77] The coalition supports a $15 an hour minimum wage, decent working conditions, and investing in employees. It provides testimonials from business owners and managers that there is no tradeoff between employee well-being and business success. Rather, for BWA members the two are positively connected. For example, the co-owner of HotBlack, an independent coffee shop in downtown Toronto, describes how he totally trusts his staff and provides decent pay and treatment.[78] A positive result of these business practices is a sense of community among employees and customers, both of whom want to keep coming back.

## Sustainable Progress

This chapter has examined healthy organization practices from the perspective of organizational sustainability. We have shown the close alignment between workers' well-being, corporate HR policies and practices, and organizational commitments to be a responsible corporate citizen and operate in ways that are sustainable. A healthy organization evolves organically, so it is in a constant state of renewal. But it does so with an eye on the distant horizon, not just on today's challenges. It also seeks innovative ways to balance the needs and aspirations of customers, shareholders, employees, workers in its supply chain, and community stakeholders.

One of the key points made in the chapter is that new directions in corporate sustainability have the potential to reposition businesses in ways that benefit all stakeholders, especially workers, their families, and their communities. This approach, in my view, is what a sustainable organization is all about. Another key point is that internal and external sustainability strategies need to be merged. A broad range of HR policies and practices – from health and safety, wellness, anti-discrimination and harassment, respect and civility, and more challenging and flexible job design – are central to business strategies that embrace the ethics of environmental and social responsibility.

We also documented how transparency and accountability for ethical and sustainable business practices have increased substantially over the past decade. As I've documented, many of the world's largest corporations now publish annual sustainability reports, making progress visible and verifiable. And there are more tools and resources to help do this, from the Corporate Knights Global 100 to the Global Reporting Initiative's Sustainability Reporting Standards, the Dow Jones Sustainability Indices, and the Corporate Human Rights Benchmark. Socially responsible companies use annual reporting systems, set targets, commit to improvement actions, and hold themselves publicly accountable for progress. And many of the organizations profiled in this chapter have undergone rigorous independent vetting in order to earn a place on one or more of the lists that recognize ethical, responsible, and sustainable business and people practices. In short, a purposeful use of relevant metrics can inform decisions and actions required to build sustainable organizations. This is the subject of chapter 8.

## CHAPTER 8

# Measuring Progress

In this chapter, I discuss the promise and pitfalls of measuring progress along your healthy organization trajectory. Throughout the book, I have drawn on various types of data – surveys, qualitative consultations, corporate information, independent rankings, and published research findings – to build a case for investing time and resources to make organizations healthier. Having the relevant metrics available contributes to good decisions, healthy change, and a positive culture. Now I will help readers to identify what they can do to improve the use of data relevant to their organization's improvement goals. To this end, the chapter addresses five questions:

1 How can you make better use of evidence to plan, implement, and monitor organizational improvements?
2 What measurement tools are available to you, and how can you adapt them to your needs?
3 What are successful practices for using surveys and corporate data as catalysts for healthy change?
4 What must you consider when integrating people metrics into a corporate performance reporting framework or sustainability report?
5 What are the basic guidelines you need to follow in order to measure workplace progress effectively?

It should now be clear how vitally important it is to measure and report results from any workplace HR, health, safety, or wellness initiative, as well as integrating these metrics into overall corporate reporting as part of your organization's commitment to sustainability and transparency. To get you into a measurement mind-set, let's revisit some relevant points from earlier chapters.

The terms "health," "wellness," and "well-being" are used interchangeably by practitioners. So the language you use has implications for your goals, and hence for any assessments you carry out and for your progress measures. Adopting a holistic and integrated approach to employee health, safety, and wellness – as I advocate – requires a range of progress measures addressing psychological, physical, and social health. If you're targeting job stress, which clearly is a huge concern in today's workplaces, you will need to assess its causes in people's jobs, work environments, and relationships with supervisors and coworkers. And as we've seen, there now is a wide range of assessment and measurement tools available to help you address psychological health and safety. From various examples I have provided, you can see how some organizations leverage their own HR, OHS, employee survey, and health benefits data to take the pulse of their workforce. Remember that any of these metrics should be broken down by employee group and work unit, to provide a finely grained picture of your workplace and workforce.

I would encourage you and your colleagues to consider any insights from the examples I provide that you can adopt to improve how you gather the evidence needed to design necessary changes, set improvement goals, and measure and report progress. To avoid getting overwhelmed by metrics – what I would label "metric madness" – look specifically for useful suggestions that can fine-tune what you are already doing and increase your chances of sustainable success in the next few years. Carefully planning what measures will be most meaningful also must determine how to make the fullest use of existing data, such as health benefit utilization, absenteeism, long-term disability, EAP utilization, and employee surveys.

Given the widespread use of employee surveys today, make sure that your survey goes beyond measuring engagement – typically the main focus of these surveys – to capture employees' overall work experience and quality of work-life. Consider my earlier discussion of how important it is to ask employees to assess the organization's health and safety climate. Furthermore, in a panel discussion at a conference on healthy outcomes, there was agreement that employee surveys should ask employees, "How are you doing?" For example, one large consulting firm asks employees on its survey how strongly they agree or disagree with the following statement: "This firm cares about my well-being." Answers to this particular question, or one like it, reveal a lot about the health of the organization.

## Connecting the Data Dots

Many organizations, especially smaller ones, are a long way from adapting the sustainability reporting frameworks that more and more large corporations use in their annual reports. However, you may not need a sophisticated corporate report card to paint a bigger picture of your organization's performance. Rather, look for easy ways to triangulate existing data – basically, connect the data dots. Triangulation looks for connections between three common data sources many organizations already have: administrative and HR data (e.g., health benefit and long-term disability utilization, absenteeism, turnover, lost-time injuries, training investments, etc.); employee input from surveys on work experiences, health risks and wellness needs, and program utilization; and performance data such as product or service quality and/or customer surveys (if relevant). The key to data triangulation is using a standardized reporting category for every type of data, such as department, functional unit, or worksite. Using a Microsoft Excel spreadsheet, you can present data from different sources side by side and look for patterns. When you look at these patterns, ask questions such as "Are units high in employee satisfaction also low in overtime utilization and absentee-ism as well as above average in customer satisfaction?"

An instructive case study is a large Canadian public sector organization that I advised on how to consolidate its health, well-ness, human resource, and engagement initiatives and measure progress with an integrated corporate scorecard. A new HR divi-sion manager wanted a solid business case for the value added of the organization's extensive wellness programs. HR also wanted to link wellness to other HR programs. After setting the stage for a common understanding of healthy workplaces in presenta-tions and discussions with the wellness and HR teams, consensus emerged about the need to be more proactive, focus more on the organizational benefits of wellness, and be able to easily commu-nicate this to business unit managers. Thus, the practical challenge was figuring how to make use of their existing data, which was plentiful but underutilized.

The organization had done a good job of measuring wellness activities, but not outcomes. Nor had it attempted to link wellness with other HR goals. The organization had lots of HR administra-tive data and results from an annual employee survey, but no cor-porate scorecard that pulled all these data points together to paint a complete picture of employee costs, productivity, health, and safety. As one of the HR managers aptly put it: "We have lots of data, but we focus on collection, not reflection." One of the first steps was to create a team that included the person in the benefits section who "owned" the data on absenteeism, disability, and health benefits, along with the staff person in HR who "owned" the employee engagement survey data. Occupational health and safety was in a separate area (labor relations), and while it regularly reported lost-time injuries and other relevant OHS measures, it was not at all proactive in looking at leading indicators of safety, such as safety culture. Breaking down these corporate silos was a prerequisite for maximizing the use of existing data.

The organization's three-year business plan for health and wellness (H&W) needed to include two kinds of metrics. The first kind assessed the evolving needs of the workforce for H&W services. The second kind of metric measured the impact of individual programs: to what extent were H&W goals being achieved by these programs and, at a corporate level, were there improvements in individual and organizational outcomes? The corporate employee survey (CES) and existing HR databases provided valuable sources of both kinds of information. A priority action was to more rigorously mine, integrate, and report this available information. Leaders also recognized that new initiatives – notably adopting a health risk assessment tool or the Standard – could be supported by available data. For example, the CES contained thirteen items identified in the Standard as measuring workplace factors relevant to psychological health and safety. The CES also included a composite index of employee satisfaction, a key outcome, which could be a proxy for psychological well-being.

Progress was not easy, but it did happen. On one hand, the project confronted engrained resistance among managers to reporting unit-level people indicators because of concerns it would reflect badly on them. Yet on the other hand, the same managers wanted to know if they were "doing the right thing." Through communication and discussion, the latter view won out because of the perceived value of an integrated reporting system that tracked health, safety, and wellness goals and the actions required to achieve these. As a start, project leads realized they needed to simplify how they communicated about these issues. They discovered that fourteen different terms were used in H&W documents, the corporate HR strategy, the corporate employee survey, and strategic planning documents:

- strengthen the workplace
- respectful workplace
- health and wellness framework

- supportive and healthy workplace
- healthy sustainable corporation
- healthy employees
- healthy workforce
- healthy organization
- healthy workplace
- individual and organizational health and wellness
- organizational health and wellness
- wellness action plan
- work culture that supports diversity, innovation, risk-taking, sustainable change
- maintaining a healthy and sufficient workforce

In order to avoid the inevitable confusion caused by this smorgasbord of terms, the project team agreed it was essential to simplify the language used to talk about goals and actions. Here is what it proposed:

> Our Health & Wellness resources, policies and programs support employees and leaders to attain optimal well-being. This happens at the personal level by individuals taking responsibility for healthy living. It also happens at the organizational level through coordinated actions that will create and maintain healthy, safe and engaging workplaces – actions that are a shared responsibility.
>
> Health means the absence of disease or illness, whereas wellness refers to a person's overall well-being in all dimensions of life, including emotional physical, environmental, social, intellectual, spiritual, and occupational. Optimal well-being means a higher quality of life overall.

The model in figure 8.1 was used to communicate how these concepts fit together and aligned with the organization's strategy.

The organization's leaders agreed to begin using an H&W performance report card, in addition to continuing to conduct

**Figure 8.1** Health and Wellness Alignment with Strategic Priorities

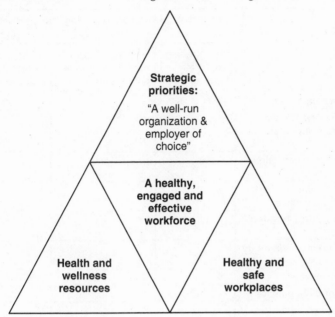

evaluations of programs in these areas (see table 8.1). The data
were integrated using a familiar tool – an Excel worksheet. The
Excel data could be reported at the corporate level or separately
for each business unit. Anyone comparing the unit-level Excel
worksheets would immediately see the relationship between these
data points. The left-hand column in table 8.1 lists all the relevant
metrics currently available from the organization's databases. The
next three columns describe the intended users, data reporting
levels, and frequency of reporting. The three measures from the
employee survey also included annual improvement targets at the
corporate and unit levels in the HR and leader reports. The Excel
graphing function was used to show trends over time. The health
and wellness team consulted widely with leaders to set and coordinate improvement targets for all the metrics below in its three-
year business plan. Over time, regular use of the report card was

Table 8.1 Health and Wellness Performance Report Card

| Metric | Report recipients, data reporting levels, reporting frequency | | |
| --- | --- | --- | --- |
| | HR – ongoing (corporate, business unit) | Leaders – Quarterly, Annual (corporate, business unit) | Public – Annual (corporate results only) |
| Lost-time injury rate | ✓ | ✓ | ✓ |
| Average days lost per workers' compensation claim | ✓ | ✓ | |
| Workers' compensation claim costs | ✓ | | |
| Average number of sick days per employee | ✓ | ✓ | ✓ |
| Total voluntary turnover rate | ✓ | ✓ | |
| Non-retirement voluntary turnover rate | ✓ | ✓ | ✓ |
| Retirement rate | ✓ | ✓ | ✓ |
| Long-term disability rate | ✓ | ✓ | |
| Long-term disability duration | ✓ | | |
| Training hours per employee | ✓ | | |
| % annual performance reviews completed | ✓ | | |
| Employee Satisfaction Index (from employee survey) | ✓ | ✓ | ✓ |
| % of employees with manageable work stress (from employee survey) | ✓ | ✓ | |
| % of employees with good work–life balance (from employee survey) | ✓ | | |

expected to create management accountability for implementing required changes.

To summarize, here are four general lessons from this case study. First, comprehensive reporting requires collaboration and cooperation among health, safety, HR, and wellness areas. Second, take stock of all relevant existing data sources and mine these before collecting any new data. Third, what may look and sound like a sophisticated report card may be easily accomplished using basic software such as Excel. And fourth, be sure to use clear, consistent, and simple language to communicate your goals and results. Doing so will help to get buy-in and active participation across the organization.

## Assessing Your Employees' Needs

Employees' health, safety, and wellness needs will vary considerably by the demographics of your workforce. Consider three examples, recognizing of course that there are other workforce characteristics that will define these needs. First, age matters. Older workers may be more resistant than younger ones to employer-sponsored health promotion initiatives. Yet helping employees to manage chronic conditions and conducting ergonomic assessments can address health issues more likely experienced by older workers, and which they may recognize as necessary to address. Second, work schedules also matter. If your organization operates 24/7, you will need to address the specific health needs of shift workers. This group is more prone to health risks such as an unhealthy diet, diabetes, physical inactivity, tobacco use, unbalanced blood glucose, hypertension, and overweight or obesity.[1] And third, gender also matters in many ways. As documented in the previous chapter, the incidence of harassment and discrimination is far higher for women than for men. On a different topic, men on average consume more alcohol and are less likely to seek help for risky drinking than women, which has led to initiatives to address risky alcohol consumption among workers in male-dominated worksites.[2]

Looking beyond demographics, emerging social trends can influence workplaces. For example, with the shifting landscape for cannabis use (now legal in Canada and a number of US states), it would be helpful to access publicly available data to understand which groups in your workforce are most likely to be users and to introduce appropriate education and policies, especially in safety- and security-sensitive industries.[3]

As you plan your organization's path forward, the initial step is to document your employees' health and wellness needs. This can be done in two complementary ways. One is to use a health risk assessment (HRA) or other method of health screening to identify high-risk individuals, then to tailor a program that will reduce those health risks. The 2016 Sanofi Canada Healthcare Survey illustrates the results of an employee HRA, as well as opportunities to make changes.[4] Among employees completing the HRA, 59 percent have at least one chronic condition, such as high blood pressure, high cholesterol, diabetes, or depression. Exercising and managing stress are the two biggest challenges the employees surveyed face in trying to stay healthy, so these would be areas in which to provide health promotion resources.

The other way is to consult with employees using a survey, focus groups, town-hall meetings, or other methods that have worked previously in your organization. Ask for their input on the sorts of health and wellness resources they consider most needed and are most likely to use. To illustrate this latter approach to assessment, consider common workplace health promotion programs examined in the national 2016 Sanofi Canada Healthcare Survey (see box 8.1). These are rank-ordered by the percentage of employees surveyed who said they would take advantage of each.[5] Top-rated (41 percent would use it) are flexible work arrangements, which underscores how some employers' HR policies are viewed by employees as health promoting. Approximately one in three respondents would make use of programs 2 through 5, and between 27 percent and 15 percent would use the remaining programs listed in box 8.1.

---

**Box 8.1 Thirteen Common Workplace Wellness Programs Ranked by Employees' Interest in Using Each**

1　Flexible work arrangements
2　Healthy foods and snacks
3　Discount for gym membership/fitness classes outside of work
4　Flu shots at work
5　Fitness center/gym at work
6　Vaccinations at work (other than flu shots)
7　Health/fitness classes or clubs during work hours
8　Access to a healthcare professional to learn about personal health and risks
9　Group programs at work (e.g., weight loss, smoking cessation, etc.)
10　Health-related challenges or goals at work
11　Access to healthcare professional coaching sessions
12　Health/wellness fairs
13　Availability of mobile health tools/personal fitness devices

Source: Sanofi Canada. (2016). *The Sanofi Canada Healthcare Survey: Canada's premier survey on health benefit plans.* https://www.sanofi.ca/-/media/Project/One-Sanofi-Web/Websites/North-America/Sanofi-CA/Home/en/About-us/The-Sanofi-Canada-Healthcare-Survey/The-Sanofi-Canada-Healthcare-Survey-2016---Full-Report.pdf

---

Don't assume that all employees are aware of existing wellness programs and resources and can easily access them. So before you consider launching a new program, it's important to communicate what is available and how employees can access these resources.

Then you can evaluate the effectiveness of these communications in terms of increasing awareness and access.

American Express (Amex) provides a telling example of an evidence-based approach to addressing employees' health needs.[6] The company launched its corporate wellness initiative, Healthy Living, in 2009, first in the US at its four major service centers, then at six other major locations around the world. The company hired a physician, Dr. Wayne Burton, to improve the health and performance of service center employees. The company had used internal data to confirm that improving employees' well-being would result in higher performance. US employees were offered an HRA and a work limitations questionnaire that measures presenteeism (both done annually), free on-site biometric screening, preventative screening, and support programs such as coaching and nutritional counseling. Amex partnered with the University of Michigan to create an integrated data warehouse that could identify needs and gaps, enabling it to tailor programs to specific groups. Employees received incentives to complete the HRA and participate in a walking program. Mental health turned out to be a critical factor in call center performance and employee well-being. Data synthesis was global, so differences across employee groups and locations could be identified and used to fine-tune programs. For example, while financial incentives helped boost HRA completion rates in the US, few incentives were needed to encourage participation among the company's India employees. In Mexico, the HRA found a high incidence of gastrointestinal problems in the workforce, so the company provided on-site fresh food and education on food safety, such as proper food refrigeration and storage. In the US, there was more emphasis on disease management through voluntary chronic disease intervention programs for workers with diabetes, migraines, or asthma. In other words, the program was designed to be culturally relevant, tailored to local needs. Within a few years, Amex's program had generated annual estimated productivity savings of $438 per participating employee in the US.

## How Leading Organizations Achieve Health and Wellness Goals

Readers may want to know what leading organizations do to achieve and maintain high standards for employee health promotion. The Employee Health and Well-Being Best Practices Scorecard, created by the Health Enhancement Research Organization (HERO), has US and international versions, available online, that can help organizations adopt workplace health and well-being best practices and to measure improvements over time.[7] The HERO scorecard is a good predictor of employers' healthcare costs, with those scoring high on the scorecard experiencing reductions in healthcare costs over a three-year period.[8] Let's now look at specific practices that are known to contribute to health and wellness goals. Here we can draw practical insights from the HERO Employee Health Management Best Practices Scorecard, which documents workplace health promotion best practices in forty-eight companies.[9]

This scorecard provides an inventory of successful workplace health promotion practices, organized into six domains: strategic planning; organizational and cultural support; programs delivered; program integration; participation strategies; and measurement/evaluation strategies. These domains, and corresponding practices, are summarized in table 8.2 below. As you review the scorecard, think about how (if at all) you would have to adapt some of the employee health management practices to workplaces not located in the US.

Consider adapting this scorecard of the most common employee health promotion practices by leading companies as a benchmark for what you can aspire to achieve. The scorecard emphasizes

Table 8.2 Prevalence of Most Common Workplace Health Promotion Practices in High-Scoring HERO Scorecard Publicly Traded US Companies

| HERO Domain | Practice | Percent reporting practice |
|---|---|---|
| Strategic Planning Practices | Conducted assessment of employee health needs within the past two years | 98% |
| | Uses a population-based approach to employee health management (EHM) to address health needs of all employees | 84% |
| Leadership Engagement & Culture | Safe work environment provided including ergonomics | 96% |
| | Well-lit and accessible stairwells | 93% |
| | Senior leadership allocates adequate budget and resources for EHM programs | 91% |
| | Physical work environment has fitness centers, walking or biking trails | 87% |
| | Healthy food options provided in cafeterias, vending machines, at catered events | 87% |
| | Lactation rooms | 87% |
| | Allow participation in EHM activities during work time | 84% |
| | Senior leaders actively participate in EHM programs | 78% |
| | Senior leadership involvement in employee communications about EHM programs | 78% |
| | Recognition and rewards for healthy behavior | 78% |
| | Flex-time or work-at-home policies | 73% |
| | Managers and supervisors encourage employee participation in EHM programs | 69% |
| Program Management Practices | EHM programs are coordinated with one or more other organizational programs (EAP, OHS, disability, absence management, etc.) | 100% |
| | Communications refers individuals to other programs as appropriate | 93% |
| | Claims data from multiple plans and sources are evaluated together to identify priorities and analyze results | 73% |
| | EHM vendors are required to share data to allow integrated reporting, predictive modeling or outreach to employees | 64% |
| EHM Programs | Health assessment | 100% |
| | Targeted, interactive lifestyle management/behavior modification programs | 100% |
| | Programs to assist employees in managing chronic diseases or conditions | 100% |
| | On-site or near-site preventative health screening | 91% |
| | Population-based health education | 91% |

(Continued)

| HERO Domain | Practice | Percent reporting practice |
|---|---|---|
| Engagement Methods | Organization educates employees about health care consumerism | 100% |
| | Some type of incentive offered for participation in health assessment | 98% |
| Measurement and Evaluation Practices | Some type of program evaluation data are collected to inform EHM program improvements | 100% |
| | Program participation data reviewed to inform EHM program improvements | 98% |
| | EHM program performance data are communicated to senior management or other key stakeholders at least annually | 89% |
| | Health care utilization and cost data analyzed to identify costly conditions and evaluate EHM impact on outcomes | 89% |
| | Population health/risk data reviewed to inform EHM program improvements | 80% |
| | Participant satisfaction data reviewed to inform EHM program improvements | 78% |
| | Process evaluation data reviewed to inform EHM program improvements | 64% |

Source: Grossmeier, J.P., Fabius, R.D., Flynn, J.P.M., Noeldner, S.P.P., Fabius, D.D., Goetzel, R.Z.P., et al. (2016). Linking workplace health promotion best practices and organizational financial performance: Tracking market performance of companies with highest scores on the HERO scorecard. *Journal of Occupational and Environmental Medicine, 58,* 20–21.

the importance of rigorous program evaluation and performance reporting as an enabler of successful healthy workplace initiatives.

## Evaluating Your Change Initiatives

While it's true that most workplace health and wellness interventions in Canada are not adequately evaluated, incorporating an evaluation framework into your plans is relatively easy. There are two kinds of evaluations. Process evaluation assesses a program's implementation, operations, and service delivery. And outcome evaluation assesses its impact on employee health status and behavior, cost-effectiveness, and other organizational benefits such as improved morale or engagement. Before you determine if a workplace health promotion intervention has had the intended effect for workers, it's useful to establish if it was properly designed and implemented. That's what process evaluation does, so it is a starting point.

While it's important to incorporate a solid evaluation framework into any change initiative, keep a practical focus and collect only the information you need to track progress, learn, and improve. In short, collect only what you can meaningfully use to guide follow-up actions. Scholarly research sets a very high benchmark in this regard, one that can provide you with useful insights about evaluation design, but that probably is not practical to emulate.

The gold-standard research design for healthy workplace interventions is the randomized control trial (RCT). While you likely may never use this design, it nonetheless is useful to understand its advantages. I briefly mentioned RCTs in chapter 6 when presenting the STAR intervention at an IT company to improve work–family balance and employees' health. An RCT design eliminates the confounding effects of what researchers call selection bias, where pre-existing differences in the groups being studied – not their participation in a wellness program – explain study results.[10] Observational studies, which are most common in workplace wellness evaluations, can't rectify this problem. For example, if your company installs an on-site fitness center, it may attract the fittest employees because they want a more convenient location for their regular workouts. Any comparison of the overall health between gym users and non-users will be skewed by users' already above-average level of fitness and exercise.

To more fully understand the advantages of an RCT, consider results from the Illinois Workplace Wellness Study, a large RCT of 5,000 employees at the University of Illinois. The Illinois study found no differences after one year between the group receiving no wellness services and those who did. However, when the researchers analyzed the data as if the study were an observational study, they (incorrectly) found improvements in the group receiving wellness services. This is a cautionary note about the limited conclusions that can be drawn from observational studies.

RCTs are pretty much a prerequisite if you want to publish the results of your evaluation in a top-tier, peer-reviewed academic journal. But that's not a relevant goal for practitioners. From a more practical perspective, Dee Edington and Jennifer Pitts, two experts in healthy workplace measurement, advocate measuring and communicating what matters.[11] They propose "realistic evaluation," citing the WHO's conclusions that RCTs are not appropriate, can be misleading if the statistics are not properly interpreted, and are overly expensive. As they state: "During thirty-four years at the University of Michigan Health Management Research Center we never designed a randomized controlled trial because we believe the requirements and assumptions needed to conduct a research trial could not be fulfilled in a worksite environment."[12]

I agree with Edington and Pitts that defining what matters requires input from employees. This underscores the importance of combining measurement with communication: collecting and distributing relevant information about progress toward the organization's goals. Focusing broadly on measures that matter for stakeholders shifts the focus away from return on investment (ROI), which tells us only whether a wellness program saves a company money. The more important question to ask is: "Do wellness programs provide value to employers and employees?"[13] Edington and Pitts note that employers usually don't evaluate the ROI from other employee programs and benefits, so why wellness? Edington and Pitts encourage employers to expand their measurement focus to what they call the "value of caring." This is based on the recognition that non-monetary compensation and people-friendly workplaces are part of a caring organization, which employees want and surely will benefit from.

## Do You Need to Calculate Return on Investment?

I caution employers not to get sidetracked trying to calculate the return on investment for specific programs. There is an abundance of evidence showing the business benefits of comprehensive workplace health promotion, which I have summarized throughout this book. More useful for employers are guidelines for how they can use their own metrics to track progress toward their own healthy workplace goals and show the overall value of their interventions – a topic I discuss below. US employers are more likely than those in Canada and other countries to calculate ROI from wellness programs because of the costly private healthcare benefits many provide to their employees and employees' families. Typical wellness programs show an average return of $3.27 for every dollar invested, mostly from reduced absenteeism savings.[14] These ROI calculations are based on comparisons between workers who participated in wellness programs with their peers who did not. Because most programs target common health risk factors, they show an ROI based on reduced obesity and smoking, two leading causes of preventable death. However, this ROI calculation leaves out other health and wellness drivers and outcomes, especially in the area of workplace mental health.

The Conference Board of Canada has estimated that fewer than 1 percent of Canadian employers rigorously evaluate financial returns from workplace wellness investments.[15] And only one in three Canadian employers measure the impacts and outcomes of workplace health promotion initiatives, which usually is enough to convince senior leaders of a program's utility. Nonetheless, several Canadian examples mirror the more extensively documented ROI in the US. BC Hydro (a large public utility in the province of British Columbia) established a return-to-work program that provided an ROI of $2 to $4 for every dollar invested.[16] CIBC, a large bank, introduced a backup childcare center for its employees. This initiative helped alleviate the stress associated with childcare worries and at the same time reduced absenteeism by 2,500 days during the first year of operation. The result was a productivity saving of $1.5 million.[17] We can speculate that this initiative also signaled to CIBC employees that the bank acknowledged their family responsibilities and wanted to provide support where appropriate – a result that would not be captured in an ROI study but could contribute to more positive results on an employee satisfaction or engagement survey.

There are many challenges to calculating a health and wellness program's ROI, not the least of which is that most positive ROI results show up after a program has been operating at least three years.[18] Before you go down this path, consider the advice of one group of experts: "Conducting a rigorous and credible ROI analysis is time-consuming, expensive, and requires a high level of expertise in statistical analysis, health services research, econometrics, and benefit plan design."[19] All of which is fine if you are able to partner with experienced researchers from a university or an independent research institute. But this is not an option for the vast majority of employers. That's why leading employers look beyond ROI to the full value of improving the overall health of their workforce.

## Measuring the Value of Investment

Rigorously evaluating a health and wellness program's process, impact, and outcomes is considered by experts to be an essential component of the program, yet only about a third of employers in the US do so.[20] This would require you to measure whether the program is operating as planned (process) and achieving its goals (impact), and to document the downstream effects of achieving program goals (outcomes). From this broader perspective, ROI's focus on the financials of health risk reduction fails to consider that many wellness initiatives are preventative in focus. Two experts, Ronald Burke and Astrid Richardsen, remind us that when it comes to evaluation methods and metrics, "the question is whether you want to achieve just ROI or whether the health improvement would be a valuable investment in and of itself."[21]

Burke and Richardsen are critical of "an inordinate focus on ROI based solely on healthcare cost containment," so they propose a much broader value proposition that covers the non-financial benefits of worksite wellness and health promotion programs.[22] Relevant measures of this "value of investment" (VOI) include job satisfaction, productivity, morale, recruitment and retention, and corporate reputation. VOI covers both the tangible and intangible benefits of a wellness program, with more emphasis on cost-effectiveness than on calculating healthcare dollars saved for every dollar invested in the program. As Burke and Richardsen advise: "The focus of wellness program evaluation should be less about how high health risks drive higher long-term healthcare costs and more about how engagement in wellness relates to higher levels of morale, team cohesion, job satisfaction and improved business results."[23] VOI can also show how wellness is critical for sustainable organizational success. Furthermore, given that employers are increasingly expanding their focus to improving employee well-being – encompassing life satisfaction, engagement, positive workplace relationships, and the meaning and sense of accomplishment derived from work – clearly needed is a much broader set of metrics than traditionally used in "business case" ROI studies.

Here are several Canadian examples of VOI, which includes improved health status for participants. A Canadian a wellness initiative that targeted high-risk employees was Tune Up Your Heart

(TUYH), a cardiovascular wellness program at Chrysler Canada's plant in Windsor, Ontario.[24] TUYH was a partnership between the company, the union, the local public health unit, healthcare professionals, researchers, and health benefits providers. It was open to employees, their family members, and retirees. The 343 employees who volunteered for TUYH received an initial cardiovascular risk assessment, followed by education and awareness-building. They then set goals for weight loss, smoking cessation, nutrition, and physical activity. Over eighteen months, TUYH participants experienced an average risk reduction of 12.7 percent, resulting in lower prescription drug costs.

An evaluation of a comprehensive wellness program, Healthy LifeWorks, in a Canadian government department found a positive relationship between risk reduction among program participants across eleven health risk categories, their absenteeism rates, and drug costs.[25] An evaluation of a three-year health promotion program using educational modules at a financial services company, called Take Care of Your Health!, documented a decline in absenteeism and turnover and improved overall health status among participants.[26] The three-year time frame and the fact that the program was tied to a wider organizational renewal initiative help explain the positive results.

The Sun Life–Ivey Canadian Wellness ROI Study found that wellness programs can improve worker health and reduce absenteeism.[27] The study focused on the relationship between cardiovascular disease (CVD) risk awareness and health behaviors. Wellness programs that are able to raise an employee's awareness of their health risks could lead them to adopt preventative health behaviors, particularly physical activity. However, these positive findings don't necessarily translate into measureable financial returns, given the study's short time frame (two years) and small sample size. The unique contribution of the Sun Life–Ivey study is its focus on the relationship between employees' CVD risk awareness and their health behaviors. Wellness programs that are able to raise an individual's awareness of their health risks could lead to preventative health behaviors being adopted.

## Understanding the Full Value of Improved Well-Being

Some corporate decision-makers don't need to be convinced of the benefits of healthy workplaces. If your organization prides itself in having strong people-oriented values, this alone can be a powerful catalyst for setting and meeting healthy workplace goals. Other employers may be influenced by their competitors' health promotion strategies, or especially by the perceived need to have wellness programs in order to attract and retain staff in a competitive labor market and to be widely known as an "employer of choice." In short, this means expanding our discussion of metrics to include less-tangible benefits and what can be called "return on values." This is when corporate support and resources for employee health promotion are clear signs that the company genuinely values and promotes the well-being of its employees, their families, and their local communities.

As I've noted, most of the published evaluations of comprehensive workplace health promotion programs have been conducted in the US, and to a much lesser extent in Europe, Australia, and Canada. A review of trends in the corporate wellness industry in the US found that wellness companies are revising their business model to emphasize value on investment, instead of the narrower cost-focused return on investment, and promoting a culture of health.[28] Increasingly, the benefits of health and wellness initiatives are being tracked using more organizationally focused metrics such as employee satisfaction, engagement, turnover, and retention. The vice president and health science officer of a health benefit plan commented about these broadening employer expectations: "It is about caring for their people and making sure they are an employer of choice and making sure they have low turnover rates and have high retention of quality personnel. It is way beyond ROI."[29]

Consistent with this trend, there's also an expanding focus on outcomes including employee well-being. For example, a two-year study directly linked the health and well-being of 11,700 employees at a *Fortune* 100 company to improved future retention, productivity, and healthcare costs.[30] This study used a rigorous, scientifically validated measure of well-being based on the Gallup-Healthways Well-Being Index. Six dimensions of well-being were measured: life evaluation (the appraisal of one's present and future life situation); emotional health (daily positive and negative emotions); physical health (chronic and acute conditions and symptoms); healthy behavior (diet, exercise, and smoking habits); work environment (satisfaction with a range workplace factors); and basic access (ability to obtain the resources needed to be safe and healthy). Overall well-being was calculated as the average of these six dimensions on a scale from 0 to 100. Measured this way, it became clear that higher levels of well-being benefited both individual employees and their employer.

This is the direction advocated by the Total Worker Health (TWH) program, discussed earlier. TWH "is designed to support policies, programs, and practices that integrate protection from work-related safety and health hazards with promotion of injury and illness prevention efforts to advance worker well-being."[31] The framework defines worker well-being as an integrative concept encompassing an individual's quality of life as influenced by their health- and the work-related environmental, organizational, and psychosocial factors to which they are exposed. TWH assesses well-being using five dimensions: workplace physical environment and safety climate; workplace policies and culture; mental and physical health status; evaluation and experiences related to the individual's quality of work-life; and external factors at home, in the community, and society that may influence a worker's well-being.

A growing trend is mining employee health claims data to provide a disease and health risk profile of the workforce. This is a useful first step in assessing employees' needs for tailored health promotion interventions. It involves identifying the main sources, or drivers, of healthcare costs. This can be done in partnership with the employer's health and disability insurance providers. The financial savings accruing from an intervention can be more easily determined than in an ROI analysis. For example, when BP America Inc. analyzed its healthcare claims, it discovered that 6 percent of employees accounted for 60 percent of claims costs, a statistic that informed the design of its corporate wellness program and that over time bought healthcare costs down by targeting this small group of workers.[32]

## Combining Leading and Lagging Indicators

Having a logic model of how the work environment, job characteristics, workplace culture, and employee health and well-being are interconnected will help you understand "what influences what." Leading indicators measure upstream factors that contribute to outcomes. By accurately measuring and then taking action to improve leading indicators – the thrust of health and safety promotion and illness and injury prevention initiatives – you can expect over time to achieve better outcomes. These outcomes can be measured using relevant lagging indicators. A well-designed employee survey, HR dashboard, or sustainability report will include both types of measures.

Here are three different examples, looking at work injuries, job satisfaction, and workplace civility.

The lost-time work injury rate is a lagging OHS indicator. However, if you also measure and report the number of OHS training hours per employee, you will be capturing a leading indicator that should contribute over time to a safer work environment and reduced injuries. Or for a more robust measure, you can use the

Institute for Work and Health's Organizational Performance Metric (see chapter 4), which provides an accurate assessment of your safety culture – the foundation of good safety performance and an accurate predictor of lost-time injuries.

Job satisfaction is a commonly used outcome measure, or lagging indicator, for overall employee well-being. However, viewed as a leading indicator, the level of job satisfaction or dissatisfaction can signal potential future problems (or successes) in the areas of engagement, absenteeism (lost productivity), or turnover. I encourage you to flip back to figure 3.2, the Ontario Hospital Association's Quality Healthcare Workplace Model, and review the distinction between drivers (leading indicators) and individual and organizational outcomes (or lagging indicators).

Employers also have a legal and moral responsibility to ensure that the workplace is free of bullying, harassment, and discrimination. You also need to measure civility – basic respect and fairness – in your workplace. Bullied workers not only experience poor mental health; they also cost employers more in terms of health plan claims for mental health–related problems.[33] Surveys are an effective tool for tracking who is experiencing incivility in its various forms: harassment, bullying, or discrimination. Surveys also help to pinpoint the underlying causes of incivility and identify what actions managers need to take to enforce a zero-tolerance policy.

Now shifting our attention to mental health, consider that antidepressant drug consumption doubled in OECD countries between 2000 and 2015, possibly reflecting reduced mental health stigma and people's greater willingness to seek help.[34] According to Express Scripts Canada, which manages health benefits including prescription drugs, 26 percent of their claimants used a mental health medication in 2018. The use of antidepressant medications is on the increase, but tracking this provides only a lagging health indicator. However, you can design your employee health risk assessment and employee survey to get at the individual and organizational drivers of psychological well-being. Doing so can inform immediate actions, because you will know the levers at your disposal most likely to influence positive psychosocial work experiences.

A Toronto-area hospital provides a good example of how one employer made effective use of mental health data. The hospital takes a very strategic, metrics-driven approach to continuously improving the workplace and employee well-being, all with better patient care as the ultimate goal. The hospital's Wellness and Mental Health Strategic Plan has key progress indicators, targets, and improvement actions. There is an effective approach to workload management that actively involves frontline staff and is tracked using annual employee survey results. The Wellness Committee regularly tracks absenteeism, drug benefit utilization, and EAP data. Noticing a jump in the use of prescription drugs for depression and related mental health issues and increased access to EAP-provided counseling for stress, it took the proactive step of establishing a Psychological Health and Safety Committee to introduce and monitor the Standard. Workload and job strain are now considered psychological health and safety issues, and these leading indicators are measured in regular employee surveys.

Taking your cue from this hospital, you also can use your employee survey to expand the assessment of factors affecting psychological health and safety. Many organizations now conduct employee surveys at regular intervals. There is untapped potential to use or modify existing surveys to assess workplace health drivers and outcomes. You also may be able to identify health, wellness, or well-being indicators (depending on your goals) that could be included in a corporate report card that gets the full attention of the executive team. Some companies already do this with lagging indicators such as job satisfaction or engagement. But given the growing interest among senior leaders in mental health issues, why not use your survey to ask employees for their assessments of key workplace factors contributing to a psychologically healthy and safe workplace? Adding a few questions about leading indicators as a new psychological health module in the survey is worth exploring with your survey vendor. Here are sample questions, but there are other similar items that would work just as well, from public-domain surveys I mentioned earlier:[35]

- The amount of work I am expected to do is reasonable for my position.
- My supervisor supports me in getting my work done.
- I am satisfied with the fairness and respect I receive on the job.
- I am satisfied with the amount of involvement I have in decisions that affect my work.
- I feel I am well rewarded in terms of praise and recognition for the level of effort I put out for my job.
- I am informed about important changes at work before they happen.

Finally, let's take a look at sleep. Several organizations I have worked with identified sleep as a significant employee health concern, based on the health needs assessments they conducted. Poor sleep can result from a number of workplace and job characteristics, particularly shift work, total weekly work hours, and a demanding workload. Some occupations – notably police, fire, emergency, and other protective services, and healthcare jobs such as nursing – typically operate on a 24/7 basis. Supporting these groups of workers to maintain good sleep patterns is an important responsibility for the employer. Tracking hours and schedules provide key leading indicators regarding sleep.

Certainly, it would be easy to include in your employee survey a validated measure of sleep quality as a key outcome, or lagging indicator, to determine the extent of the problem. A meta-analysis of 152 studies of sleep quality and quantity confirmed that poor sleep negatively influences job performance, safety behavior, and health. Workload affects sleep quality, as does working a night shift and an irregular shift.[36] Fortunately, sleep quality (which is more important than quantity) can be measured using a single questionnaire item: "How do you evaluate this week's sleep?" The question is answered on a four-point Likert scale (where 1 is very poor and 4 is very good).[37] If sleep is an issue for your workforce, think about adding this diagnostic measure to your employee survey.

## Guidelines for Evaluating Healthy Organization Change Initiatives

As a way of summarizing this discussion of evaluation and measurement, I thought it would be useful to lay out guidelines for planning the evaluation component of your healthy organization strategy or of a specific workplace intervention. An intervention is any new program, practice, or initiative intended to improve work environments, employee health and wellness, and organizational performance. What's critical is being able to track progress, learn from these results, and continue to improve efforts aimed at a healthier and more productive workplace.

1 *Be goal-focused.* Always keep your objectives front and center. It helps to create a shared vision of the kind of work environment you are striving to create. If you are having difficulty figuring out how to evaluate a program, perhaps it has too many goals or fuzzy goals. Don't let the tools or methods drive the process. Rather, always keep your eye on the objectives of the intervention and use only evaluation tools that specifically address these.

2 *Model your vision.* Every step of the intervention process must contribute to your organization's (or team's) vision of a healthy work environment. Evaluation is not just data collection, but an opportunity for collaborative learning and organizational

development. A robust evaluation process will give managers, employees, committees, and teams more control over improvements in their environment. It will also contribute to their ongoing learning and capacity to undertake future change.

3 *Take a positive approach.* Evaluation should help the organization improve. It should encourage group learning and workplace innovation. Avoid the use of measures for punitive actions, such as using absenteeism data to target specific groups through an absenteeism management program that does not address underlying causes, or inferring that managers of specific units where survey results show low morale are poor managers. Evaluation data should encourage constructive discussions among stakeholders, beginning with the question "How can we better support the employees in this team or work unit to be healthy, safe, and productive?"

4 *Create a model.* A model maps out your common-sense understanding of how specific changes should improve quality of work-life and contribute to other organizational goals. Establishing a "causal relationship" in scientific terms is difficult, but you can still build a convincing case, and a logically laid-out model will help do this. See figure 8.1, above, and the Quality Healthcare Workplace Model in figure 3.2.

5 *Integrate.* Look for opportunities to integrate different kinds of measures, creating a composite picture of how the intervention contributes not only to employees but also to organizational goals such as product quality, customer satisfaction, and operational excellence. Connecting the data dots in this way makes your evaluation far more compelling to decision-makers.

6 *Make meaningful and actionable use of data.* Think of the end user. Collect and analyze only the data you need and are prepared to act upon. Ask employees, managers, and health and safety and wellness committees for their input in this regard. Report your findings in ways that support learning, action planning,

and change implementation. Who will use the evaluation information and for what purposes? The knowledge generated by the evaluation must be a catalyst for actions in support of a higher-quality work environment. As an impetus for action, consider translating some of the indicators into costs, such as costs of lost-time injuries or absenteeism or the cost to replace an employee who voluntarily leaves.

7 *Mine existing data.* Most organizations already have data that can be useful for evaluations on outcomes such as absenteeism, time-loss injuries, incidence and length of disability, prescription drug utilization, and voluntary turnover. Try to analyze and report these data in ways that assess the impact of an intervention, and look for ways to make connections to surveys of employees and customers. This can be done by using a uniform reporting unit, such as a worksite, functional unit, or employee group based on demographics and/or job type.

## Sustainability Reporting

Voluntary reporting and standard-setting is becoming more common for workplace and employee health, safety, and well-being and for corporate sustainability. As I've emphasized, the Standard is designed this way, as is the range of health, safety, and CSR standards from the International Organization for Standardization (ISO). The ISO 26000, launched in 2010, provides guidelines for social responsibility reporting that can be used by organizations of all sizes. The GRI Sustainability Reporting Standards, which I outlined earlier in chapter 7, have become the leading sustainability reporting framework.[38] A limitation of the ISO and GRI reporting frameworks is that neither provides a way to monitor and assess whether or not a company is living up to its claims or has followed the reporting process laid out in the frameworks. It is "self-declared compliance."[39] Independent verification would strengthen the credibility of CSR reports, and there are third-party certifications that can do this. All the more reason to be accurate and fully transparent in reporting your sustainability performance.

Research shows that a company's treatment of its employees affects financial performance. This link can be seen in US companies that received the annual C. Everett Koop National Health Award, described in chapter 2.[40] Koop Award winners are a diverse group of corporations with well-established corporate health promotion initiatives. These companies achieved a double win: above-average stock market performance and high employee job satisfaction, which is a proxy for overall well-being. The latter indicator reflects how these companies treat their employees, which is a crucial dimension of corporate social responsibility. While most US businesses have corporate health promotion programs, very few are as effective or as comprehensive as Koop Award–winning companies. According to researchers who studied these companies, "Koop Award winners spend many years, even decades, in crafting and fine-tuning their programs to become best-practice for other companies to emulate."[41] In other words, effectively promoting employees' health and well-being takes ongoing and long-term effort, commitment, investments, measurement, and continuous improvement.

There's growing recognition by multinational corporations that their employees' health is linked to community health. And sustainability reporting is being used by employers to articulate company values, improve employee engagement by reinforcing pride and purpose in their work, break down organizational silos, and improve operational performance. However, more attention must be given to including leading employee indicators in sustainability reports to show what actions are being taken to promote health and safety and prevent illness, injuries, or fatalities. Most companies include standard OHS indicators (such as lost-time injury rates) in their sustainability reporting, but these are over-the-shoulder looks back into the past.

Returning to our earlier example of Adidas, its 2018 annual report provides lots of information on its policies and programs for employees. The report outlines the company's people strategy, which includes actions on diversity and inclusion, leadership development, employee collaboration and learning, performance management, wages and benefits, and work–life integration.[42] The latter includes providing the option of flexible working times and places, developing leadership competencies related to work–life integration, and offering family-oriented services. Employee engagement is a key measure of its people strategy's success, reflecting its goal of being an employer of choice. Here's how Adidas describes its employee engagement goal: "We have set ourselves the goal of becoming the best sports company in the world by becoming a truly consumer-centric organization and putting our people at the heart of everything we do. When it comes to measuring up to these ambitions, our consumers and people are the best sources of data." Regarding the latter, in 2017 the company launched its monthly "People Pulse" survey of all office employees who have email accounts, assessing their experiences working for the company. Answers to one question from the Pulse survey – "On a scale of 1–10, how likely are you to recommend Adidas as a place to work?" – are a key performance indicator reported to the executive team. As well, the survey offers opportunities for employees to provide their feedback and input on a variety of issues, including its strategy. In 2018, there was a 90 percent participation rate in the survey.

A compelling reason for companies to integrate key people metrics and environmental and other CSR metrics into a unified, annual public report is that this is increasingly what employees want. In the minds of a growing number of workers, especially millennials (people under age 35), a close connection to their employer implies that the company will not only treat them well but will operate by high ethical and environmental standards. As mentioned earlier, the growing climate rebellion inside Amazon, with thousands of employees joining Amazon Employees for Climate Justice, is an organized effort to lobby Jeff Bezos, the company's founder and CEO, and the company's board to take more determined action to mitigate environmental damage and shrink the company's massive carbon footprint.[43] Granted, these highly skilled young tech workers are in a privileged labor market position that gives them the security to feel empowered to take on their employer. Yet the actions of Amazon employees' grassroots climate change initiative may well be the tip of the iceberg, giving voice to concerns that millions of other young (and older) workers have about the slow, or negligible, response of their employers to climate change. So while Amazon's CEO and board have so far resisted pressure to disclose its emissions – a basic requirement of sustainability reporting – other companies that do so will no doubt be viewed in a much more positive light by current and prospective employees. This sort of values congruence is sure to become a significant source of employee loyalty and motivation in the future.

Indeed, the largest audience for a corporation's sustainability report is its own employees. This is another reason why more employers are integrating health and safety metrics into sustainability reporting. Innovative reporting practices by companies such as Anglo American (mining), Heineken (beverages), LafargeHolcim (a Swiss multinational manufacturer of building materials), and Newmont Mining Corporation – all on the Dow Jones Sustainability Indices – view employee health and safety through the lens of sustainability.[44] This is a holistic view of employee health, safety, and wellness that encompasses physical, mental, social, and financial well-being. It also demonstrates a better understanding of how non-communicable diseases – ranging from heart disease and diabetes to depression – impact business performance. And it shows growing recognition by corporate executives of the many benefits of sustainability reporting, including the following: higher employee engagement through pride and purpose; better stakeholder relations with local communities, civil society organizations, and regulators; and enhanced business value by demonstrating to investors that the company is ably managing risks and identifying future opportunities.

## Conclusion

As organizations do a better job measuring and reporting key people indicators, including employee well-being, we can expect better decisions about people goals and how best to achieve these. The point of collecting any of the measures discussed in this chapter is, first, to learn whether the time, energy, and resources you have invested in changes are having the desired results, and second, to track how your organization is advancing toward its healthy organization goals. Meaningful people metrics and evaluation tools help an organization to track its progress on workforce and workplace improvement goals by creating transparency and accountability for the required actions. The result, over time, will be more human-centered and therefore sustainable organizations.

As we've seen, organizations at the vanguard of strengthening the links between employee well-being and sustainable business success make effective use of metrics. In other words, decisions in this regard are evidence based, using the organizations' own evidence. They set goals, track progress toward those goals, report results, and are transparent about their actions. Yet despite significant advances in corporate environmental impact reporting in the past decade, more must be done to integrate relevant measures of employee well-being into these public reports.[45] The stage is set for this to happen. The big challenge for companies now is figuring out how to incorporate the well-being of their workers as a priority goal in their business strategy. The end result will be a much more complete and accurate picture of how the organization as a complex human system is functioning. That's what's most critical for sustainable success.

## CHAPTER 9

# A Practical Guide to Creating a Healthier Organization

This final chapter provides an action-oriented summary of key insights and practical suggestions I have provided throughout the book. My intent is to offer readers a guide for planning and implementing a healthy organization strategy, regardless of their starting point.

As I stated at the beginning, I am aware that organizations are at different places on a healthy organization trajectory. And for each of you, that path looks somewhat different, reflecting the distinctive circumstances of your organization – its size, industry, location, workforce demographics, current people challenges, and more. Some of you will already have a healthy organization strategy mapped out, so you will be thinking in tactical terms about a staged implementation. Others will be looking for ideas than can help to launch a strategy that builds on successful OHS and wellness programs. Others may not have taken any formal action yet, beyond addressing legislated OHS requirements, and so may want to explore how to incrementally expand their focus and activities to give equal emphasis to the "health" in "health and safety." So I'm not offering a prescriptive guide. Rather, I am challenging you to think about where you are at and where you want to go next, discuss your options with coworkers, and then develop an action plan. In sum, I firmly believe that you have to find your own way forward.

I encourage you to apply or adapt the ideas, suggestions, and resources I have presented throughout the book. Please use them in any way that is helpful, adapting entire sections, using figures or checklists as organizational development tools, or pulling together pieces from different sections to meet your specific needs. Some of the content can be adapted for use in action-planning sessions with change agents and in leadership training. As you and your coworkers tailor these suggestions to fit your organization's immediate needs and goals, you will find considerable room for creativity. As my various examples have shown, regardless of your position, as a committed change agent you can have positive influences within your own sphere in the organization.

My approach to action in this chapter reflects my observations of numerous organizations at workshops I have facilitated, watching what happens when employees and managers jointly craft a healthy path forward for their organization. When designing these workshops, I try to learn as much as I can about the organization, its goals, and the challenges faced by change agents. The starting points and direction of the strategy design process reflect these different realities. In fact, the people in the organization codesign the workshop with me. For example, if you have just refreshed your corporate values, that can provide a natural stepping stone for framing a vibrant workplace vision (or healthy workplace or healthy organization vision – you choose the most appropriate language). And if you have at hand results from a recent employee survey, then an alternate starting point is to discuss priority survey follow-up actions. Finally, for organizations that have a robust sustainability or CSR reporting framework, the timing and opportunity may be good to forge closer links with HR, OHS, and wellness that include employee well-being metrics and goals.

## Healthy Organization Assessment

The big question I would like to focus your attention on now is: How far you have progressed along a healthy organization trajectory? The tool in table 9.1 can help you determine where your

Table 9.1  Healthy Organization Assessment

*To what extent do you disagree or agree that each of these statements describes your organization? Put the number of your response to the right of each statement:*
1 = Strongly disagree
2 = Disagree
3 = Neither agree nor disagree
4 = Agree
5 = Strongly agree

| | Your response: |
|---|---|

**Vibrant Workplace**
a) Employees are empowered to be innovative in their jobs.
b) Working relationships are based on mutual respect.
c) Employees are supported to learn and to develop their abilities.
d) Employees' contributions are valued and recognized.
e) Managers believe that employee well-being is key to performance.

Section Score: /25

**Inspired Employees**
a) Employees actively collaborate in the interests of customers or clients.
b) Employees seek opportunities to contribute their skills and abilities.
c) Employees are passionate about meeting customer or client needs.
d) Employees do their work with enthusiasm.
e) Employees feel they have a personal stake in the future of the organization.

Section Score: /25

**Inclusive Leadership**
a) Managers encourage employees to take initiative in their job.
b) Managers listen to employees' suggestions for how to create a better workplace.
c) Employees have taken action to improve their immediate work environment.
d) Employees feel responsible for living the organization's values.
e) Employees are trusted to do what is best for customers and clients.

Section Score: /25

**Positive Culture**
a) The organization has strong people-focused values.
b) Employees know and personally identify with the values of the organization.
c) Supervisors are selected based on their people skills.
d) Employees are involved in planning and implementing change.
e) There is a sense of community in the workplace.

Section Score: /25

*(Continued)*

*To what extent do you disagree or agree that each of these statements describes your organization? Put the number of your response to the right of each statement:*
1 = Strongly disagree
2 = Disagree
3 = Neither agree nor disagree
4 = Agree
5 = Strongly agree

|  | Your response: |
|---|---|
| **Sustainable Success** | |
| a) The organization supports community causes and employee volunteering. | |
| b) Clear ethical principles guide relationships with community stakeholders. | |
| c) The organization acts in environmentally responsible ways. | |
| d) The organization has a long-range plan for renewing its workforce. | |
| e) Managers are committed to sustainable business practices. | |
| Section Score: | /25 |
| **Total Score (Add the Section Scores):** | **/125** |

organization is on its path to promoting employee well-being and achieving sustainable performance into the future. The Healthy Organization Assessment focuses on the building blocks of a healthy organization – vibrant workplaces, inspired employees, inclusive leadership, and positive culture – and the concept of sustainable success.[1] All these topics have been discussed in previous chapters. You can use the tool in table 9.1 individually, or you and your colleagues can fill it in as a team or at a wellness or OHS committee meeting. I've also used it in many corporate workshops as both a leadership development and a planning tool. Use your results to help strategize how to move further down your healthy organization path. The assessment will focus your attention on identifying the strengths you can build on, where improvements need to be made, and potential barriers to change that you will need to overcome.

## Guidelines for Interpreting Your Results

To calculate your score for each section in the survey, and an overall score, add the points for each question in the response column. There are no right or wrong answers. Rather, the survey is intended to generate thinking and discussions that will lead to healthy organization actions.

Scores in each section range from 5 to 25 and between 25 and 125 for the survey. Use the following grid to locate your scores:

| Score Range | Getting Started | Gaining Momentum | Strong Foundation |
|---|---|---|---|
| Each Section | 5–12 | 13–17 | 18–25 |
| Survey Total | 25–60 | 65–85 | 90–125 |

**Getting Started**: Scores in this range suggest that there is little being done in your organization to support a healthy trajectory. So you need to carefully identify starting points.

**Gaining Momentum**: Scores in this range suggest there is modest momentum toward a healthy organization, that some action is being taken, and that you have strengths to build on.

**Strong Foundation**: Scores in this range suggest there are strong healthy organization building blocks in place and a sustainable approach to business success. Your challenge will be to ensure that this progress can be maintained and further leveraged.

It is useful to look at how you rated in each section. Look for differences in scores across sections, discussing and trying to understand reasons for them.

## Tapping into Available Resources

In earlier chapters, I have described many resources and tools that can help you to assess and report the determinants and outcomes of employee health, safety, and well-being. For me, an obvious sign of how much progress has been made in the past decade addressing workplace health, safety, and wellness is the fact that few of these resources existed when I was writing the first edition of this book. There now are many publicly available resources to choose from that provide assessment and action-planning tools that can be adapted for use in different types of organizations. Here are just a few:

- The Mental Health Commission of Canada, the Canadian Standards Association, and the Bureau de normalisation du Québec have created the National Standard of Canada for Psychological Health and Safety in the Workplace, along with its implementation guide, and the Guarding Minds @ Work employee and organizational assessment tools.[2]
- The European Network for Workplace Health Promotion provides a self-assessment questionnaire, Healthy Employees in Healthy Organizations, to assess and improve your workplace health promotion efforts.[3]
- The Institute for Work and Health has created a short safety culture survey, the Organizational Performance Metric.[4]
- The Harvard School of Public Health's Center for Work, Health and Well-Being provides a tool for assessing the integration of health, safety, and well-being initiatives.[5]
- The state of Queensland, Australia, has developed the People at Work survey for assessing psychosocial hazards in the workplace.[6]
- The City of London Healthy Workplace Charter Self-Assessment can be used to assess best practices as endorsed by Public Health England for improving employee health and well-being.
- Public Health England offers a workplace health needs assessment to find out employees' health status and needs, plus other resources.[7]
- The HERO Scorecard, mentioned earlier, provides a way to compare your practices with what leading organizations are doing (US based).

- WELCOA offers a range of assessment tools, including a job satisfaction survey, a health culture audit, a health risk assessment, and a health needs assessment.[8] (Access to WELCOA resources requires an annual fee for membership. All other resources listed above are free.)

Also on the topic of measurement, while I've cautioned against going overboard with metrics, I have also provided numerous examples of how key individual and organizational factors are being measured. To emphasize, select only measures that are directly relevant for your goals and that will be meaningful for all stakeholder groups. To mention just a few: the thirteen workplace factors associated with a psychologically healthy and safe workplace; relevant Great Place to Work Institute measures for psychological health and safety; items from Rethinking Work surveys that measure a wide range of critical employee perceptions, work values, and workplace factors associated with employee health, safety, job performance, and quality of work-life; behavioral checklists for psychological capital and transformational leadership; measures of engagement; and examples of sustainability reporting used by leading corporations. You may find that your corporate employee survey covers some or many of the same topics, or that your HR dashboard or annual CSR report includes similar indicators. However, if you see information gaps, there are plenty of examples in this book of how you can measure what's missing.

## Tracking Your Healthy Organization Actions

I'm providing an Action Checklist for Building Healthier Organizations, which I have used with a wide variety of organizations.[9] The checklist in table 9.2 is a tool designed to help change agents during all stages of developing, implementing, and improving a comprehensive healthy organization change agenda. It addresses enabling

Table 9.2  Action Checklist for Building Healthier Organizations

| Healthy Workplace Improvement Action | Planned (✓ when plan is finalized) | Ongoing (✓ if implementation is underway) | Implemented (✓ when program or change is implemented) |
|---|---|---|---|
| 1. Set up a committee or HR/OHS/ wellness unit to plant seeds, propose options, and circulate a vision. | | | |
| 2. Build alliances across the organization to create a shared vision of a healthy workplace from which actions can flow. | | | |
| 3. Use a broad definition of employee and workplace health to mine existing data for strengths, gaps, and opportunities. | | | |
| 4. Tie healthy organization goals into the corporate strategic plan, values, vision, mission, HR plan, CSR strategy, and performance reporting. | | | |
| 5. Build a case that a healthier work environment will address other priority issues (e.g., retention, workload, engagement, learning, work–life balance). | | | |
| 6. Shift your thinking: this is long-term cultural change and not a quick-fix "program." | | | |
| 7. Develop language and guiding principles that resonate with all stakeholders. | | | |
| 8. Identify and involve a senior management champion. | | | |
| 9. Meet with senior management to identify needs, build the case, and get commitment and resources to develop a healthy workplace strategic direction. | | | |
| 10. Initiate frank discussions with senior management about trust-building through all healthy organization changes. | | | |

(Continued)

| Healthy Workplace Improvement Action | Planned (✓ when plan is finalized) | Ongoing (✓ if implementation is underway) | Implemented (✓ when program or change is implemented) |
|---|---|---|---|
| 11. Assess change readiness, identify and remove barriers, and support momentum. | | | |
| 12. Design ways to help line managers "own" the process so they become accountable for improvements. | | | |
| 13. Engage line managers in discussions of their role, perceived challenges, and needed supports. | | | |
| 14. Have the same discussion with HR, OHS, OD, and CSR practitioners. | | | |
| 15. If applicable, establish and maintain open dialogue with union(s) and include union reps on the committee. | | | |
| 16. Refine the healthy workplace vision: include its focus and state the case for "why we need to do this." | | | |
| 17. Consult with employees about priority healthy workplace needs and required actions. | | | |
| 18. Engage other change agents formally and informally as the change strategy evolves and rolls out. | | | |
| 19. Communicate, communicate, and communicate to the workforce. | | | |
| 20. Think ahead to measurement and accountability. Strive for two to three priority goals with measurable outcomes. Don't take on too much! | | | |

the conditions for change, the change process, and the scope and focus of interventions. Individual change agents, committees, teams, training workshops, or informal networks in an organization can use this checklist.

You can adjust the actions listed in the checklist and the sequence in which you do them, adding other items to fit your organization's specific context and goals. The checklist also provides you with a guide to the issues you will need to fully consider, discuss, and learn from. I would encourage you to view the checklist as a set of principles for how to make improvements. You may need to regularly revisit the checklist, updating it as you make progress.

## Overcoming Change Barriers

It is dispiriting indeed when your best-laid plans run into a brick wall of resistance. Being able to anticipate what these barriers will be is essential for making progress. The tools I presented above will get you thinking about barriers. So too will table 6.1, as you work through the change readiness checklist looking for potential sources of resistance. Now let's recap key points from earlier discussions so you can feel well equipped to remove or get around change barriers.

Just as the Institute for Work and Health's research on break-through OHS change emphasized, for change to happen someone needs to educate and raise awareness in the workforce that there are better ways of doing things. From this perspective, what may first appear to be resistance by some people in your organization may simply be that they have never had the opportunity to consider a viable alternative. If it is becoming more obvious to you and your coworkers that the workplace increasingly poses risks to workers' psychological health and safety, just knowing that there are useful resources available – such as the Standard – that other organizations are using successfully to reduce these risks could be one of those "ah-ha!" moments and a catalyst for remedial action. A good number of the workshops I run are designed to do just that. In a similar vein, I have seen organizations with strong OHS programs and a well-functioning OHS committee, but where a traditional OHS focus on physical injuries still prevails. If this sounds familiar, what would it take to expand your approach to OHS and incorporate psychological health and safety? Again, new knowledge and targeted training can provide a nudge to a more integrated and comprehensive approach to health and safety.

As we saw in chapter 4, the level of mutual trust in a workplace is either a barrier or an enabler to positive change. To avoid the conundrum of low trust–no change, and to break out of that downward spiral, approach every single action you and others take to develop a healthy organization strategy as an opportunity to rebuild trust. Critical here will be demonstrating respect and caring for others in every interaction. Also important in this regard is having open channels of communication, listening to others' concerns and suggestions, and turning words into actions that will make a difference. Furthermore, one of the surest ways to build change momentum is to encourage the active participation of as many employees and managers as possible at each stage. This not only creates ownership for the change and its goals, but also can dissolve lingering cynicism employees, middle managers, or frontline supervisors may harbor based on the failure of past change initiatives, or changes that senior leaders promised but did not deliver. As I'm sure you've witnessed, cynicism and trust are close cousins in workplaces, conspiring to defeat change initiatives.

Echoing extensive academic research on healthy workplaces, I've emphasized how culture and leadership are big enablers of change. And by the same token, they can be impediments to needed changes. The assessment tools in this chapter can help pinpoint the greatest sources of resistance in this regard. Resistance speaks to the importance of taking an incremental approach to change by leveraging existing strengths and designing next steps to address the most widely acknowledged health, safety, and wellness needs – all the while looking for compelling examples of how moving in this direction will contribute to future success.

An entry point in this regard could be shifting the content of upcoming leadership development sessions to address much-needed people skills. You may be able to do this in a non-threatening way by framing it as resilience-building, a topic that now has the attention of corporate leaders. And frank discussions of resilience open the door to a wider range of healthy organization topics, from stress and burnout to psychological capital and a transformational style of people leadership. Consider the same approach if your organization is developing a comprehensive sustainability or CSR strategy, particularly one focused on reducing the company's carbon footprint. As noted, corporate sustainability approaches have expanded to include a company's social and environmental impacts on internal as well as external stakeholders – providing an ideal opportunity for addressing employee well-being.

Finally, based on our discussion of work trends, we know that heavy workloads and time pressures define the experience of a good number of workers. In a perverse way, while these very workers may be pushed to the point of burnout, the very causes of this disable them from doing anything about it. This came into sharp relief in a nonprofit organization that asked me to help them document their "workload problem" and develop solutions. A workload committee was set up with what initially appeared to be a high level of commitment to get to the root of the problem. However, when it came to rolling up their sleeves and devoting a day or more to planning a path forward, it took months to fit this into everyone's schedule. Then the light went on; there was collective recognition that "we need to make time to find time," which essentially meant reducing work hours. So if time scarcity is a barrier to positive changes in your organization, you may need to help people who want to get involved in making change shuffle their work priorities and push some of their work onto the back burner. Or, to use the Standard as an example, present specific improvements not as brand-new initiatives – which many managers would not welcome – but rather as something that can be seamlessly woven into existing plans and work processes.

## Conclusion

My hope is that *Creating Healthy Organizations* provides a stimulus for change and a new lens for understanding and acting upon emerging workplace and workforce challenges. Ideally, it will give you and your coworkers more control over shaping a better future for your organization. Your version of a healthy organization should be both aspirational and evolving: the bar edges up the more you do and the more you learn about what works and what doesn't. That's what creating healthy organizations is all about. Moving further along a healthy organization trajectory, plotting a future course, and keeping everyone moving in that direction requires commitment and persistence by you and many others in your organization. That is why I have emphasized the importance of inclusive leadership, healthy change as a shared responsibility, and the need for managers and employees to co-create vibrant workplaces. As your next step, why not take a handful of the ideas from this book that resonated most with you back to your coworkers, start a discussion, and collectively explore the possibilities.

# Notes

## Introduction

1 *Business Wire*. (6 August 2018). Electronic Arts and NFL connect esports to millions with the new Madden NFL 19 Championship Series. https://www.businesswire.com/.../Electronic-Arts-NFL-Connect-Esports-Millions-New

2 Brock, T. (26 May 2017). The problem of treating play like work – how esports can harm well-being. *The Conversation*. http://webcache.googleusercontent.com/search?q=cache:XFQa-UfPW4YJ:theconversation.com/the-problem-of-treating-play-like-work-how-esports-can-harm-well-being-78366+&cd=9&hl=en&ct=clnk&gl=ca

3 *Economist*. (10 November 2018). The price of free, 18.

4 Chua, K. (11 September 2017). *5 most common health concerns for esport athletes. Rappler.com*. https://www.rappler.com/technology/.../181571-esports-common-health-concerns

5 World Health Organization. (September 2018). Gaming disorder. https://www.who.int/features/qa/gaming-disorder/en/

6 Howarth, A., Quesada, J., Silva, J., Judycki, S., and Mills, P.R. (2018). The impact of digital health interventions on health-related outcomes in the workplace: A systematic review. *Digital Health*. https://doi.org/10.1177/2055207618770861

7 Health Enhancement Research Organization (HERO). (February 2017). *Wearables in wellness: Employer case studies on use of wearable tracking devices in wellness programs*. https://hero-health.org/wp-content/uploads/2017/02/Wearables_Case-Study-Report_Final-2.pdf

8 *Economist*. (31 March 2018). Smile, you're on camera, 9–10; Pfeffer, J. (4 December 2018). Warning: AI may be hazardous to employee health.

*Forbes*. https://www.forbes.com/sites/insightsteam/2018/12/04/warning-ai-may-be-hazardous-to-employee-health/#4f1c810acbc9

9  See: Lowe, G., and Graves, F. (2016). *Redesigning work: A blueprint for Canada's future well-being and prosperity*. Toronto: University of Toronto Press; *Benefits Canada*. (28 May 2019). Survey finds half of U.S. workers report most stress comes from finances. https://www.benefitscanada.com/news/survey-finds-half-of-u-s-workers-report-most-stress-comes-from-finances-130693?utm_source=EmailMarketing&utm_medium=email&utm_campaign=Daily_Newsletter&oft_id=59613255&oft_k=fkB2TklU&oft_lk=bJjmNI&oft_d=636960312416600000&fpid=406788&m32_fp_id=V7l8bS&ctx=newsletter&m32_fp_ctx=DI_MASTER_Relational

10  Han, K.M., Chang, J., Won, E., Lee, M.S., and Ham, B.J. (2017). Precarious employment associated with depressive symptoms and suicidal ideation in adult wage workers. *Journal of Affective Disorders, 218*, 201–209; Mojtehedzadeh, S. (20 March 2017). Precarious jobs scar employees' mental health: Survey. *Toronto Star*. https://www.thestar.com/news/gta/2017/03/20/precarious-jobs-scar-employees-mental-health-survey.html

11  Statistics Canada. (28 May 2019). *Study: Self-employed Canadians: Who and why?* https://www150.statcan.gc.ca/n1/daily-quotidien/190528/dq190528f-eng.pdf

12  Tait, C., and Leeder, J. (20 May 2019). With high stress, anxiety and depression, 40 per cent of Canadian farmers uneasy about seeking help. *Globe and Mail*. https://www.theglobeandmail.com/canada/alberta/article-with-high-stress-anxiety-and-depression-40-per-cent-of-canadian/

13  Conger, K., and Scheiber, N. (11 September 2019). California bill makes app-based companies treat workers as employees. *New York Times*. https://www.nytimes.com/2019/09/11/technology/california-gig-economy-bill.html

14  Paterson, J. (4 June 2018). Mental-health focus leads to culture change at CGI Group. *Benefits Canada*. https://www.benefitscanada.com/news/mental-health-focus-leads-to-culture-change-at-cgi-group-115075?utm_source=EmailMarketing&utm_medium=email&utm_campaign=Daily_Newsletter

15  Burnett-Nichols, H. (19 December 2017). Tending the roots of employee wellness: A look at workplace gardens. *Benefits Canada*. https://www.benefitscanada.com/news/tending-the-roots-of-employee-wellness-a-look-at-workplace-gardens-107908?utm_source=EmailMarketing&utm_medium=email&utm_campaign=Daily_Newsletter

16  Burnett-Nichols, H. (10 October 2017). FreshBooks adapts workplace perks with childcare guarantee as employees have kids. *Benefits Canada*. https://www.benefitscanada.com/news/how-freshbooks-changed-workplace-perks-as-employees-became-parents-104617

17  Burke, R.J., and Richardsen, A.M. (2014). Corporate programs: A summary of best practices and effectiveness. In R.J. Burke and A.M. Richardsen (Eds.), *Corporate wellness programs: Linking employee and organizational health*. Cheltenham, UK: Edward Elgar, 351.

18  Edington, D.W., and Pitts, J.S. (2016). *Shared values shared results: Positive organizational health as a win-win philosophy*. Edington Associates, 6. This case study is provided by Dr. Wayne Burton.

19  NIOSH. (2018). *Total Worker Health: Planning, assessment, and evaluation resources*. http://www.cdc.gov/niosh/twh/tools.html

20  Goetzel, R.Z., Ozminkowski, R.J., Bowen, J., and Tabrizi, M.J. (2008). Employer integration of health promotion and health protection programs. *International Journal of Workplace Health Management, 1*, 109–122.

21  Vision Zero. (2018). *Vision Zero American launch*. http://visionzero.global /vision-zero-american-launch

22  Loeppke, R.R., Hohn, T., Baase, C., Burton, W.N., Eisenberg, B.S., Ennis, T., et al. (2015). Integrating health and safety in the workplace. *Journal of Occupational and Environmental Medicine, 57*(5), 585–597. doi:10.1097 /JOM.0000000000000467.

23  Ibid., 591.

24  Ibid., 592.

25  UK Department for Business, Energy and Industrial Strategy. (11 July 2017). *Good work: The Taylor review of modern working practices*. https://www.gov .uk/government/publications/good-work-the-taylor-review -of-modern-working-practices

26  Australasian Faculty of Occupational and Environmental Medicine (AFOEM) and Royal Australasian College of Physicians. (October 2011). *Realising the health benefits of work: A Position Statement*. https://www .racp.edu.au/docs/default-source/default-document-library/afoem -pos-aus-nz-con-health-benefits-work-pack.pdf?sfvrsn=0

27  See: Baynton, M.A., and Fournier, L. (2017). *The evolution of workplace mental health in Canada: Toward a standard for psychological health and safety*. Great-West Life Assurance Company: Friesens. https://www.workplaces-trategiesformentalhealth.com/pdf/articles/Evolution_Book.pdf; Samra, J. (2017). *The evolution of workplace mental health in Canada: Research report (2007–2017)*. https://www.hrpa.ca/Documents/Public/Thought-Leadership /The-Evolution-of-Workplace-Mental-Health-in-Canada.pdf

28  Mental Health Commission of Canada. https://www.mentalhealthcom-mission.ca/English

29  Canadian Standards Association. http://shop.csa.ca/en/canada/landing -pages/z1003-psychological-health-and-safety-in-the-workplace/page /z1003-landing-page

30 Deloitte. (2019). *Leading the social enterprise: Reinvent with a human focus. 2019 Deloitte Global Human Capital Trends.* https://www2.deloitte.com/insights /us/en/focus/human-capital-trends.html

31 Ahmad, S. (2015). Green human resource management: Policies and practices. *Cogent Business and Management.* https://doi.org/10.1080/23311975 .2015.1030817

32 Kamarulzaman, N., Saleh, A.A., Hashim, S.Z., Hashim, H., and abdul-Ghani, A.A. (2011). An overview of the influence of physical office environments towards employee. *Procedia Engineering, 20,* 262–268.

33 Singh, A., Syal, M., Grady, S.C., and Korkmaz, S. (2010). Effects of green buildings on employee health and productivity. *American Journal of Public Health, 100,* 1665–1668.

34 Scott, K. (5 December 2017). Building a sustainable campus in Silicon Valley. *Microsoft blog.* https://blogs.microsoft.com/blog/2017/12/05/building -sustainable-campus-silicon-valley/

35 Stadin, M., Nordin, M., Brostrom, A., Magnusson Hanson, L.L., Westerlund, H., and Fransson, E.I. (2016). Information and communication technology demands at work: The association with job strain, effort-reward imbalance and self-rated health in different socio-economic strata. *International Archives of Occupational and Environmental Health, 89,* 1049–1058.

36 Karmel, J.D. (2017). *Dying to work: Death and injury in the American workplace.* Ithaca, NY: ILR Press, 5.

37 Pfeffer, J. (2018). *Dying for a paycheck: How modern management harms employee health and company performance – and what we can do about it.* New York: Harper Business, 8.

38 Cocker, F., Sanderson, K., and LaMontagne, A.D. (2017). Estimating the economic benefits of eliminating job strain as a risk factor for depression. *Journal of Occupational and Environmental Medicine, 59,* 12–17.

39 Farnacio, Y., Pratt, M.E., Marshall, E.G., and Graber, J.M. (2017). Are workplace psychosocial factors associated with work-related injury in the US workforce? National Health Interview Survey, 2010. *Journal of Occupational and Environmental Medicine, 59*(10), e164–e171.

40 Lowe, G., and Graves, F. (2016). *Redesigning work: A blueprint for Canada's future well-being and prosperity.* Toronto: University of Toronto Press.

41 Conference Board of Canada. (16 November 2017). *Wellness initiatives: Trends in organizational health management.* https://www.conferenceboard. ca/e-library/abstract.aspx?did=9106&AspxAutoDetectCookie Support=1

42 Sanofi Canada. (2016). *The Sanofi Canada Healthcare Survey: Canada's premier survey on health benefit plans.* https://www.benefitscanada.com/wp-content /uploads/2017/05/SanofiCanadaHealthCareSurvey2017.pdf

## Chapter 1

1  Malzon, R.A., and Lindsay, G.B. (1992). *Health promotion at the worksite: A brief survey of large organizations in Europe.* Copenhagen: World Health Organization, Regional Office for Europe. European Occupational Health Series No. 4, 9.

2  World Health Organization. (n.d.). *Constitution.* https://www.who.int /about/who-we-are/constitution

3  *British Medical Journal.* (2011). How should we define health? http://www .bmj.com/content/343/bmj.d4163

4  D'Andreamatteo, A., Ianni, L., Lega, F., and Sargiacomo, M. (2015). Lean in healthcare: A comprehensive review. *Health Policy, 119,* 1197–1209; Moraros, J., Lemstra, M., and Nwankwo, C. (2016). Lean interventions in healthcare: Do they actually work? A systematic literature review. *International Journal for Quality in Health Care, 28,* 150–165.

5  Putnam, L. (2015). *Workplace wellness that works: 10 Steps to infuse well-being and vitality into any organization.* Hoboken, NJ: Wiley, 273.

6  Biswas, A., Severin, C.N., Smith, P.M., Steenstra, I.A., Robson, L.S., and Amick, B.C. (2018). Larger workplaces, people-oriented culture, and specific industry sectors are associated with co-occurring health protection and wellness activities. *International Journal of Environmental Research and Public Health, 15*(12), 2739. doi:10.3390/ijerph15122739

7  *Benefits Canada.* (30 July 2018). 71% of global employers offer wellness programs: Survey. https://www.benefitscanada.com/news/71-of-global -employers-offer-workplace-wellness-programs-survey-117528?utm_source =EmailMarketing&utm_medium=email&utm_campaign=Daily_News letter&oft_id=36465988&oft_k=YQ4EzXDv&oft_lk=Dmmk85&oft_d =636752042108100000&cx_tcm_la_eid=406788

8  *Economist.* (10 November 2018). Time to perk up, 71.

9  Paterson, J. (4 October 2016). Should Canada follow France's lead in clamping down on off-hours email? *Benefits Canada.* https://www .benefitscanada.com/human-resources/other/should-canada-follow -frances-lead-in-clamping-down-on-off-hours-email-88120?print

10  Malachowski, C., Kirsh, B., and McEachen, E. (2017). The sociopolitical context of Canada's National Standard for Psychological Health and Safety in the Workplace: Navigating policy implementation. *Healthcare Policy, 12,* 10–17.

11  American Psychological Association, Center for Organizational Excellence. http://www.apaexcellence.org/

12  International Organization for Standardization. (2018). ISO 45001:2018. *Preview: Occupational health and safety management systems – requirements with guidance for use.* https://www.iso.org/standard/63787.html

13  International Organization for Standardization. ISO/WD 45003. *Occu-pational health and safety management – psychological health and safety in the workplace – guidelines.* https://www.iso.org/standard/64283.html

14  Heads Up: Better Mental Health in the Workplace. https://www.headsup.org.au/

15  R U OK. (29 May 2017). *World-first study into workplace psychological safety launched.* https://www.ruok.org.au/world-first-study-into-workplace-psychological-safety-launched

16  State of Victoria. (2018). *Healthy workplaces.* http://www.achievementprogram.health.vic.gov.au/workplaces/what-it-is

17  Alberta Health Services. (2019). *Building healthy workplaces together.* https://workplaces.healthiertogether.ca/

18  Greater London Authority. (2015). *London Healthy Workplace Charter Self-Assessment Framework.* https://www.london.gov.uk/sites/default/files/self-assessment_framework.pdf

19  https://hero-health.org/hero-scorecard/; https://www.welcoa.org/

20  *Canadian Occupational Safety.* (18 October 2018). Announcing the 2018 Canada's Safest Employers. https://www.cos-mag.com/personal-process-safety/38088-announcing-the-2018-canadas-safest-employers/

21  State of California Commission on Health and Safety and Workers' Compensation. (2010). *The whole worker: Guidelines for integrating occupational health and safety with workplace wellness programs.* http://www.dir.ca.gov/chswc/WOSHTEP/Publications/WOSHTEP_TheWholeWorker.pdf

22  Yang, S. (9 November 2017). *Path to sustainability: Applying sustainability principles to the World Bank's internal operations.* World Bank. https://www.worldbank.org/en/about/what-we-do/crinfo

23  World Bank. (2017). *Sustainability review 2017.* Washington, DC: World Bank. https://openknowledge.worldbank.org/handle/10986/28457

24  *Fortune.* (n.d.). Fortune *100 Best. 60: SAS Institute.* http://fortune.com/best-companies/sas-institute/

25  Great Place to Work USA. (n.d.). *World's Best Workplaces 2018.* https://www.greatplacetowork.com/best-workplaces/worldsbest/2018; SAS Institute. (n.d.). *SAS Institute Canada is no. 10 on the 2019 Best Workplaces in Canada.* https://www.sas.com/en_ca/news/press-releases/2019/april/sas-institute-canada-is-no--10-on-the-2019-best-workplaces-in-ca.html. Also see: Crowley, M.C. (22 January 2013). How SAS became the world's best place to work. *Fast Company.* https://www.fastcompany.com/3004953/how-sas-became-worlds-best-place-work

26  SAS Institute. (n.d.). *SAS Institute Canada Inc. made it to the 2019 List of Best Workplaces for Women.* https://www.sas.com/en_us/news/press-releases/2019/march/sas-institute-canada-inc-2019-list-of-best-workplaces-for-women.html

27  Great Place to Work Canada. (n.d.). *Report: Empowering women for innovation and business success.* https://www.greatplacetowork.ca/en/resources
   /reports/636-empowering-women-for-innovation-and-business-success
28  Urban Systems. (10 May 2019). *A great place to work is created by great people.*
   https://urbansystems.ca/a-great-place-to-work-is-created-by
   -great-people/
29  https://urbansystems.ca/about-us/
30  City of Kelowna. (2018). *Journey home.* https://www.kelowna.ca/our
   -community/addressing-homelessness/journey-home
31  Urban Systems Foundation. (2016). http://urbanblair.wpengine.com/wp
   -content/uploads/2016/06/2016-Guiding-Principles.pdf
32  urbanmatters.ca
33  Urban Systems. (16 February 2017). *8 Steps to embed a culture of social
   innovation in your organization.* https://urbansystems.ca/are-you-a
   -change-maker-8-steps-to-embed-a-culture-of-social-innovation-in-your
   -organization/
34  Kaspin, L.C., Gorman, K.M., and Miller, R.M. (2013). Systematic review of
   employer-sponsored wellness strategies and their economic and health-
   related outcomes. *Population Health Management, 16,* 14–21.
35  Connors, D. (2018). *A better place to work: Daily practices that transform
   culture.* Well-Advised Publishing.
36  Kent, K., Goetzel, R.Z., Roemer, E.C., Prasad, A., and Freundlich, N. (2016).
   Promoting healthy workplaces by building cultures of health and applying strategic communications. *Journal of Occupational and Environmental
   Medicine, 58,* 114–122.
37  Seppälä, E., and Cameron, K. (1 December 2015). Proof that positive work
   cultures are more productive. *Harvard Business Review.* https://hbr.org
   /2015/12/proof-that-positive-work-cultures-are-more-productive
38  European Network for Workplace Health Promotion. (n.d.). Healthy
   employees in healthy organisations. https://www.enwhp.org/?i=portal
   .en.mission-and-vision
39  Pfeffer, J. (2018). *Dying for a paycheck: How modern management harms
   employee health and company performance – and what we can do about it.* New
   York: Harper Business, 35.
40  Quoted in Macey, W.H., and Schneider, B. (2008). The meaning of
   employee engagement. *Industrial and Organizational Psychology, 1,* 7.
41  Wigert, B., and Agrawal, S. (12 July 2018). Employee burnout, part 1:
   The 5 main causes. *Gallup Workplace.* https://www.gallup.com/work-
   place/237059/employee-burnout-part-main-causes.aspx
42  World Health Organization. (28 May 2019). Burn-out an "occupational phenomenon": *International Classification of Diseases.* https://www.who.int
   /mental_health/evidence/burn-out/en/

43  Robroek, S.J.W., van de Vathorst, S., Hilhorst, M.T., and Burdorf, A. (2012). Moral issues in workplace health promotion. *International Archives of Occupational and Environmental Health, 85,* 327–331; Crawford, J.O., Graveling, R.A., Cowie, H.A., and Dixon, K. (2010). The health, safety and health promotion needs of older workers. *Occupational Medicine, 60,* 184–192.

44  Drucker, P.F. (1999). *Management challenges for the 21st century.* New York: HarperCollins.

45  Gephart, M.A., Marsick, V.J., Van Buren, M.E., and Spiro, M.S. (December 1996). Learning organizations come alive. *Training and Development,* 35–45.

46  Garvin, D.A. (1999). *Learning in action.* Boston: Harvard Business School Press, 42.

47  Senge, P.M. (1990). *The fifth discipline: The art and practice of the learning organization.* New York: Currency Doubleday.

48  Fuller, J.B., Raman, M., Wallenstein, J.K., and de Chalendar, A. (2019). Your workforce is more adaptable than you think. *Harvard Business Review, 97*(3), 118–126.

49  Ibid., 126.

50  Phua, F., and Rowlinson, S. (2004). How important is cooperation to construction project success? A grounded empirical quantification. *Engineering, Construction and Architectural Management, 11,* 45.

51  Berry, L.L. (2004). Leadership lessons from Mayo Clinic. *Organizational Dynamics, 33,* 228–242.

52  Harter, J.K., Hayes, T.L., and Schmidt, F.L. (2002). Business-unit-level relationship between employee satisfaction, employee engagement, and business outcomes: A meta-analysis. *Journal of Applied Psychology, 87,* 268–279.

53  Long, M. (16 October 2018). *Employees are happier, healthier and more productive in LEED green buildings.* U.S. Green Building Council (USGBC). https://www.usgbc.org/articles/employees-are-happier-healthier -and-more-productive-leed-green-buildings

54  WELL Building Institute. https://www.wellcertified.com/

55  Libby, B. (8 April 2019). Using CLT, Hacker Architects helps connect a workplace to its surrounding nature preserve. *Metropolis.* https:// www.metropolismag.com/architecture/hacker-architects-first- tech-federal-credit-union-office/

56  Engineered Wood Association. (2018). *First Tech Federal Credit Union: The building that wanted to be mass timber.* https://www.structurlam.com /wp-content/uploads/2018/07/First-Tech-CU-case-study-1.pdf

57  Olanipekun, A.O., Xia, B., and Skitmore, M. (2016). Green building incentives: A review. *Renewable and Sustainable Energy Reviews, 59*, 1611–1621; Leder, S., Newsham, G.R., Veitch, J.A., Mancini, S., and Charles, K.E. (2016). Effects of office environment on employee satisfaction: A new analysis. *Building Research and Information, 44*, 34–50.

## Chapter 2

1  For information see: Health Promotion Board. (n.d.). *Singapore HEALTH Award.* https://www.hpb.gov.sg/workplace/singapore-health-award
2  Health Promotion Board. (n.d.). *Essential guide to workplace health promotion.* https://www.hpb.gov.sg/workplace/workplace-programmes /useful-information-for-organisations/essential-guide-to-workplace -health-promotion
3  Ang, J. (28 May 2018). 60% of Singaporean staff experience above average stress levels. *Humanresourcesonline.net.* https://www.humanresourcesonline .net/60-of-singaporean-staff-experience-above-average-stress-levels/
4  Siow, L.S. (27 August 2016). S'pore workplace stress on the rise: Survey. *Business Times.* https://www.businesstimes.com.sg/government-economy /spore-workplace-stress-on-the-rise-survey. The survey was carried out among 2,100 mid-level and senior-level professionals in the three locations, including 1,000 participants from Singapore.
5  Rand Corporation. (2012). *A review of the U.S. workplace wellness market, 5.* http://www.rand.org/pubs/occasional_papers/OP373.html
6  Sears, L.E., Shi, Y., Coberley, C.R., and Pope, J.E. (2013). Overall well-being as a predictor of health care, productivity, and retention outcomes in a large employer. *Population Health Management, 16*(6), 397–405. http:// online.liebertpub.com/doi/abs/10.1089/pop.2012.0114
7  Goetzel, R.Z., Henke, R.M., Tabrizi, M., Pelletier, K.R., Loeppke, R., Ballard, D.W., et al. (2014). Do workplace health promotion (wellness) programs work? *Journal of Occupational and Environmental Medicine, 56*, 929.
8  Pelletier, K.R. (2011). A review and analysis of the clinical and cost-effectiveness studies of comprehensive health promotion and disease management programs at the worksite: Update VIII 2008 to 2010. *Journal of Occupational and Environmental Medicine, 53*, 1310–1331.
9  Pelletier, K.R. (2005). A review and analysis of the clinical and cost-effectiveness studies of comprehensive health promotion and disease management programs at the worksite: Update VI 2000–2004. *Journal of Occupational and Environmental Medicine, 47*, 1051–1058.

10   Chari, R., Chang, C.C., Sauter, S.L., Petrun Sayers, E.L., Cerully, J.L., Schulte, P., et al. (2018). Expanding the paradigm of occupational safety and health: A new framework for worker well-being. *Journal of Occupational and Environmental Medicine, 60,* 589–593

11   Ibid., 590.

12   Harvard School of Public Health, Center for Work, Health, and Well-Being. (2012). *SafeWell Practice Guidelines: An integrated approach to worker health. Version 2.* http://centerforworkhealth.sph.harvard.edu/resources /safewell-resources

13   State of California Commission on Health and Safety and Workers' Compensation (CHSWC). (2010). *The whole worker: Guidelines for integrating occupational health and safety with workplace wellness programs.* http://www. dir.ca.gov/chswc/WOSHTEP/Publications/WOSHTEP_TheWhole-Worker.pdf

14   Robroek, S.J.W., van de Vathorst, S., Hilhorst, M.T., and Burdorf, A. (2012). Moral issues in workplace health promotion. *International Archives of Occupational and Environmental Health, 85,* 327–331; Crawford, J.O., Graveling, R.A., Cowie, H.A., and Dixon, K. (2010). The health, safety and health promotion needs of older workers. *Occupational Medicine, 60,* 184–192.

15   European Network for Workplace Health Promotion. (2018). *Models of good practice.* https://www.enwhp.org/?i=portal.en.8th-initiative-work-in-tune -with-life-models-of-good-practice

16   Goetzel, R.Z., and Ozminkowski, R.J. (2008). The health and cost benefits of work site health-promotion programs. *Annual Review of Public Health, 29,* 303–322.

17   Jacobs, M., and Pienaar, J. (2017). Stress, coping and safety compliance in a multinational gold mining company. *International Journal of Occupational Safety and Ergonomics, 23,* 152–161.

18   Farnacio, Y., Pratt, M.E., Marshall, E.G., and Graber, J.M. (2017). Are workplace psychosocial factors associated with work-related injury in the US workforce? National Health Interview Survey, 2010. *Journal of Occupational and Environmental Medicine, 59,* e164–e171.

19   Smith, T.A. (2018). An assessment of safety climate, job satisfaction and turnover intention relationships using a national sample of workers from the USA. *International Journal of Occupational Safety and Ergonomics, 24,* 27–34.

20   Dorner, T.E., Alexanderson, K., Svedberg, P., Tinghog, P., Ropponen, A., and Mittendorfer-Rutz, E. (2016). Synergistic effect between back pain and common mental disorders and the risk of future disability pension: A nationwide study from Sweden. *Psychological Medicine, 46,* 425–436.

21  Steptoe, A., and Kivimäki, M. (2013). Stress and cardiovascular disease: An update on current knowledge. *Annual Review of Public Health, 34,* 337–354.

22  Kouvonen, A., Manty, M., Lallukka, T., Lahelma, E., and Rahkonen, O. (2016). Changes in psychosocial and physical working conditions and common mental disorders. *European Journal of Public Health, 26,* 458–463.

23  Sultan-Taïeb, H., Chastang, J.F., Mansouri, M., and Niedhammer, I. (2013). The annual costs of cardiovascular diseases and mental disorders attributable to job strain in France. *BMC Public Health, 13,* 748.

24  Kivimäki, M., and Siegrist, J. (2016). Work stress and cardiovascular disease: Reviewing research evidence with a focus on effort-reward imbalance at work. In J. Siegrist and M. Wahrendorf (Eds.), *Work stress and health in a globalized economy: The model of effort-reward Imbalance* (pp. 89–101). New York: Springer International Publishing.

25  Chu, A.H.Y., Koh, D., Moy, F.M., and Mueller-Riemenschneider, F. (2014). Do workplace physical activity interventions improve mental health outcomes? *Occupational Medicine, 64,* 235–245.

26  Wieland, L., Skoetz, N., Pilkington, K., Vempati, R., D'Adamo, C.R., and Berman, B.M. (2017). Yoga treatment for chronic non-specific low back pain. *Cochrane Database of Systematic Reviews, 1,* CD010671. doi:10.1002/14651858.CD010671.pub2.

27  Carnide, N., Franche, R.L., Hogg-Johnson, S., Côté, P., Breslin, F.C., Severin, C.N., et al. (2016). Course of depressive symptoms following a workplace injury: A 12-month follow-up update. *Journal of Occupational Rehabilitation, 26,* 204–215.

28  Goetzel, R.Z., Fabius, R.M., Fabius, D.D., Roemer, E.C.P., Thornton, N.B., Kelly, R.K.P., et al. (2016). The stock performance of C. Everett Koop Award winners compared with the Standard and Poor's 500 Index. *Journal of Occupational and Environmental Medicine, 58,* 9–15. Also see The Health Project. (n.d.). Award information. http://thehealthproject.com/award-information-2/

29  Grossmeier, J.P., Fabius, R.D., Flynn, J.P.M., Noeldner, S.P.P., Fabius, D.D., Goetzel, R.Z., et al. (2016). Linking workplace health promotion best practices and organizational financial performance: Tracking market performance of companies with highest scores on the HERO Scorecard. *Journal of Occupational and Environmental Medicine, 58,* 16–23.

30  Ibid, 22.

31  Sears, L.E., Shi, Y., Coberley, C.R. and Pope, J.E. (2013). Overall well-being as a predictor of health care, productivity, and retention outcomes in a large employer. *Population Health Management, 16*(6), 397–405. http://online.liebertpub.com/doi/abs/10.1089/pop.2012.0114

32   Lee, L.Y., and Tan, E. (2012). The influences of antecedents on employee creativity and employee performance: A meta-analytic review. *Interdisciplinary Journal of Contemporary Research in Business, 4,* 984–996.

33   Gilboa, S., Shirom, A., Fried, Y., and Cooper, C. (2008). A meta-analysis of work demand stressors and job performance: Examining main and moderating effects. *Personnel Psychology, 61,* 227–271.

34   Ton, Z. (January–February 2012). Some companies are investing in their workers and reaping healthy profits. *Harvard Business Review,* 125–131.

35   Lowe, G., and Graves, F. (2016). *Redesigning work: A blueprint for Canada's future well-being and prosperity.* Toronto: University of Toronto Press.

36   Ibid.

37   Oshio, T., Inoue, A., and Tsutsumi, A. (2017). Does work-to-family conflict really matter for health? Cross-sectional, prospective cohort and fixed -effects analyses. *Social Science and Medicine, 175,* 36–42.

38   Bellavia, G.M., and Frone, M.R. (2005). Work-family conflict. In J. Barling, E.K. Kelloway, and M.R. Frone (Eds.), *Handbook of work stress* (pp. 113–147). Thousand Oaks, CA: Sage; Gilboa, S., Shirom, A., Fried, Y., and Cooper, C. (2008). A meta-analysis of work demand stressors and job performance: Examining main and moderating effects. *Personnel Psychology, 61,* 227–271.

39   Duxbury, L., and Higgins, C. (2017). *Something's got to give: Balancing work, childcare, and eldercare.* Toronto: University of Toronto Press.

40   Bajwa, U., Gastaldo, D., Di Ruggiero, E., and Knorr, L. (2018). The health of workers in the global gig economy. *Globalization and health, 14,* 124.

41   International Labour Organization. (14 November 2016). *Non-standard employment around the world: Understanding challenges, shaping prospects.* https://www.ilo.org/wcmsp5/groups/public/---dgreports/---dcomm /---publ/documents/publication/wcms_534326.pdf

42   Conger, K., and Scheiber, N. (11 September 2019). California passes landmark bill to remake gig economy. *New York Times.* https://www.nytimes .com/2019/09/11/technology/california-passes-landmark-bill-to-remake -gig-economy.html?smid=nytcore-ios-share

43   Bliese, P.D., Edwards, J.R., and Sonnentag, S. (2017). Stress and well-being at work: A century of empirical trends reflecting theoretical and societal influences. *Journal of Applied Psychology, 102,* 390. Also see: Karasek, R., and Theorell, T. (1990). *Healthy work: Stress, productivity, and the reconstruction of working life.* New York: Basic Books; Siegrist, J. (1996). Adverse health effects of high-effort/low-reward conditions. *Journal of Occupational Health Psychology, 1,* 27–41; Maslach, C., Schaufeli, W.B., and Leiter, M.P. (2001). Job burnout. *Annual Review of Psychology, 52,* 397–422.

44   See, for example: Vahtera, J., Kivimaki, M., Pentti, J., and Theorell, T. (2000). Effect of change in the psychosocial work environment on sickness

absence: A seven year follow up of initially healthy employees. *Journal of Epidemiology and Community Health, 54*, 484–493; Marmot, M. (1994). Work and other factors influencing coronary health and sickness absence. *Work & Stress, 8*, 191–201; Mustard, C.A., Lavis, J., and Ostry, A. (2006). New evidence and enhanced understandings: Labour market experiences and health. In J. Heymann, C. Hertzman, M. Barer, and R. Evans (Eds.), *Healthier societies: From analysis to action* (pp. 173–201). New York: Oxford University Press.

45  Bakker, A.B., Demerouti, E., and Sanz-Vergel, A.I. (2014). Burnout and work engagement: The JD–R approach. *Annual Review of Organizational Psychology and Organizational Behavior, 1*, 389–411.

46  See: Schaufeli, W.B., Leiter, M.P., and Maslach, C. (2009). Burnout: 35 years of research and practice. *Career Development International, 14*(3), 204–220.

47  Havermans, B.M., Schlevis, R.M., Boot, C.R., Brouwers, E.P., Anema, J., and van der Beek, A.J. (2016). Process variables in organizational stress management intervention evaluation research: A systematic review. *Scandinavian Journal of Work, Environment and Health, 42*(5), 371–381.

48  Kuster, A.T., Dalsbo, T.K., Luong Thanh, B.Y., Agarwal, A., Durand-Moreau, Q.V., and Kirkehei, I. (2017). Computer-based versus in-person interventions for preventing and reducing stress in workers. *Cochrane Database of Systematic Reviews, 8*, CD011899. http://dx.doi.org/10.1002/14651858.CD011899.pub2

49  Robertson, I.T., Cooper, C.L., Sarkar, M., and Curran, T. (2015). Resilience training in the workplace from 2003 to 2014: A systematic review. *Journal of Occupational and Organizational Psychology, 88*, 533–562.

50  Vanhove, A.J., Herian, M.N., Perez, A.L.U., Harms, P.D., and Lester, P.B. (2016). Can resilience be developed at work? A meta-analytic review of resilience-building programme effectiveness. *Journal of Occupational and Organizational Psychology, 89*, 278–307.

51  Institute for Work and Health. (2018). *Evidence-informed guide to supporting people with depression in the workplace.* https://www.iwh.on.ca/tools-and -guides/evidence-informed-guide-to-supporting-people-with -depression-in-workplace

52  Wan Mohd Yunus, W.M.A., Musiat, P., and Brown, J.S.L. (2018). Systematic review of universal and targeted workplace interventions for depression. *Occupational and Environmental Medicine, 75*, 66–75.

53  Callander, E.J., Lindsay, D.B., and Scuffham, P.A. (2017). Employer benefits from an early intervention program for depression: A cost-benefit analysis. *Journal of Occupational and Environmental Medicine, 59*, 246–249.

54  Okechukwu, C.A., Souza, K., Davis, K.D., and de Castro, A.B. (2014). Discrimination, harassment, abuse, and bullying in the workplace:

Contribution of workplace injustice to occupational health disparities. *American Journal of Industrial Medicine, 57*, 573–586; Einarsen, S., and Nielsen, M.B. (2015). Workplace bullying as an antecedent of mental health problems: A five-year prospective and representative study. *International Archives of Occupational and Environmental Health, 88*, 131–142.

55  *Canadian HR Reporter*. (1 May 2017). Sexual harassment "national crisis." http://www.hrreporter.com/sharedwidgets/systools/_printarticle_.aspx?articleid=33285

56  Schwartz, T., and McCarthy, C. (October 2007). Manage your energy, not your time. *Harvard Business Review*. https://hbr.org/2007/10/manage-your-energy-not-your-time

57  For overviews see: Samra, J. (2017). *The evolution of workplace mental health in Canada: Research report (2007–2017)*. Great-West Life Centre for Mental Health in the Workplace. https://www.hrpa.ca/Documents/Public/Thought-Leadership/The-Evolution-of-Workplace-Mental-Health-in-Canada.pdf; Baynton, M.A., and Fournier, L. (2017). *The evolution of workplace mental health in Canada: Toward a standard for psychological health and safety*. Great-West Life Assurance Company: Friesens. https://www.workplacestrategiesformentalhealth.com/pdf/articles/Evolution_Book.pdf

58  https://www.mentalhealthcommission.ca/English

59  https://www.workplacestrategiesformentalhealth.com

60  https://letstalk.bell.ca/en/

61  Mental Health Commission of Canada. (n.d.). *Opening minds*. https://www.mentalhealthcommission.ca/English/opening-minds

62  Canadian Standards Association. (2013). *National Standard for Psychological Health and Safety in the Workplace*. https://store.csagroup.org/ccrz__ProductList?cartID=&operation=quickSearch&searchText=National%20Standard%20for%20Psychological%20Health%20and%20Safety%20in%20the%20Workplace&searchFilter=all&portalUser=&store=&cclcl=en_US

63  Guarding Minds @ Work. (2012). *A workplace guide to psychological health and safety*. http://www.guardingmindsatwork.ca/info; Mental Health Commission of Canada. (2012). *Psychological health and safety: An action guide for employers*. https://www.mentalhealthcommission.ca/English/media/3050

64  Canadian Standards Association. (2013). *National Standard for Psychological Health and Safety in the Workplace*. https://store.csagroup.org/ccrz__ProductList?cartID=&operation=quickSearch&searchText=National%20Standard%20for%20Psychological%20Health%20and%20Safety%20in%20the%20Workplace&searchFilter=all&portalUser=&store=&cclcl=en_US

65  Guarding Minds @ Work. (2012). *A workplace guide to psychological health and safety*. http://www.guardingmindsatwork.ca/info

66  Kelloway, E.K. (2017). Mental health in the workplace: Towards evidence-based practice. *Canadian Psychology/Psychologie canadienne, 58*, 1–6; LaMontagne, A.D., Martin, A., Page, K.M., Reavley, N.J., Noblet, A.J., Milner, A.J., et al. (2014). Workplace mental health: Developing an integrated intervention approach. *BMC Psychiatry, 14*, 131.

67  Memish, K., Martin, A., Bartlett, L., Dawkins, S., and Sanderson, K. (2017). Workplace mental health: An international review of guidelines. *Preventive Medicine, 101*, 213–222.

68  Malachowski, C., Kirsh, B., and McEachen, E. (2017). The sociopolitical context of Canada's National Standard for Psychological Health and Safety in the Workplace: Navigating policy implementation. *Healthcare Policy, 12*(4), 10–17.

69  Sheikh, M.S., Smail-Crevier, R., and Wang, J. (2018). A cross-sectional study of the awareness and implementation of the National Standard of Canada for Psychological Health and Safety in the Workplace in Canadian employers. *Canadian Journal of Psychiatry, 63*(12), 842–850. https://doi.org/10.1177/0706743718772524

70  Mental Health Commission of Canada. (n.d.). *Case study research project*. https://www.mentalhealthcommission.ca/English/case-study-research-project.

71  Health and Safety Executive. (n.d.). *Work-related stress*. http://www.hse.gov.uk/stress/

72  Mellor, N., Mackay, C., Packham, C., Jones, R., Palferman, D., Webster, S., et al. (2011). "Management Standards" and work-related stress in Great Britain: Progress on their implementation. *Safety Science, 49*, 1040–1046.

73  Zoni, S., and Lucchini, R.G. (2012). European approaches to work-related stress: A critical review on risk evaluation. *Safety and Health at Work, 3*(1), 43–49.

74  *OHS News*. (8 June 2018). http://content.safetyculture.com.au/news/index.php/06/nsw-government-invests-55m-workplace-mental-health/#.WzhNcK2B3eQ

75  Queensland Government, WorkCover Queensland. (6 December 2018). *Overview of People at Work*. https://www.worksafe.qld.gov.au/injury-prevention-safety/mentally-healthy-workplaces/guidance-and-tools/people-at-work/overview

76  Queensland Government. (18 March 2019). *Work health and safety act 2011*. https://www.legislation.qld.gov.au/view/html/inforce/2019-03-18/act-2011-018

77  https://mentallyhealthyworkplacealliance.org.au/

78  SafeWork Australia. (n.d.). Mental health. https://www.safeworkaustralia .gov.au/topic/mental-health

## Chapter 3

1  Sharp, I. (2009). *Four Seasons: The story of a business philosophy*. Toronto: Viking Canada.

2  Younglai, R. (17 August 2018). Beyond the Saudi spat, Isadore Sharp sees a bright future for Four Seasons. *Globe and Mail*. https://www.theglobeandmail .com/business/article-four-seasons-founder-isadore-sharp-is-caught-in-a -diplomatic-row/

3  Association of Workers' Compensation Boards of Canada. (2018). About AWCBC. http://awcbc.org/?page_id=2

4  Conference Board of Canada. (16 November 2017). *Wellness initiatives: Trends in organizational health management*. https://www.conferenceboard. ca/e-library/abstract.aspx?did=9106&AspxAutoDetectCookieSupport=1

5  See, for example: Samra, J. (2017). *The evolution of workplace mental health in Canada: Research report (2007–2017)*. https://www.hrpa.ca /Documents/Public/Thought-Leadership/The-Evolution-of-Workplace -Mental-Health-in-Canada.pdf; Canadian Standards Association. (2013). *National Standard for Psychological Health and Safety in the Workplace*. https:// store.csagroup.org/ccrz__ProductList?cartID=&operation=quickSearch &searchText=National%20Standard%20for%20Psychological%20Health%20 and%20Safety%20in%20the%20Workplace&searchFilter=all&portalUser= &store=&cclcl=en_US; Great-West Life Centre for Mental Health in the Workplace. https://www.workplacestrategiesformentalhealth.com; Guarding Minds @ Work https://www.guardingmindsatwork.ca/info; Mental Health Commission of Canada. (n.d.). *Case study research project*. https://www .mentalhealthcommission.ca/English/case-study-research-project

6  The survey was conducted by EKOS Research Associates in October 2018. Employees, self-employed, temporary, and contract workers are included (but not the unemployed). The sample size is 1,388, which pro- vides a margin of error of +/- 2.6 percentage points at a 95 percent level of confidence.

7  Patterson, M.G., West, M.A., Shackleton, V.J., Dawson, J.F., Lawthom, R., Maitlis, S., et al. (2005). Validating the organizational climate measure: Links to managerial practices, productivity and innovation. *Journal of Organizational Behavior, 26*, 379–408. Also see: Schneider, B., Gonzalez-Roma, V., Ostroff, C., and West, M.A. (2017). Organizational

climate and culture: Reflections on the history of the constructs in the *Journal of Applied Psychology. Journal of Applied Psychology, 102,* 468–482.

8   Neal, A., West, M.A., and Patterson, M.G. (2005). Do organizational climate and competitive strategy moderate the relationship between human resource management and productivity? *Journal of Management, 31,* 492–512.

9   Cooklin, A., Joss, N., Husser, E., and Oldenburg, B. (2017). Integrated approaches to occupational health and safety: A systematic review. *American Journal of Health Promotion, 31,* 401–412; Fabius, R.M., Loeppke, R.R., Hohn, T., Fabius, D., Eisenberg, B., Konicki, D.L., et al. (2016). Tracking the market performance of companies that integrate a culture of health and safety: An assessment of Corporate Health Achievement Award applicants. *Journal of Occupational and Environmental Medicine, 58,* 3–8.

10   Chari, R., Chang, C.C., Sauter, S.L., Petrun Sayers, E.L., Cerully, J.L., Schulte, P., et al. (2018). Expanding the paradigm of occupational safety and health: A new framework for worker well-being. *Journal of Occupational and Environmental Medicine, 60,* 589–593

11   Torp, S., Grimsmo, A., Hagen, S., Duran, A. and Gudbergsson, S.B. (2012). Work engagement: A practical measure for workplace health promotion? *Health Promotion International.* http://heapro.oxfordjournals.org/content /early/2012/06/11/heapro.das022.full

12   Spreitzer, G., and Porath, C. (January–February 2012). Creating sustainable performance. *Harvard Business Review,* 93–99.

13   Ton, Z. (January–February 2012). Some companies are investing in their workers and reaping healthy profits. *Harvard Business Review,* 125–131.

14   Quinn, R.E., and Thakor, A.V. (2018). Creating a purpose-driven organiza-tion. *Harvard Business Review, 96*(5), 20.

15   Robinson, J. (27 November 2012). Wellbeing is contagious (for better or worse). *Gallup Business Journal.* http://businessjournal.gallup.com /content/158732/wellbeing-contagious-better-worse.aspx

16   Robison, J. (19 March 2013). How to create a culture of organizational wellbeing. *Gallup Business Journal.* http://businessjournal.gallup.com /content/159080/create-culture-organizational-wellbeing.aspx

17   Kanter, R.M. (July 2013). Surprises are the new normal; resilience is the new skill. *Harvard Business Review.* https://hbr.org/2013/07/surprises-are -the-new-normal-r.html

18   Vanhove, A.J., Herian, M.N., Perez, A.L.U., Harms, P.D., and Lester, P.B. (2016). Can resilience be developed at work? A meta-analytic review of

resilience-building programme effectiveness. *Journal of Occupational and Organizational Psychology, 89*, 278–307.

19 Seligman, M. (2012). *Flourish: A visionary new understanding of happiness and wellbeing*. New York: Simon and Schuster.

20 Luthans, F., Avolio, B.J., Avey, J.B., and Norman, S.M. (2007). Positive psychological capital: Measurement and relationship with performance and satisfaction. *Personnel Psychology, 60*, 541–572; Avey, J.B., Reichard, R.J., Luthans, F., and Mhatre, K.H. (2011). Meta-analysis of the impact of positive psychological capital on employee attitudes, behaviors, and performance. *Human Resource Development Quarterly, 22*, 127–152.

21 McFarlane, S., and Haskell, M. (September 2014). *Organisational resilience*. Presentation at the Occupational Healthy and Safety Industry Group (OHSIG) Conference, Auckland, NZ.

22 Christchurch City Council. (n.d.). *Future projects*. https://www.ccc.govt. nz/the-council/future-projects/

23 Burry, M. (13 September 2016). Christchurch City Council to commit 10 percent of spending to resilience. *RNZ (Radio New Zealand)*. https:// www.rnz.co.nz/news/national/313225/chch-city-council-to-commit -10-percent-of-spending-to-resilience

24 Healthy Christchurch. (27 March 2013). *Tips from Dr. Rob Gordon*. https:// www.healthychristchurch.org.nz/news/earthquake/2013/3/tips -from-dr-rob-gordon

25 McFarlane, S., and Haskell, M. (September 2014). *Organisational resilience*. Presentation at the Occupational Health and Safety Industry Group (OHSIG) Conference, Auckland, NZ.

26 West, M.A., and Dawson, J.F. (2012). *Employee engagement and NHS performance*. London: The King's Fund. https://www.kingsfund.org.uk/sites /default/files/employee-engagement-nhs-performance-west-dawson -leadership-review2012-paper.pdf

27 See: Lowe, G. (September 2012). *The relationship between employee engagement and human capital performance*. Ontario Hospital Association. http://www.longwoods.com/blog/wp-content/uploads/2012/09/ OHA-The-Relationship-Between-Employee-Engagement-and-Human -Capital-Performance-Report-Final-Sept-13-2012.pdf; Lowe, G. (2012). How employee engagement matters for hospital performance. *Healthcare Quarterly, 15*(2), 29–39.

28 Gibbons, J., and Schutt, R. (2010). *A global barometer for measuring employee engagement*. Research Working Group Report No. 1460-09-RR. New York: Conference Board; Macey, W.H., and Schneider, B. (2008). The meaning of employee engagement. *Industrial and Organizational Psychology, 1*, 3–30.

29 Standard social science practices were followed in constructing the EES engagement scale. Scale items were selected based on frequency

distributions, correlations, face and construct validity considerations, and factor analysis. Factor loadings for the six items range between .77 and .89 (i.e., these items measure the same underlying concept – engagement), and Cronbach's reliability alpha ($\alpha$) is .92.

30  West, M.A., and Dawson, J.F. (2012). *Employee engagement and NHS performance*. London: The King's Fund, 20. https://www.kingsfund.org.uk /sites/default/files/employee-engagement-nhs-performance-west -dawson-leadership-review2012-paper.pdf

31  https://www.rvh.on.ca/SitePages/main.aspx

## Chapter 4

1  Scudamore, B. (16 May 2018). Why good culture matters for your business – and how to get it. *Globe and Mail*. https://www.theglobeandmail.com /report-on-business/careers/leadership-lab/why-good-culture-matters -for-your-business-and-how-to-get-it/article29690328/

2  Berry, L.L., and Seltman, K.D. (2008). *Management lessons from the Mayo Clinic: Inside one of the world's most admired service organizations*. New York: McGraw-Hill, 58.

3  *Stuff.co.nz*. (6 October 2017). Japanese woman dies after working 159 hours overtime. http://fw.to/GzOQX3f

4  *Economist*. (24 March 2018). Employers and the government are trying to tackle overtime, 99.

5  Schein, E.H. (1990). Organizational culture. *American Psychologist, 45*(2), 109–119.

6  Malone, G.K. (9 August 2018). Hundreds of Manitoba civil servants have experienced harassment, report finds. *The Globe and Mail*. https://www .theglobeandmail.com/canada/article-hundreds-of-manitoba-civil -servants-have-experienced-harassment

7  Quoted in *The Economist*. (8 June 2019). Charity begins at work, 60.

8  McVeigh, K. (6 February 2019). Amnesty International has toxic working culture, report finds. *Guardian*. https://www.theguardian.com/world/2019 /feb/06/amnesty-international-has-toxic-working-culture-report-finds; Konterra Group. (January 2019). *Amnesty International staff wellbeing review*. Amnesty International. https://www.amnesty.org/en/documents/org60 /9763/2019/en/; *BBC.com*. (29 May 2019). Amnesty loses five bosses after report on "toxic workplace." https://www.bbc.com/news/uk-48431652

9  Konterra Group. (January 2019). *Amnesty international staff wellbeing review*, 15. Amnesty International. https://www.amnesty.org/en/documents /org60/9763/2019/en/

10  Duxbury, L., and Higgins, C. (2017). *Something's got to give: Balancing work, childcare, and eldercare*. Toronto: University of Toronto Press, 276.

11  Ibid., 276.
12  US Centers for Disease Control and Prevention. (n.d.). *Workplace health glossary*. https://www.cdc.gov/workplacehealthpromotion/tools-resources/glossary/glossary.html
13  Kent, K., Goetzel, R.Z., Roemer, E.C., Prasad, A., and Freundlich, N. (2016). Promoting healthy workplaces by building cultures of health and applying strategic communications. *Journal of Occupational and Environmental Medicine, 58*, 114–122.
14  International Corporate Health Leadership Council. (2016). *Creating a culture of health for a global organization: Framework and practices*. http://www.ichlc.org/about-the-council/
15  Wellness Council of America. (n.d.). *WELCOA's 7 benchmarks: Creating a culture of health*. https://www.welcoa.org/wp/wp-content/uploads/2014/09/welcoa-creating-a-culture-of-health.pdf
16  *Benefits Canada*. (13 June 2018). Benefits plan sponsors continuing to focus on cost management: Sanofi survey. https://www.benefitscanada.com/news/benefits-plan-sponsors-continuing-to-focus-on-cost-management-sanofi-survey-115282?print
17  Sanofi Canada. (2016). *The Sanofi Canada Healthcare Survey: Canada's premier survey on health benefit plans*, 18–19. https://www.sanofi.ca/-/media/Project/One-Sanofi-Web/Websites/North-America/Sanofi-CA/Home/en/About-us/The-Sanofi-Canada-Healthcare-Survey/The-Sanofi-Canada-Healthcare-Survey-2017---Full-Report.pdf
18  Fabius, R.M., Loeppke, R.R. M., Hohn, T.C., Fabius, D.D., Eisenberg, B.C., Konicki, D.L., et al. (2016). Tracking the market performance of companies that integrate a culture of health and safety: An assessment of Corporate Health Achievement Award applicants. *Journal of Occupational and Environmental Medicine, 58*, 3–8.
19  Ibid., 7.
20  Zohar, D. (2014). Safety climate: Conceptualization, measurement, and improvement. In B. Schneider and K.M. Barbera (Eds.), *The Oxford handbook of organizational climate and culture* (pp. 317–334). Oxford: Oxford University Press; Schneider, B., Gonzalez-Roma, V., Ostroff, C., and West, M.A. (2017). Organizational climate and culture: Reflections on the history of the constructs in the *Journal of Applied Psychology*. *Journal of Applied Psychology, 102*, 468–482.
21  Nordlöf, H., Wiitavaara, B., Winblåd, U., Wijk, K., and Westerling, R. (2015). Safety culture and reasons for risk-taking at a large steel-manufacturing company: Investigating the worker perspective. *Safety Science, 73*, 126–135.
22  Cagno, E., Micheli, G.J.L., Jacinto, C., and Masi, D. (2014). An interpretive model of occupational safety performance for small- and medium-sized enterprises. *International Journal of Industrial Ergonomics, 44*, 60–74.

23   Amick, B., Farquhar, A., Grant, K., Hunt, S., Kapoor, K., Keown, K., et al. (2011). *Benchmarking organizational leading indicators for the prevention and management of injuries and illnesses: Final report*. Toronto: Institute for Work and Health. https://www.iwh.on.ca/scientific-reports/benchmarking -organizational-leading-indicators-for-prevention-and-management-of

24   Go to the IWH website to download the OPM tool, instructions on how to administer and score it, benchmarks, and follow-up questions to help guide improvements in safety performance: https://www.iwh.on.ca /tools-and-guides/iwh-organizational-performance-metric

25   CSA Group and Bureau de normalisation du Québec. (2013). CAN/ CSA-Z1003-13/BNQ 9700-803/2013. *National Standard of Canada: Psychological health and safety in the workplace – prevention, promotion, and guidance to staged implementation*, 19. https://www.csagroup.org /documents/codes-and-standards/publications/CAN_CSA-Z1003-13 _BNQ_9700-803_2013_EN.pdf

26   Great Place to Work Institute. (n.d.). Fortune *100 Best Companies to Work for 2017*. https://www.greatplacetowork.com/best-workplaces/100 -best/2017

27   Great Place to Work Institute. (n.d.). *Best Workplaces Canada 2018*. https:// www.greatplacetowork.ca/en/best-workplaces/best-workplaces -in-canada-1000-employees

28   Great Place to Work Institute. (n.d.). *Financial performance*. https://www .greatplacetowork.ca/en/culture-consulting/financial-performance

29   CSA Group. (n.d.). *Psychological health and safety in the workplace*. http:// shop.csa.ca/en/canada/landing-pages/z1003-psychological -health-and-safety-in-the-workplace/page/z1003-landing-page.

30   Fried, J., and Hansson, D.H. (2018). *It doesn't have to be crazy at work*. New York: Harper Business, 82.

31   Colquitt, J.A., Scott, B.A., and LePine, J.A. (2007). Trust, trustworthiness, and trust propensity: A meta-analytic test of their unique relationships with risk taking and job performance. *Journal of Applied Psychology, 92*, 909–927.

32   Solomon, R.C., and Flores, F. (2001). *Building trust in business, politics, relationships and life*. New York: Oxford University Press, 5.

33   Quoted in Pitts, G. (30 October 2007). Community-ship v. the decision maker. *Globe and Mail Report on Business*, B2.

34   Values. (n.d.). In *Oxford English dictionary online*. Accessed on the University of Alberta Library website, 21 November 2019.

35   Kanter, R.M. (January 2008). Transforming giants: What kind of company makes it its business to make the world a better place? *Harvard Business Review*, 43–52.

36  Collins, J.C., and Porras, J.I. (1994). *Built to last: Successful habits of visionary companies.* New York: HarperCollins.

37  https://www.olympic.org/vancouver-2010. Also see Brethour, P. (28 May 2007). Shaped by the crucible of culture. *Globe and Mail Report on Business*, B3.

38  George, B. (18 January 2012). How IBM's Sam Palmisano redefined the global corporation. *Harvard Business Review.* https://hbr.org/2012/01/how-ibms-sam-palmisano-redefin.html; Hemp, P., and Stewart, P.A. (December 2004). Leading change when business is good. *Harvard Business Review.* https://hbr.org/2004/12/leading-change-when-business-is-good

## Chapter 5

1  Yakowicz, W. (4 August 2014). Lessons from leadership guru Warren Bennis. *Inc.com.* https://www.inc.com/will-yakowicz/7-leadership-lessons-from-late-warren-bennis.html. Also see: Bennis, W. (2009). *On becoming a leader.* New York: Basic Books.

2  Mintzberg, H. (November 2004). Enough leadership. *Harvard Business Review*, 22.

3  Kouzes, J.M., and Posner, B.Z. (2017). *The leadership challenge: How to make extraordinary things happen in organizations* (6th ed.). San Francisco: John Wiley.

4  Mohan, P. (30 August 2019).These CEOs work 40 hours or less a week (and think you should too). *Fast Company.* https://www.fastcompany.com/90385364/these-ceos-work-40-hours-or-less-a-week-and-think-you-should-too

5  TOMS Canada. https://www.toms.ca/

6  Mycoskie, B. (2016). The founder of TOMS on reimagining the company's mission. *Harvard Business Review, 94*(1), 41–44.

7  Meinert, D. (27 June 2019). TOMS founder Blake Mycoskie encourages self-help after depression diagnosis. SHRM. https://www.shrm.org/resourcesandtools/hr-topics/employee-relations/pages/toms-founder-blake-mycoskie-self-help-depression.aspx

8  Dixon, G. (27 March 2019). Winning workplaces put flexibility first. *Globe and Mail.* https://www.theglobeandmail.com/business/careers/workplace-award/article-winning-workplaces-put-flexibility-first

9  West, M., Dawson, J., Admasachew, L., and Topakas, A. (August 2011). *NHS staff management and health service quality.* Results from the NHS Staff Survey and related data. https://www.gov.uk/government/publications/nhs-staff-management-and-health-service-quality

10  Ibid.

11  Ibid., 15.

12  Rath, T., and Harter, J. (2010). *Wellbeing: The five essential elements.* New York: Gallup Press, 133–136.

13  Zilio, M. (31 July 2018). The Phoenix pay system debacle is on track to cost taxpayers $2.2-billion. *Globe and Mail.* https://www.theglobeandmail.com/politics/article-phoenix-pay-system-problems-on-track-to-cost-government-22-billion/

14  Lee, L.Y., and Tan, E. (2012). The influences of antecedents on employee creativity and employee performance: A meta-analytic review. *Interdisciplinary Journal of Contemporary Research in Business, 4*, 984–996.

15  Spreitzer, G.M., and Porath, C. (January–February 2012). Creating sustainable performance. *Harvard Business Review,* 4.

16  Pfeffer, J. (2018). *Dying for a paycheck: How modern management harms employee health and company performance – and what we can do about it.* New York: Harper Business, 164.

17  Fullan, M. (2001). *Leading in a culture of change.* San Francisco: Jossey-Bass.

18  Wheatley, M.J. (2005). *Finding our way: Leadership for an uncertain time.* San Francisco: Berrett-Koehler.

19  Goleman, D. (2006). *Emotional intelligence.* New York: Bantam, 149.

20  Wigert, B., and Agrawal, S. (12 July 2018). Employee burnout, part 1: The 5 main causes. *Gallup Workplace.* https://www.gallup.com/workplace/237059/employee-burnout-part-main-causes.aspx

21  Hellebuyck, M., Nguyen, T., Halphern, M., Fritze, D., and Kennedy, J. *Mind the workplace.* Mental Health America. http://www.mentalhealthamerica.net/sites/default/files/Mind per cent20the per cent20Workplace per cent20- per cent20MHA per cent20Workplace per cent20Health per cent20 Survey per cent202017 per cent20FINAL.PDF

22  Klie, S. (17 January 2011). "Problem" managers a big problem: Survey. *Canadian HR Reporter.* http://www.hrreporter.com/articleview/8783-problem-managers-a-big-problem-survey

23  Government of Canada, Treasury Board of Canada Secretariat. (2019). *2018 Public Service Employee Survey.* https://www.canada.ca/en/treasury-board-secretariat/services/innovation/public-service-employee-survey/2018.html

24  Ammerman, C., and Groysberg, B. (21 December 2017). Why sexual harassment persists and what organizations can do to stop it. *Harvard Business Review.* https://hbr.org/2017/12/why-sexual-harassment-persists-and-what-organizations-can-do-to-stop-it

25  https://www.cdc.gov/niosh/twh/totalhealth.html

26 Anger, W.K., Kyler-Yano, J., Vaughn, K., Wipfli, B., Olson, R., and Blanco, M. (2018). Total Worker Health intervention for construction workers alters safety, health, well-being measures. *Journal of Occupational and Environmental Medicine, 60*, 700–709.

27 Gayed, A., Milligan-Saville, J.S., Nicholas, J., Bryan, B.T., LaMontagne, A.D., Milner, A., et al. (2018). Effectiveness of training workplace managers to understand and support the mental health needs of employees: A systematic review and meta-analysis. *Occupational and Environmental Medicine, 75*, 462–470.

28 Boini, S., Colin, R., and Grzebyk, M. (2017). Effect of occupational safety and health education received during schooling on the incidence of workplace injuries in the first 2 years of occupational life: A prospective study. *BMJ Open, 7*(7), e015100. http://dx.doi.org/10.1136/bmjopen-2016-015100.

29 Robertson, I.T., Cooper, C.L., Sarkar, M., and Curran, T. (2015). Resilience training in the workplace from 2003 to 2014: A systematic review. *Journal of Occupational and Organizational Psychology, 88*, 533–562.

30 Vanhove, A.J., Herian, M.N., Perez, A.L.U., Harms, P.D., and Lester, P.B. (2016). Can resilience be developed at work? A meta-analytic review of resilience-building programme effectiveness. *Journal of Occupational and Organizational Psychology, 89*, 278–307.

31 Flint-Taylor, J., and Cooper, C.L. (2017). Team resilience: Shaping up for the challenges ahead. In M.F. Crane (Ed.), *Managing for resilience: A practical guide for employee wellbeing and organizational performance* (pp. 129–149). New York: Routledge.

32 McEwen, K., and Boyd, C.M. (2018). A measure of team resilience: Developing the resilience at work team scale. *Journal of Occupational and Environmental Medicine, 60*, 258–272.

33 Crane, M.F. (2017). A manager's introductory guide to resilience. In M.F. Crane (Ed.), *Managing for resilience: A practical guide for employee wellbeing and organizational performance* (pp. 1–12). New York: Routledge.

34 https://www.asebp.ca/about

35 Luthans, F., Avolio, B.J., and Avey, J.B. (n.d.). Psychological capital questionnaire. *Mind Garden*. http://www.mindgarden.com/products/pcq.htm

36 Luthans, F., Youssef, C.M., and Avolio, B.J. (2007). *Psychological capital*. New York: Oxford University Press. Also see Avey, J.B., Reichard, R.J., Luthans, F., and Mhatre, K.H. (2011). Meta-analysis of the impact of positive psychological capital on employee attitudes, behaviors, and performance. *Human Resource Development Quarterly, 22*(2), 127–152; Ledesma, J. (2014). Conceptual frameworks and research models on resilience in leadership. *SAGE Open, 4*(3). https://doi.org/10.1177%2F2158244014545464; Youssef-Morgan, C.M., and Stratman, J.L. (2017). Psychological capital: Developing resilience

by leveraging the HERO within leaders. In M.F. Crane (Ed.), *Managing for resilience: A practical guide for employee wellbeing and organizational performance* (pp. 53–68). New York: Routledge.

37  Youssef-Morgan, C.M., and Stratman, J.L. (2017). Psychological capital: Developing resilience by leveraging the HERO within leaders. In M.F. Crane (Ed.), *Managing for resilience: A practical guide for employee wellbeing and organizational performance* (pp. 53–68). New York: Routledge, 60.

38  Bass, M.B., and Avolio, B.J. (n.d.). Multifactor leadership questionnaire. *Mind Garden*. http://www.mindgarden.com/products/mlqr.htm#mlq3605x

39  See for example: Geijsel, F., Sleegers, P., Leithwood, K., and Jantzi, D. (2003). Transformational leadership effects on teachers' commitment and effort toward school reform. *Journal of Educational Administration, 41,* 228–256; Leithwood, K., and Jantzi, D. (2000). The effects of transformational leadership on organizational conditions and student engagement with school. *Journal of Educational Administration, 38,* 112–129; Onorato, M. (2013). Transformational leadership style in the educational sector: An empirical study of corporate managers and educational leaders. *Academy of Educational Leadership Journal, 17,* 33–47.

40  Robson, L.S., Amick III, B.C., Moser, C., Pagell, M., Mansfield, E., Shannon, H.S., et al. (2016). Important factors in common among organizations making large improvement in OHS performance: Results of an exploratory multiple case study. *Safety Science, 86,* 211–227. Also see: Institute for Work and Health. (January 2014). Breakthrough change in OHS: Case study series. https://www.iwh.on.ca/tools-and-guides/breakthrough-change-in-ohs-case-study-series

41  Ibid., 222.

42  Lai, J. (13 October 2017). *Ronald McDonald House Charities of Southern and Central Alberta workplace wellness framework.* Healthy Workplaces for Helping Professions Conference, Edmonton, Alberta.

43  Berry, L.L., and Seltman, K.D. (2008). *Management lessons from the Mayo Clinic: Inside one of the world's most admired service organizations.* New York: McGraw Hill, 65.

## Chapter 6

1  Goh, J., Pfeffer, J., Zenios, S.A., and Rajpal, S. (2015). Workplace stressors and health outcomes: Health policy for the workplace. *Behavioral Science and Policy, 1,* 48.

2  Kaspin, L.C., Gorman, K.M., and Miller, R.M. (2013). Systematic review of employer-sponsored wellness strategies and their economic and health-related outcomes. *Population Health Management, 16,* 14–21.

3   Robroek, S.J., van Lenthe, F.J., van Empelen, P., and Burdorf, A. (2009). Determinants of participation in worksite health promotion programmes: A systematic review. *International Journal of Behavioral Nutrition and Physical Activity, 6*, 26.

4   Beckhard, R. (1997). The healthy organization: A profile. In F. Hesselbein, M. Goldsmith, and R. Beckhard (Eds.), *The organization of the future* (pp. 325–328). San Francisco: Jossey-Bass.

5   Buono, A.F., and Kerber, K.W. (2010). Creating a sustainable approach to change: Building organizational change capacity. *S.A.M. Advanced Management Journal, 75*(2), 4–14.

6   Ibid., 13.

7   Axelrod, R.H. (2000). *Terms of engagement: Changing the way we change organizations*. San Francisco: Berrett-Koehler.

8   Ibid.

9   World Health Organization. (n.d.). *Health promotion*. https://www.who.int /healthpromotion/fact-sheet/en/

10   Sutton, R.I. (2007). *The no asshole rule: Building a civilized workplace and surviving one that isn't*. New York: Random House.

11   Conger, K., Wakabayashi, D., and Benner, K. (31 October 2018). Google faces internal backlash over handling of sexual harassment. *New York Times*. https://www.nytimes.com/2018/10/31/technology/google-sexual -harassment-walkout.html

12   Wakabayashi, D., Griffith, E., Tsang, A., and Conger, K. (1 November 2018). Google walkout: Employees stage protest over handling of sexual harassment. *New York Times*. https://www.nytimes.com/2018/11/01/technology /google-walkout-sexual-harassment.html

13   Conger, K., and Wakabayashi, D. (22 April 2019). Google employees say they faced retaliation after organizing walkout. *New York Times*. https:// www.nytimes.com/2019/04/22/technology/google-walkout-employees -retaliation.html

14   Kotter, J.P. (1996). *Leading change*. Boston: Harvard Business School Press.

15   Connors, D. (2019). *A better place to work: Daily practices that transform culture*. Well-Advised Publishing.

16   Hackman, R.J., and Edmondson, A.C. (2008). Groups as agents of change. In T.G. Cummings (Ed.), *Handbook of organization development* (pp. 167– 186). Thousand Oaks, CA: Sage.

17   Pfeffer, J., and Sutton, R.I. (2000). *The knowing-doing gap: How smart companies turn knowledge into action*. Boston: Harvard Business School Press.

18   Felter, E.M., Nolan, B.A., Colombi, A. Albert, S.M., and Pringle, J.L. (2013). We're working hard, but is it hardly working? Why process is

critical in the delivery of worksite health promotion programs. *Journal of Occupational and Environmental Medicine, 55,* 586–592.

19  Dickson-Swift, V., Fox, C., Marshall, K., Welch, N., and Willis, J. (2014). What really improves employee health and wellbeing: Findings from regional Australian workplaces. *International Journal of Workplace Health Management, 7,* 138–155.

20  Loch, C.H., Sting, F.J., Bauer, N., and Mauermann, H. (March 2010). How BMW is defusing the demographic time bomb. *Harvard Business Review,* 99–102. Also see: Impact Lab. (19 February 2011). *BMW opens new car plant where the workforce is all aged over 50.* http://www.impactlab.net/2011/02/19/bmw-opens-new-car-plant-where-the-workforce-is-all-aged-over-50/

21  Holman, D., and Axtell, C. (2016). Can job redesign interventions influence a broad range of employee outcomes by changing multiple job characteristics? A quasi-experimental study. *Journal of Occupational Health Psychology, 21,* 284–295.

22  Gallup. (2017). *State of the American workplace.* https://news.gallup.com/reports/199961/7.aspx?utm_source=SOAWlaunch&utm_campaign=StateofAmericanWorkplace-Launch&utm_medium=email&utm_content=nonpeek

23  Sanofi Canada. (2016). *The Sanofi Canada Healthcare Survey: Canada's premier survey on health benefit plans.* https://www.sanofi.ca/-/media/Project/One-Sanofi-Web/Websites/North-America/Sanofi-CA/Home/en/About-us/The-Sanofi-Canada-Healthcare-Survey/The-Sanofi-Canada-Healthcare-Survey-2016---Full-Report.pdf

24  Dobush, G. (20 February 2019). This company swears by a 4-day work week. Now it has advice on how your employer can make the switch. *Fortune.* http://fortune.com/2019/02/20/four-day-work-week-research-benefits/

25  Haar, J. (July 2018). Overview of the Perpetual Guardian 4-day (paid 5) work trial. Auckland University of Technology. https://static1.squarespace.com/static/5a93121d3917ee828d5f282b/t/5b4e4237352f53b0cc369c8b/1531855416866/Final+Perpetual+Guardian+report_Professor+Jarrod+Haar_July+2018.pdf. Also see: Nadkarni, A. (3 October 2018). Company makes four-day working week permanent after trial. *Sydney Morning Herald.* https://www.smh.com.au/business/workplace/company-makes-four-day-working-week-permanent-after-trial-20181003-p507fo.html

26  Harr, ibid., 10.

27  Ibid., 7.

28  Graham-McLay, C. (19 July 2018). A 4-day workweek? A test run shows a surprising result. *New York Times*. https://www.nytimes.com/2018/07/19/world/asia/four-day-workweek-new-zealand.html

29  Lee, J. (28 August 2017). B.C. company bests flexible working with five-hour workday. *Benefits Canada*. https://www.benefitscanada.com/news/b-c-company-bests-flexible-working-with-five-hour-workday-102890?print

30  Moen, P., Kelly, E.L., Fan, W., Lee, S.R., Almeida, D., Kossek, E.E., et al. (2016). Does a flexibility/support organizational initiative improve high-tech employees' well-being? Evidence from the Work, Family, and Health Network. *American Sociological Review, 81*, 134–164. Also see: Dominus, S. (25 February 2016). Rethinking the work-life equation. *New York Times Magazine*. https://www.nytimes.com/2016/02/28/magazine/rethinking-the-work-life-equation.html

31  Ibid., 158.

32  Gallup. (2017). *State of the American workplace*. https://news.gallup.com/reports/199961/7.aspx?utm_source=SOAWlaunch&utm_campaign=StateofAmericanWorkplace-Launch&utm_medium=email&utm_content=nonpeek

33  Institute for Work and Health. (December 2017). *IWH model on breakthrough change used as foundation for WSPS small business strategy*. https://www.iwh.on.ca/impact-case-studies/iwh-model-on-breakthrough-change-used-as-foundation-for-wsps-small-business-strategy

34  Beer, M. (2003). Building organizational fitness. In S. Chowdhury (Ed.), *Organization 21C: Someday all organizations will lead this way* (pp. 311–328). Upper Saddle River, NJ: Financial Times Prentice Hall.

35  Barber, F., and Strack, R. (June 2005). The surprising economics of a "people business." *Harvard Business Review*, 84.

## Chapter 7

1  Heaps, T.A.A. (22 January 2018). Knights of the (clean capitalism) realm. *Corporate Knights*. http://www.corporateknights.com/channels/leadership/knights-clean-capitalism-realm-15166614/

2  Lyon, T.P., Delmas, M.A., Maxwell, J.W., Bansal, P., Chiroleu-Assouline, M., Crifo, P., et al. (2018). CSR needs CPR: Corporate sustainability and politics. *California Management Review, 60*, 5–24.

3  Ibid. Also see: Reguly, E. (16 March 2018). U.K.'s Unilever loss is social capitalism's gain. *Globe and Mail*. https://www.theglobeandmail.com/report-on-business/international-business/uks-unilever-loss-is-social-capitalisms-gain/article38296725/

4  Reguly, ibid. Also see: Sorkin, A.R. (15 January 2018). BlackRock's message: Contribute to society, or risk losing our support. *New York Times*. https:// www.nytimes.com/2018/01/15/business/dealbook/blackrock-laurence -fink-letter.html

5  De Stefano, F., Bagdadli, S., and Camuffo, A. (2018). The HR role in corporate social responsibility and sustainability: A boundary-shifting literature review. *Human Resource Management, 57*, 549–566.

6  Kunz, M.B. (2018). Corporate social responsibility reporting in *Fortune* 500 corporate websites: Review and analysis. *International Journal of Business and Public Administration, 15*, 30–51.

7  Voegtlin, C., and Greenwood, M. (2016). Corporate social responsibility and human resource management: A systematic review and conceptual analysis. *Human Resource Management Review, 26*, 181–197.

8  Pfeffer, J. (2018). *Dying for a paycheck: How modern management harms employee health and company performance – and what we can do about it*. New York: Harper Business, 7.

9  Goetzel, R.Z.P., Fabius, R.M., Fabius, D.D., Roemer, E.C.P., Thornton, N.B., Kelly, R.K.P., et al. (2016). The stock performance of C. Everett Koop Award winners compared with the Standard and Poor's 500 Index. *Journal of Occupational and Environmental Medicine, 58*, 9–15.

10  Monachino, M.S., and Moreira, P. (2014). Corporate social responsibility and the health promotion debate: An international review on the potential role of corporations. *International Journal of Healthcare Management, 7*, 53–59.

11  De Stefano, F., Bagdadli, S., and Camuffo, A. (2018). The HR role in corporate social responsibility and sustainability: A boundary-shifting literature review. *Human Resource Management, 57*, 559.

12  Godkin, L. (2015). Mid-management, employee engagement, and the generation of reliable sustainable corporate social responsibility. *Journal of Business Ethics, 130*, 15–28.

13  Zibarras, L.D., and Coan, P. (2015). HRM practices used to promote pro-environmental behavior: A UK survey. *International Journal of Human Resource Management, 26*, 2121–2142.

14  Mirvis, P. (2012). Employee engagement and CSR: Transactional, relational, and developmental approaches. *California Management Review, 54*, 105.

15  Ibid., 93–117.

16  United Nations. (n.d.). *About the Sustainable Development Goals*. https:// www.un.org/sustainabledevelopment/sustainable-development -goals/

17   Wang, H., Tong, L., Takeuchi, R., and George, G. (2016). Corporate social responsibility: An overview and new research directions. *Academy of Management Journal, 59,* 534.

18   Global Reporting Initiative. (n.d.). *About GRI.* https://www.globalreporting.org/information/about-gri/Pages/default.aspx

19   Global Reporting Initiative. (n.d.). *Consolidated set of GRI Sustainability Reporting Standards.* https://www.globalreporting.org/standards/gri-standards-download-center/?g=455cdad7-6ef4-4602-a549-798c0266301a https://www.globalreporting.org/information/about-gri/Pages/default.aspx

20   Global Reporting Initiative. (n.d.). *GRI 403: Occupational Health and Safety 2018,* 6. https://www.globalreporting.org/standards/gri-standards-download-center/gri-403-occupational-health-and-safety-2018/

21   Sancroft. (2017). *Maximizing the value of occupational health and safety and workplace wellness reporting for a global workforce.* Report commissioned by the International SOS Foundation. https://sancroft.com/2017/09/27/international-sos-foundation-and-sancroft-launch-occupational-health-safety-and-workplace-wellness-reporting-guidelines-for-a-global-workforce/

22   Flammer, C. (2015). Does corporate social responsibility lead to superior financial performance? A regression discontinuity approach. *Management Science, 61,* 2549–2568; Wang, Q., Dou, J., and Jia, S. (2015). A meta-analytic review of corporate social responsibility and corporate financial performance: The moderating effect of contextual factors. *Business and Society, 55,* 1083–1121.

23   *Economist.* (22 August 2019). I'm from a company, and I'm here to help. https://www.economist.com/node/21770324?frsc=dg per cent7Ce

24   Corporate Knights. (n.d.). https://www.corporateknights.com/us/about-us/; Dow Jones Sustainability Indices. https://www.robecosam.com/csa/indices/

25   Safi, M., and Rushe, D. (24 April 2018). Rana Plaza, five years on: Safety of workers hangs in balance in Bangladesh. *Guardian.* https://www.theguardian.com/global-development/2018/apr/24/bangladeshi-police-target-garment-workers-union-rana-plaza-five-years-on; International Labour Organization. (n.d.). *The Rana Plaza accident and its aftermath.* https://www.ilo.org/global/topics/geip/WCMS_614394/lang--en/index.htm

26   Safi and Rushe, ibid.

27   Bacchi, U. (11 November 2018). Most big companies failing UN human rights test, labour ranking shows. *Globe and Mail.* https://www.theglobeandmail.com/world/article-most-big-companies-failing-un

-human-rights-labour-test-ranking-shows/; Corporate Human Rights Benchmark. *2018 Key Findings*. https://www.corporatebenchmark.org/

28   Corporate Human Rights Benchmark, ibid.

29   Bacchi, U. (11 November 2018). Most big companies failing UN human rights test, labour ranking shows. *Globe and Mail*. https://www.theglobeandmail.com/world/article-most-big-companies-failing-un-human-rights-labour-test-ranking-shows/; Corporate Human Rights Benchmark, ibid.

30   Hymann, Y. (9 April 2016). Nike vs Adidas – who's more ethical? *Good on You*. https://goodonyou.eco/nike-vs-adidas-whos-more-ethical/

31   Radeke, J., and Coles, T.L. (14 March 2018). Better corporate governance can end slavery in supply chains. *Corporate Knights*. https://www.corporateknights.com/channels/workplace/better-corporate-governance-can-end-slavery-supply-chains-15210036/

32   Epstein, M.J., Buhovac, A.R., and Yuthas, K. (2010). Why Nike kicks butt in sustainability. *Organizational Dynamics, 39*, 353–356.

33   Nike Inc. 2016–2017. *Maximum performance minimum impact*. FY16/17 Sustainable Business Report. https://s1.q4cdn.com/806093406/files/doc_downloads/2018/SBR-Final-FY16-17.pdf

34   Ibid., 4.

35   Milstead, M. (6 March 2018). Nike and Adidas make the list of top 100 places to work 2018. *Running Shoes Guru*. https://www.runningshoesguru.com/2018/03/nike-and-adidas-make-the-list-of-top-100-places-to-work-2018/

36   Kauflin, J. (3 December 2017). The happiest companies to work for in 2018. *Forbes*. https://www.forbes.com/sites/jeffkauflin/2017/12/03/the-happiest-companies-to-work-for-in-2018/#247a6c6e47c2

37   Bernstein, J. (16 January 2018). Why Nike sees social responsibility as an opportunity to innovate. *Fast Company*. https://www.fastcompany.com/40509030/why-nike-sees-social-responsibility-as-an-opportunity-to-innovate

38   Cowley, S. (23 July 2018). Nike will raise wages for thousands after outcry over inequality. *New York Times*. https://www.nytimes.com/2018/07/23/business/nike-wages-raises.html

39   Morgeson, F.P., Aguinis, H., Waldman, D.A., and Siegel, D.S. (2013). Extending corporate social responsibility research to the human resource management and organizational behavior domains: A look to the future. *Personnel Psychology, 66*, 805–824. See this entire issue of *Personnel Psychology* for research on an HR/OB perspective on CSR.

40  Jones, D.A., Willness, C.R., and Madey, S. (2014). Why are job seekers attracted by corporate social performance? Experimental and field tests of three signal-based mechanisms. *Academy of Management Journal, 57*, 383–404.

41  Hansen, S., Dunford, B., Boss, A., Boss, R., and Angermeier, I. (2011). Corporate social responsibility and the benefits of employee trust: A cross-disciplinary perspective. *Journal of Business Ethics, 102*, 29–45.

42  Pfeffer, J. (2018). *Dying for a paycheck: How modern management harms employee health and company performance – and what we can do about it.* New York: Harper Business.

43  Tian, Q., and Robertson, J.L. (2019). How and when does perceived CSR affect employees' engagement in voluntary pro-environmental behavior? *Journal of Business Ethics, 155*, 399–412.

44  City of Vancouver. (n.d.). *Active transportation promotion and enabling plan: Background report.* https://vancouver.ca/files/cov/active-transportation-promotion-and-enabling-full-plan.pdf; Petrunoff, N., Wen, L.M., and Rissel, C. (2016). Effects of a workplace travel plan intervention encouraging active travel to work: Outcomes from a three-year time-series study. *Public Health, 135*, 38–47. Also see: Scheepers, C.E., Wendel-Vos, G.C.W., den Broeder, J.M., van Kempen, E.E.M.M., van Wesemael, P.J.V., and Schuit, A.J. (2014). Shifting from car to active transport: A systematic review of the effectiveness of interventions. *Transportation Research Part A: Policy and Practice, 70*, 264–280.

45  Grene, S. (22 January 2018). New Year's resolution. *Corporate Knights.* https://www.corporateknights.com/channels/workplace/new-years-resolution-15166116/; Lorinc, J. (24 May 2018). Off to work. *Corporate Knights.* https://www.corporateknights.com/channels/workplace/off-to-work-15271380/

46  Ingram Micro. (n.d.). *Corporate social responsibility.* http://corp.ingrammicro.com/About-Us/Social-Responsibility.aspx

47  United Nations Development Programme. (n.d.). *Sustainable Development Goals.* https://www.undp.org/content/dam/undp/library/corporate/brochure/SDGs_Booklet_Web_En.pdf

48  Chari, R., Chang, C.C., Sauter, S.L., Petrun Sayers, E.L., Cerully, J.L., Schulte, P., et al. (2018). Expanding the paradigm of occupational safety and health: A new framework for worker well-being. *Journal of Occupational and Environmental Medicine, 60*, 590.

49  World Health Organization. (2010). *Healthy workplaces: A model for action.* Geneva: World Health Organization, 6.

50  Smith, B. (17 January 2017). Cisco workers get five days to give back under formalized volunteer policy. *Benefits Canada.* https://www.benefitscanada.com/news/a-look-at-ciscos-formal-policy-around-volunteer-work-92547

?utm_source=EmailMarketing&utm_medium=email&utm_campaign
=Daily_Newsletter

51  Cisco. (2018). *Corporate social responsibility report*. https://www.cisco.
com/c/en/us/about/csr/csr-report.html

52  Ranosa, R.R. (5 September 2018). Starbucks to pay employees for charity work.
*Human Resources Director*. https://www.hcamag.com/ca/news/general
/starbucks-to-pay-employees-for-charity-work/120306

53  Nault, L. (30 April 2018). Managing health and safety for volunteers. *Canadian
Occupational Safety*. https://www.cos-mag.com/personal-process-safety
/columns/managing-health-and-safety-for-volunteers/

54  Berry, L.L., and Seltman, K.D. (2008). *Management lessons from the Mayo
Clinic: Inside one of the world's most admired service organizations*. New York:
McGraw-Hill, 9.

55  Ibid, 38–39.

56  Wang, H., Tong, L., Takeuchi, R., and George, G. (2016). Corporate social
responsibility: An overview and new research directions. *Academy of
Management Journal, 59*, 537.

57  Taft, M. (10 June 2019). Inside the growing climate rebellion at Amazon.
*Fast Company*. https://www.fastcompany.com/90361180/inside-the
-growing-climate-rebellion-at-amazon

58  *Human Resources Director*. (16 July 2019). Amazon Prime Day: Workers
hold worldwide protests. https://www.hcamag.com/ca/news/general
/amazon-prime-day-workers-hold-worldwide-protests/172809

59  Maldonado, S. (15 August 2019). U.S. tech industry becomes hotbed for
employee activism. *Globe and Mail*. https://www.theglobeandmail.com
/business/technology/article-us-tech-industry-becomes-hotbed-for
-employee-activism/

60  Dow Jones Sustainability Indices. https://www.robecosam.com/csa
/indices/?r

61  Corporate Knights. (2018). *2018 Global 100 issue*. https://www
.corporateknights.com/magazines/2018-global-100-issue/

62  Aziz, A. (29 October 2018). The power of purpose: How Adidas will make
$1 billion helping solve the problem of ocean plastic. *Forbes*. https://www.
forbes.com/sites/afdhelaziz/2018/10/29/the-power-of-purpose-how
-adidas-will-make-1-billion-helping-solve-the-problem-of-ocean-plastic
/#18d037d0d215

63  Gonzalez, R. (22 April 2019). Adidas commits to sustainability with
100% recyclable shoe. *PSFK*. https://www.psfk.com/2019/04/adidas
-sustainability-recyclable-shoe.html; Danziger, P.N. (18 July 2019). Adidas
challenges the fashion industry in sustainability, pledging only recycled
plastic by 2024. *Forbes*. https://www.forbes.com/sites/pamdanziger

/2019/07/18/adidas-challenges-the-fashion-industry-in-sustainability
-pledging-only-recycled--plastic-by-2024/#50a79e0d1049

64  Adidas. (2018). *Annual report 2018*. https://report.adidas-group.com
/fileadmin/user_upload/adidas_Annual_Report_GB-2018-EN.pdf

65  Ibid., 80.

66  Leonhardt, D. (20 April 2017). O'Reilly, ousted. *New York Times*. https://
www.nytimes.com/2017/04/20/opinion/oreilly-ousted.html

67  Lanthier, S., Bielecky, A., and Smith, P.M. (2018). Examining risk of workplace violence in Canada: A sex/gender-based analysis. *Annals of Work
Exposures and Health, 62*, 1012–1020.

68  O'Kane, J. (18 December 2017). Canadian executives say sexual harassment isn't an issue at their companies. *Globe and Mail*.

69  Scheiber, N., and Creswel, J. (14 December 2017). When HR is part of the
workplace-harassment problem. *Globe and Mail*.

70  Human Resources Professional Association. (12 April 2018). *Doing our
duty: Preventing sexual harassment in the workplace*. https://www.hrpa.ca
/Documents/Public/Thought-Leadership/Doing-Our-Duty.PDF; Savage,
M. (10 June 2018). A third of women say they have faced sexual harassment at work. *Guardian*. https://www.theguardian.com/uk-news/2018/
jun/10/third-of-women-say-they-have-faced-sexual-harassment-at-work;
McCurry, J. (2 March 2016). Nearly a third of Japan's women "sexually
harassed at work." *Guardian*. https://www.theguardian.com/world/2016
/mar/02/japan-women-sexually-harassed-at-work-report-finds

71  Mastoras, J. (March 2016). New sexual harassment protections and
employer obligations in Ontario. Norton Rose Fulbright. https://www
.nortonrosefulbright.com/en-ca/knowledge/publications/8ac8ea1a
/new-sexual-harassment-protections-and-employer-obligations-in-ontario

72  Organisation for Economic Co-operation and Development. (n.d.).
*Work-life balance*. http://www.oecdbetterlifeindex.org/topics/
work-life-balance/

73  U.S. Travel Association. (8 May 2018). *State of American vacation 2018*.
https://www.ustravel.org/research/state-american-vacation-2018;
*Economist*. (24 November 2018). Take a break, 56.

74  Cain Miller, C. (26 April 2019). Women did everything right. Then work got
"greedy." How America's obsession with long hours has widened the gender gap. *New York Times*. https://www.nytimes.com/2019/04/26/upshot
/women-long-hours-greedy-professions.html?smid=nytcore-ios-share

75  *Benefits Canada*. (3 May 2017). Just 38 per cent of U.S. employers offer paid
parental leave. https://www.benefitscanada.com/news/just-38-of-u-s
-employers-offer-paid-parental-leave-97322

76  Burch, S. (10 April 2018). Triggering sustainability transformations. *Corporate Knights*. https://www.corporateknights.com/channels /workplace/triggering-sustainability-transformations-15233364/. Also see: University of Waterloo. (4 April 2018). *New ENV study shows Canadian small businesses leading the way in sustainability*. https:// uwaterloo.ca/environment/news/new-env-study-shows-canadian -small-businesses-leading-way

77  https://betterwayalliance.ca/

78  Better Way Alliance. (n.d.). *Indie coffee shop HotBlack Coffee shares secret to success* [Video]. https://betterwayalliance.ca/i-totally-trust-my-staff -hotblack-coffee-toronto/

## Chapter 8

1   Arne, L., and Moreno, C. (2014). Workplace interventions: A challenge for promoting long-term health among shift workers. *Scandinavian Journal of Work, Environment and Health, 40*, 539–541.

2   Lee, N.K., Roche, A.M., Duraisingam, V., Fischer, J., Cameron, J., and Pidd, K. (2014). A systematic review of alcohol interventions among workers in male-dominated industries. *Journal of Men's Health, 11*, 53–63.

3   Statistics Canada. (2019). *Table 13-10-0383-01 Prevalence of cannabis use in the past three months, self-reported*. https://www150.statcan.gc.ca/t1/tbl1/en /tv.action?pid=1310038301

4   Sanofi Canada. (2016). *The Sanofi Canada Healthcare Survey: Canada's premier survey on health benefit plans*. https://www.sanofi.ca/-/media/Project /One-Sanofi-Web/Websites/North-America/Sanofi-CA/Home/en /About-us/The-Sanofi-Canada-Healthcare-Survey/The-Sanofi-Canada -Healthcare-Survey-2016---Full-Report.pdf

5   Ibid., 21.

6   Edington, D.W., and Pitts, J.S. (2016). *Shared values shared results: Positive organizational health as a win-win philosophy*. Edington Associates, 291–294.

7   Health Enhancement Research Organization. (n.d.). *HERO Scorecard*. https://hero-health.org/hero-scorecard/

8   Goetzel, R.Z., Henke, R.M., Benevent, R., Tabrizi, M.J., Kent, K.B., Smith, K.J., et al. (2014). The predictive validity of the HERO Scorecard in determining future health care cost and risk trends. *Journal of Occupational and Environmental Medicine, 56*, 136–144.

9   Grossmeier, J.P., Fabius, R.D., Flynn, J.P.M., Noeldner, S.P.P., Fabius, D.D., Goetzel, R.Z.P., et al. (2016). Linking workplace health promotion best practices and organizational financial performance: Tracking market

performance of companies with highest scores on the HERO Scorecard. *Journal of Occupational and Environmental Medicine, 58,* 16–23.

10  Carroll, A.E. (6 August 2018). Workplace wellness programs don't work well. Why some studies show otherwise. *New York Times.* https://www.nytimes .com/2018/08/06/upshot/employer-wellness-programs-randomized -trials.html

11  Edington, D.W., and Pitts, J.S. (2016). *Shared values shared results: Positive organizational health as a win-win philosophy.* Edington Associates.

12  Ibid., 261.

13  Ibid., 245.

14  Baicker, K., Cutler, D., and Song, Z. (2010). Workplace wellness programs can generate savings. *Health Affairs, 29,* 304–311.

15  Chenier, L., Hoganson, C., and Thorpe, K., et al. (2012). *Making the business case for investments in workplace health and wellness.* Ottawa: Conference Board of Canada.

16  Stewart, N. (2010). *Creating a culture of health and wellness in Canadian organizations.* Ottawa: Conference Board of Canada, 17.

17  Conference Board of Canada. (2008). *Healthy people, healthy performance, healthy profits: The case for business action on the socio-economic determinants of health.* Ottawa: Conference Board of Canada.

18  Goetzel, R.Z., Henke, R.M., Tabrizi, M., Pelletier, K.R., Loeppke, R., Ballard, D.W., et al. (2014). Do workplace health promotion (wellness) programs work? *Journal of Occupational and Environmental Medicine, 56,* 927–934.

19  Ibid., 929.

20  Grossmeier, J., Terry, P.E., and Anderson, D.R. (2014). Broadening the metrics used to evaluate corporate wellness programs – the case for understanding the total value of the investment. In R.J. Burke and A.M. Richardsen (Eds.), *Corporate wellness programs: Linking employee and organizational health.* Cheltenman, UK: Edward Elgar, 297.

21  Burke, R.J., and Richardsen, A.M. (2014). Corporate programs: A summary of best practices and effectiveness. In R.J. Burke and A.M. Richardsen (Eds.), *Corporate wellness programs: Linking employee and organizational health.* Cheltenman, UK: Edward Elgar, 359.

22  Ibid., 298.

23  Ibid., 303.

24  Chung, M., Melnyk, P., Blue, D., Renaud, D., and Breton, M.-C. (2009). Worksite health promotion: The value of the Tune Up Your Heart Program. *Population Health Management, 12,* 297–304.

25  Makrides, L., Smith, S., Allt, J., Farquharson, J., Szpilfogel, C., Curwin, S., et al. (2011). The Healthy LifeWorks Project: A pilot study of the economic

analysis of a comprehensive workplace wellness program in a Canadian government department. *Journal of Occupational and Environmental Medicine, 53,* 799–805.

26  Renaud, L., Kishchuk, N., Juneau, M., Nigam, A., Tétreault, K., and Leblanc, M.C. (2008). Implementation and outcomes of a comprehensive worksite health promotion program. *Canadian Journal of Public Health, 99,* 73–77.

27  Sun Life Financial. (2016). *Sun Life-Ivey Canadian Wellness ROI Study update.* https://www.sunlife.ca/static/canada/Sponsor/About%20Group%20Benefits/Group%20benefits%20products%20and%20services/Health%20and%20wellness/Wellness%20ROI%20Study/Files/PDF7224-E.pdf

28  Abraham, J., and White, K.M. (2017). Tracking the changing landscape of corporate wellness companies. *Health Affairs, 36,* 222–228.

29  Ibid., 227.

30  Sears, L.E., Shi, Y., Coberley, C.R., and Pope, J.E. (2013). Overall well-being as a predictor of health care, productivity, and retention outcomes in a large employer. *Population Health Management, 16,* 397–405.

31  Chari, R., Chang, C.C., Sauter, S.L., Petrun Sayers, E.L., Cerully, J.L., Schulte, P., et al. (2018). Expanding the paradigm of occupational safety and health: A new framework for worker well-being. *Journal of Occupational and Environmental Medicine, 60,* 589–593.

32  Geisel, J. (2012). Employee buy-in powers health drive. *Business Insurance, 46,* 14.

33  Sabbath, E.L., Williams, J.A.R., Boden, L.I., Tempesti, T., Wagner, G.R., Hopcia, K., et al. (2018). Mental health expenditures: Association with workplace incivility and bullying among hospital patient care workers. *Journal of Occupational and Environmental Medicine, 60,* 737–742.

34  Spiridon, A. (10 May 2019). Are claims trends for antidepressants sustainable? *Benefits Canada.* https://www.benefitscanada.com/news/are-claims-trends-for-antidepressants-sustainable-129770

35  Answered on 5-point "strongly agree–strongly disagree" response scale. These questionnaire items are from: Shain, M. (n.d.). *Towards a psychologically safer workplace: An employer's guide.* Great-West Life Centre for Mental Health in the Workplace. https://www.workplacestrategiesformentalhealth.com/pdf/Employer_Guide_w_HP_0.pdf

36  Burch, J.B., Tom, J., Zhai, Y., Criswell, L., Leo, E., and Ogoussan, K. (2009). Shiftwork impacts and adaptation among health care workers. *Occupational Medicine, 59,* 159–166.

37  I have recoded the item responses so that higher scores represent better sleep quality. Hahn, V.C., Binnewies, C., Sonnentag, S., and Mojza, E.J. (2011). Learning how to recover from job stress: Effects of a recovery training program on recovery, recovery-related self-efficacy, and well-being. *Journal of Occupational Health Psychology, 16*, 202–216.

38  Sethi, S.P., Rovenpor, J.L., and Demir, M. (2017). Enhancing the quality of reporting in corporate social responsibility guidance documents: The roles of ISO 26000, Global Reporting Initiative and CSR-Sustainability Monitor. *Business and Society Review, 122*, 154.

39  Ibid., 153.

40  Goetzel, R.Z.P., Fabius, R.M., Fabius, D.D., Roemer, E.C.P., Thornton, N.B., Kelly, R.K.P., et al. (2016). The stock performance of C. Everett Koop Award winners compared with the Standard and Poor's 500 Index. *Journal of Occupational and Environmental Medicine, 58*, 9–15.

41  Ibid., 14.

42  Adidas. (2018). *Annual report 2018*. https://report.adidas-group.com /fileadmin/user_upload/adidas_Annual_Report_GB-2018-EN.pdf

43  Taft, M. (10 June 2019). Inside the growing climate rebellion at Amazon. *Fast Company*. https://www.fastcompany.com/90361180/inside-the -growing-climate-rebellion-at-amazon

44  Sancroft. (2017). *Maximising the value of occupational health and safety and workplace wellness reporting for a global workforce: A practical guide for internationally operating employers*. London: International SOS Foundation. https://www.internationalsosfoundation.org/OH-Sustainability -Reporting

45  Pfeffer, J. (2018). *Dying for a paycheck: How modern management harms employee health and company performance – and what we can do about it*. New York: Harper Business, 22.

## Chapter 9

1  The tool is available as a downloadable PDF at www.grahamlowe.ca. Additional resources are available on this website.

2  https://www.mentalhealthcommission.ca/English/what-we-do /workplace/national-standard; https://www.guardingmindsatwork.ca/

3  https://www.enwhp.org/?i=portal.en.tools-questionnaires-and-guidance

4  https://www.iwh.on.ca/tools-and-guides/iwh-organizational-performance -metric

5  http://centerforworkhealth.sph.harvard.edu/resources/workplace -integrated-safety-and-health-wish-assessment

6  https://www.worksafe.qld.gov.au/injury-prevention-safety/mentally
   -healthy-workplaces/guidance-and-tools/people-at-work/overview
7  https://publichealthmatters.blog.gov.uk/2018/08/01/making-it-easier
   -to-get-employee-wellbeing-right/
8  https://www.welcoa.org/resources/
9  You can download the checklist from www.grahamlowe.ca.

# Index

The letter *t* following a page number denotes a table; the letter *f* denotes a figure.